The Trans-Pacific Partnership, China and India

The United States and 11 other countries from both sides of the Pacific are currently negotiating the Trans-Pacific Partnership (TPP). The agreement is expected to set new benchmark for international trade through its comprehensive coverage of issues and binding regulations. It is expected to eventually mature into a regional trade agreement covering the entire Asia-Pacific. As of now, it does not include China and India, the two largest emerging markets and regional economies.

The TPP has generated controversy for its excessive emphasis on trade issues, which have remained unresolved or unaddressed at the WTO due to differences between developed and emerging markets. It has also been criticized for adopting a negotiating style reflecting the US regulatory approach to international trade and also as a geo-political strategy of the United States for supporting its strategic rebalancing towards Asia. From both economic and geo-political perspectives, the TPP has various significant implications for China and India that are examined in the book.

This book sheds light on how China and India's entries in the TPP are mutually beneficial and how both countries can gain from the TPP by gaining preferential access to large markets and using it as an opportunity for introducing more outward-oriented reforms. The book also cautions that the United States must reconcile to the rebalancing of economic power within the grouping that will occur following the entries of China and India. Otherwise, the TPP and China and India might walk divergent paths, and trade and regional integration in Asia-Pacific may not ever converge. This book will interest anyone who wishes to learn more about the TPP and its future implications and challenges, and China and India's roles in global and regional trade.

Amitendu Palit is an economist specializing in comparative economic studies, international trade, regional developments and public policies. His current research is on China–India comparative economic development, trade and regional architectures in the Asia-Pacific and the political economy of economic reforms. He has worked for several ministries in India, particularly the Ministry of Finance, where he worked for a decade. He has several academic publications to his credit. His latest book *China India Economics: Challenges, Competition and Collaboration* was published in 2011.

The Trans-Pacific Partnership, China and India

Economic and political implications

Amitendu Palit

Routledge
Taylor & Francis Group

LONDON AND NEW YORK

First published 2014
by Routledge
2 Park Square, Milton Park, Abingdon, Oxon OX14 4RN

and by Routledge
711 Third Avenue, New York, NY 10017

Routledge is an imprint of the Taylor & Francis Group, an informa business

© 2014 Amitendu Palit

British Library Cataloguing in Publication Data
A catalogue record for this book is available from the British Library

Library of Congress Cataloging in Publication Data
Palit, Amitendu.
The Trans-Pacific Partnership (TPP), China and India : economic and
political implications / Amitendu Palit.
  pages cm
  Includes bibliographical references and index.
  1. Free trade–Pacific Area. 2. China–Commercial policy
  3. China–Foreign economic relations. 4. India–Commercial policy.
  5. India–Foreign economic relations. I. Title.
  HF2570.7.P35 2015
  337.51054–dc23   2013047746

ISBN: 978-0-415-85457-3 (hbk)
ISBN: 978-1-315-77227-1(ebk)

Typeset in Times New Roman
by Wearset Ltd, Boldon, Tyne and Wear

For my parents
Kalyani and Dibyendu Palit

Contents

Figures

Tables

Acknowledgements

I am indebted to many for their help and support, without which this book would not have been possible. My sincere thanks to the Institute of South Asian Studies (ISAS) in the National University of Singapore (NUS) for encouraging me to pursue the research for this book and supporting it in various respects. I am grateful to Deborah Elms, Head, Temasek Centre for Trade and Negotiations, Singapore; Professor M. Sornarajah, C.J. Koh Professor of Law, NUS; Dr Wang Jiangyu, Associate Professor of Law, NUS; Dr Jie Huang, Associate Professor, Shanghai University of International Business and Economics (SUIBE), China; Dr Sarah Tong, Senior Research Fellow, East Asia Institute (EAI), NUS; Dr Biswajit Dhar, Director General, Research and Information Systems (RIS), India; Dr S. Narayan, Head (Research), ISAS, NUS; Professor Abhijit Das, Head, Centre for WTO Studies (CWS), Indian Institute for Foreign Trade (IIFT), India; and Dr Murali Kallummal, Associate Professor, CWS, IIFT, India, for the valuable perspectives they have shared with me during my research. My sincere thanks to my good friends and academic colleagues – Professor Guo Xuetang, SUIBE, China; Professor Renato Balderrama, Universidad Autonoma De Neuvo Leone (UANL), Mexico; and Professor Penelope Prime, Georgia State University (GSU) and Director, China Research Center, GSU – for facilitating my interactions with experts during my visits to their institutes, as well as for their useful insights on my research.

The idea of writing this book took shape following the keynote address I delivered at the 3rd Annual Conference of the International Association for Asia Pacific Studies (IAAPS) at the Chinese University of Hong Kong (CUHK) in November 2012. I thank the IAAPS for the opportunity, as well as Professor(s) Lim Tai Wei, Stephen Nagy and Brian Mercurio of the CUHK for the useful discussions that we had on the TPP. I also had equally useful discussions at the Korea Institute for International Economic Policy (KIEP), Seoul during my visit and wish to express my deep gratitude to the faculty.

I have learnt an enormous amount on trade issues in the Asia-Pacific from the several conversations that I have had with See Chuk Mun, Adjunct Research Associate Professor, ISAS, NUS. My sincere thanks to Mr. See and I look forward to learning more from him in future. My sincere thanks also to Yongling Lam, Editor, Taylor & Francis, for her meticulous and smooth handling of this book. Finally, as with all my research efforts, this book could finally happen due to the patience, perseverance and encouragement of my wife Parama. All errors and shortcomings in the work remain entirely mine.

Abbreviations

AoA	Agreement on Agriculture
ACTA	Anti-Counterfeit Trade Agreement
APEC	Asia Pacific Economic Cooperation
APTA	Asia-Pacific Trade Agreement
ASEAN	Association of Southeast Asian Nations
BIT	Bilateral investment treaty
BRICS	Brazil, Russia, India, China, South Africa
CBM	Confidence building measure
CECA	Comprehensive Economic Cooperation Agreement
CEPA	Comprehensive Economic Partnership Agreement
CEPEA	Comprehensive Economic Partnership for East Asia
CJK	China, Japan, Korea
CLMV	Cambodia, Laos, Myanmar, Vietnam
CPC	Communist Party of China
DDA	Doha Development Agenda
DPJ	Democratic Party of Japan
EAEG	East Asian Economic Group
EAFTA	East Asia Free Trade
EAS	East Asia Summit
EU	European Union
FTA	Free trade agreement
FTAAP	Free Trade Area for the Asia-Pacific
GATS	General Agreement on Trade in Services
GATT	General Agreement on Tariffs and Trade
GI	Geographical indication
GLC	Government-linked company
GPA	Government Procurement Agreement
GPL	Government Procurement Law
ILO	International Labour Organization
IP	Intellectual property
ISD	Investor–state dispute
ITIF	Information Technology and Innovation Foundation
KORUS	Korea–United States Free Trade Agreement

LDP	Liberal Democratic Party
MFN	Most Favoured Nation
MSME	Micro, small and medium enterprises
NAFTA	North American Free Trade Agreement
NAM	Non-aligned movement
NASSCOM	National Association of Software and Service Companies
NME	Non market economy
NTB	Non-tariff barrier
NTM	Non-tariff measure
OECD	Organisation for Economic Cooperation and Development
OPEC	Organization of Petroleum Exporting Countries
P3	Pacific 3 Closer Economic Partnership
PHP	Preferential Handling Procedure
PPP	Purchasing power parity
PTA	Preferential trade agreement
RCEP	Regional Comprehensive Economic Partnership
ROO	Rules of origin
RTA	Regional trade agreement
S&D	Special and differential
SASAC	State-owned Assets Supervision and Administration Commission
SEI	Strategic emerging industry
SME	Small and medium enterprises
SOE	State-owned enterprises
SPS	Sanitary and phytosanitary standards
TAC	Treaty of Amity and Cooperation
TBT	Technical barriers to trade
TISA	Trade in Services Agreement
TPA	Trade Promotion Authority
TPP	Trans-Pacific Partnership
TPSEP	Trans-Pacific Strategic Economic Partnership
TRIPS	Trade-Related Intellectual Property Rights
TTIP	Transatlantic Trade and Investment Partnership
USTR	United States Trade Representative
WTO	World Trade Organization

1   Why TPP, China and India

In one of his speeches during his last year as the director general of the World Trade Organization (WTO), Pascal Lamy drew attention to the 'rising weight of influence of emerging economies' and how such influence has 'shifted the balance of power'.[1] His specific reference was to the rise of emerging market economies like China, India and Brazil who were 'no longer policy takers' and were influencing the course and evolution of international trade in several significant ways.

The rise of emerging markets is one of the most significant contemporary geo-political developments, with profound implications for world trade. The biggest impact of the development has been to introduce a decisive multi-polarity in global trade negotiations by dragging the balance of economic power in world trade, traditionally skewed in favour of the United States and EU, closer to an equilibrium. While the emerging markets are yet to acquire the ability to conclusively dominate trade talks and swing outcomes in their favour, their robust economic growth trajectories and rapidly rising shares in global trade, have given them the clout to successfully resist global trade rules being shaped according to developed country preferences. The effect of their strategic rise has been felt most by the WTO, where there was little progress on implementation of the Doha Development Agenda (DDA) and multilateral trade liberalization for several years till the Bali Ministerial in December 2013 due to irreconcilable differences between the developed and emerging market economies.

The changing geo-political balance and the concomitant sluggishness at the WTO has had two major consequences for world trade. The first is a tendency to search for trade liberalization and market access outside the WTO framework. The inclination has led to a sharp increase in regional and bilateral trade agreements, popularly referred to as preferential trade agreements (PTAs), free trade agreements (FTAs) and regional trade agreements (RTAs).[2] No part of the world has experienced the proclivity more than the Asia-Pacific region. While contributing to the growth of a dense and overlapping matrix of trade agreements between economies from the region, resembling the Asian 'noodle bowl' version of what Jagdish Bhagwati described as the 'spaghetti bowl', these agreements have been spurred by the urge to closely integrate regional supply chains through additional preferential market access provisions. While the industrially mature

Asian economies like Japan, Korea and Singapore have been involved in several FTAs and RTAs, China and India have shown considerable proactivity in this regard in recent years and have signed several FTAs and are simultaneously engaged in multiple negotiations with various partners.

The second consequence of the geo-political shift in global economic power towards emerging markets has been a marked disinclination on the part of the United States to provide leadership to multilateral trade talks and the implementation of the DDA (Panagariya 2013). This unwillingness has arguably, been impelled by the realization that its ability to dominate the multilateral trade agenda has ebbed considerably. Time and again, the United States' unsuccessful attempt to frontload the WTO's trade agenda with the WTO plus and extra issues (e.g. intellectual property (IP), government procurement, labour and environment standards) that have either remained unresolved at the WTO or are not part of its work programme, has stirred it to work for its preferred trade agenda outside the WTO. A part of the motivation has been reflected in an increase in the number of FTAs that it has signed or is negotiating. The most substantive manifestation has been in its commitment to mega-regional trade agreements, with the two most important initiatives being the Transatlantic Trade and Investment Partnership (TTIP) and the Trans-Pacific Partnership (TPP). Between the two, the TPP is at a much-advanced stage of negotiations and is expected to conclude soon. While the TTIP is a RTA envisaged between the United States and EU across the Atlantic, the TPP is a RTA aiming to connect countries across both sides of the Pacific. Taken together, the two comprise two arms of the US trade strategy spanning across the Atlantic and the Pacific.

Unlike the TTIP, the TPP has acquired substantial strategic dimensions, both economic and geo-political. From an economic perspective, it is seen as shaping as an agreement that not only includes issues that the United States has had problems in tabling and pursuing at the WTO, but also as a framework modelled on US trade regulations. The immediate inference of such a perspective is that the TPP is not an inclusive grouping; it is inimical to the trade interests of emerging markets in many respects and probably an attempt to impose US trade rules and regulations on the Asia-Pacific without taking note of emerging market sensitivities. From a geo-political perspective, an oft-repeated negative perception about the TPP has been its branding as a security and foreign policy instrument of the United States for consolidating its strategic presence in the region by pulling together a group of 'like-minded' partners and allies.

One of the most conspicuous features of the TPP – and an important factor contributing to its 'anti-emerging market' perception – is the exclusion of China and India. The situation might well change over time and the future might see the TPP including the two largest Asian economies and emerging markets within its fold. As of now, however, the TPP's stated vision of growing into a 'high quality twenty-first century' trade framework for the entire Asia-Pacific seems unrealizable unless it includes China and India. On the other hand, for China and India too, the TPP is an exceptionally significant development. Neither country can afford to overlook its implications, both economic and strategic, given that they aspire to lead the world economy in the coming decades by being among the largest players in global trade and commerce.

This book studies the economic and political implications of the TPP for China and India across several aspects including the possibilities of trade diversion, the consequences for Asian regionalism and the political economy dynamics. In the process, it tries to identify the economic and strategic distance between the TPP and China and India in terms of their regulatory and institutional contrasts and the domestic political economy complexities in the two countries likely to influence perceptions on the TPP. The book also explores the possible strategies of both countries for joining the TPP. The larger context of the examination is based on gathering deeper insights on two fundamental questions: Are the TPP, and China and India, mutually exclusive; and how feasible is it for China and India to join the TPP in the foreseeable future.

The TPP, China and India: mutually indispensable

The sheer economic size of the United States compared with other members, as will be discussed in Chapter 2, was bound to make it the driving force of the agreement. It is hardly surprising therefore that the TPP's interests and ambitions are considered broadly similar to those of the United States and it is being identified as a trade framework symbolizing the US agenda in global trade. Notwithstanding the entry of Japan, the third largest economy in the world, the United States still accounts for 57.1 per cent and 59.6 per cent, measured in nominal and PPP terms respectively, of the economic size of the current TPP bloc. With around three-fifths of the TPP's economic output, the balance of economic power in the TPP is disproportionately in favour of the United States. The slant enables it to have a significant say in shaping the TPP in terms of deciding the negotiating agenda and the course of negotiations. As the largest economy in the TPP, the United States is able to leverage access to its own market as a negotiating chip for obtaining WTO plus market access commitments from other members. The problem with this current characteristic of the TPP is its low credibility as an inclusive trade framework by accommodating heterogeneous economic interests. Such credibility can come only with a more diverse grouping representing trade preferences other than those of the United States.

The economic balance within the TPP would change significantly with the entry of China and India. From almost 60 per cent of the market size of the TPP that the United States has now, its share would drop to 41.8 per cent and 36.3 per cent in nominal and PPP terms if the TPP were to include China and India. As a group by themselves, China and India would comprise 26.9 per cent and 39.1 per cent of the market size of the TPP in nominal and PPP terms.[3] From a multilateral perspective, and particularly those of emerging markets, the TPP would acquire a more egalitarian look and would be conceived of much less as an instrument for advancing US trade interests fashioned by US business lobbies and interest groups. More emerging markets might be encouraged to join the TPP, imparting it a truly plurilateral character. On the other hand, the rather drastic change in economic balance would influence the ability of the United States to decisively dominate the TPP agenda. Whether the United States is prepared to accept such an eventuality is important, as that would be significant in determining the room for emerging markets in the TPP. The likelihood of the United States insisting on a high 'entry fee' in the form of commitment to major changes in domestic regulations is quite strong. This would ensure that the United States influenced domestic regulations in China and India in its preferred manner for guaranteeing preferential access of American businesses in these markets, notwithstanding the lesser influence it might have on TPP decisions following China and India's entries.

In a sense, China and India's entries in the TPP can imply significant diplomatic dividends for the United States. By inviting China in particular to the TPP, the United States would be able to dispel the notions of it being a geo-strategic ploy to contain China by stitching an alliance of US allies, partners and friends. It would also send out positive signals about the United States being keen on making the TPP a genuinely comprehensive trade framework for integrating the Asia-Pacific, as opposed to a design for serving the narrow objectives of supporting its rebalancing strategy towards the region. Both these impressions would serve to strengthen the prospects of greater geo-political stability in the region. By including China and India, the United States would also be able to convince the global trade community about its willingness to engage in trade talks with two countries with whom it has had huge differences on various trade issues and has been at loggerheads in the WTO. Indeed, it could help in addressing the impression that the United States is no longer committed to the WTO because of the influence being wielded by emerging markets; negotiating with China and India at the TPP would convey the United States' alacrity to work with emerging markets, notwithstanding such talks taking place outside the WTO.

The inclusion of China and India would greatly enhance the scope of trade creation within the TPP given the preferential access that bloc members will obtain in the two large markets. At present, the 12-member TPP accounts for around 40 per cent of the global GDP in nominal terms and 35 per cent in nominal terms; these shares would increase to 54 per cent and 64 per cent respectively upon China and India's entries.[4] Needless to say, trade liberalization effected across such a large economic area by eliminating barriers and rationalizing standards and regulations would create enormous trade opportunities within the bloc.

Much as the TPP and the United States stand to benefit by including China and India, clear benefits are visible on the part of the latter as well. The TPP is being negotiated at a time when the world economy is still trying to come to terms with the global economic crisis of 2008. Since the crisis, China and India have also experienced slowdowns in their economic growth, largely due to lack of export demand from economically sluggish Western markets. Indeed, from 2008 onward, GDP growths in both countries have dropped below their long-term average growth rates from 1990 onward (Figure 1.1). Both countries need greater external demand for rejuvenating their economic growths: an important prerequisite in this regard is getting access to new markets. The TPP provides an opportunity to China and India for obtaining preferential access in the large NAFTA market, which has 25.8 per cent (nominal) and 22.9 per cent (PPP) shares in global GDP and around 15 per cent shares in global merchandise and commercial services trades. Neither country has FTAs with NAFTA members till now. For China, the TPP also provides the additional opportunity of obtaining similar access to the Japanese market with which it does not have an FTA. On the other hand, for India, the TPP can provide greater preferential access in the Latin American markets of Chile and Peru, and also in ASEAN (Association of Southeast Asian Nations) members like Malaysia and Vietnam, over and above what it currently has through existing bilateral and regional agreements. Staying out of the TPP can imply adverse prospects for both, with export competitors like Malaysia and Vietnam gaining deeper access in the NAFTA and other TPP member markets; and new standards implemented across the TPP emerging as trade-obstructing barriers. The prospects of trade diversion in this regard for both are discussed in Chapter 3. Minimizing such possibilities, and ensuring their domestic producers get access to supply chains created within the TPP by connecting industries from both sides of the Pacific, should be an important priority for China and India.

The lack of progress on the DDA at the WTO has forced China and India to search for preferential market access through bilateral FTAs and RTAs. Most of these, however, while being relatively exhaustive in coverage of goods, only partially cover trade in services and WTO plus and WTO extra issues. For realizing greater benefits from world trade, both countries need to become part

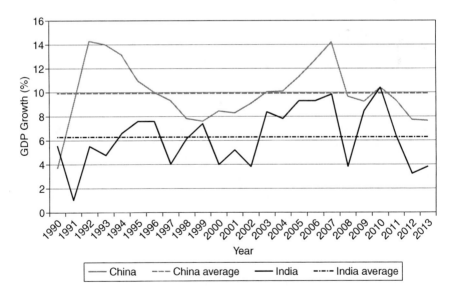

Figure 1.1 GDP Growth trajectories (%) for China and India (source: IMF, World Economic Outlook Database. The changes are for GDP growth in nominal terms).

of trade frameworks focusing on these issues, as otherwise they are likely to fall behind in global trade in services and also become less important players in cross-border flows of investments and finance. In many of the WTO plus areas, China and India have their own views and defensive interests. These interests need to be rationalized in their external trade policies and domestic regulations in a manner that preserves their domestic priorities while maximizing gains from external trade. This can happen only if they become part of frameworks like the TPP that are extensively discussing WTO plus and new generation trade issues and approach these matters constructively. They can no longer afford to sidestep these issues in external trade negotiations as some of their major trade partners, who are already in the TPP, will insist on discussing these issues in the bilateral pacts they have, or are negotiating, with China and India. Both countries must accept the inevitability of future world trade being dominated more by non-traditional issues and should look at the TPP as an opportunity for contributing their own perspectives on these issues, and introducing appropriate changes in domestic regulations. By maintaining a distance from the TPP, both countries risk the possibility of being continued to be labelled as 'reluctant' participators in the global agenda for trade liberalization, an impression they have acquired among the developed world and many of their other trade partners due to their occasionally strong defensive postures at the WTO.

As a mega-regional trade deal, the TPP is expected to move towards the Free Trade Area for the Asia-Pacific (FTAAP) by including more economies within its fold. As discussed in Chapter 4, this is a new strand of economic integration initiated in the region, different from the intra-Asian, ASEAN-centric integration initiatives prevailing in the region since the Asian financial crisis of 1997. The intra-Asian initiatives have had China and India playing important roles, particularly at the East Asia Summit (EAS) and the more recent Regional Comprehensive Economic Partnership (RCEP) involving ASEAN and its FTA partners. The RCEP is proceeding parallel to the TPP and may diverge from it if the two become shaped according to structural and issue-based characteristics of the ASEAN and US FTAs. The divergence and possible conflict between the two frameworks will be even greater if the RCEP and the TPP evolve as spheres of strategic influence between China and the United States (Palit 2013b). These adverse outcomes can be avoided if China and India join the TPP. Their entry in the TPP would increase the proportion of common members between the two agreements and would facilitate their eventual merger, paving the way for the FTAAP. In the medium term, China and India's presences in both the TPP and the RCEP can enable the two frameworks to be complementary to each other by connecting trans-Pacific and Asian businesses through common value chains. Multinationals from both sides of the Pacific can take advantage of the specific benefits of both agreements by dispersing their production along these value chains. As countries with major stakes in the economic integration of the region, China and India can hardly afford to confine themselves only to the Asian track of the RCEP and avoid the TPP; they need to consider the latter as a priority too.

China and India in the TPP: feasible?

Notwithstanding the entries of China and India in the TPP being mutually beneficial in several respects, the distance between the TPP and the two countries
remains significant. There are constraints impeding the entries of both countries,
some of which are specific to their individual circumstances, while others are
common. The former, specifically for China, includes the strategic discomfort of
being part of an agreement often interpreted as a US foreign policy and security
tool for containing China. While India does not suffer from such concerns, like
China, it has to overcome the compulsions of domestic politics for agreeing to
greater outward-oriented policy measures and market access commitments and
implementing far-reaching regulatory changes for joining the TPP.

Domestic politics will indeed be the toughest challenge for both China and
India in aspiring to join not only the TPP, but in negotiating all their future trade
agreements having comprehensive coverage and including the WTO plus and
WTO extra issues. The FTAs and RTAs signed by both countries to date include
only limited provisions on these issues, though both have displayed the willingness to commit to the General Agreement on Trade in Services (GATS) plus
market accesses in their recent FTAs. As they negotiate bilaterally with TPP
partners like Australia and New Zealand, and with other members at the RCEP,
they will be facing issues that they can expect to face later at the TPP. These
negotiations should be taken as preparatory grounds for both countries in convincing their domestic constituencies about the importance of greater integration
with the world economy and introducing reforms accordingly.

The above, of course, is much easier said than done in both cases. China's
biggest hurdle to domestic reforms and meeting the TPP's standards are its SOEs
and their political and economic clout. An entrenched incentive structure
between top managements of the SOEs and political leaders at provincial and
central levels has perpetuated the significance of these enterprises. Reforming
SOEs is critical for introducing further reforms in competition policy, government procurement and investment policies – all major issues being negotiated at
the TPP. While the SOEs represent a major interest group and hurdle to reforms,
the pro-reform new Chinese leadership has to convince different political factions within the CPC about such reforms not damaging the inclusive nature of
policies followed by China for the past few years with greater focus on distribution than growth. Both China and India, interestingly, have gone through almost
a decade of emphatic policy preference for inclusive growth, which has resulted
in the state playing bigger roles in both economies. In India, the manifestation
has been primarily through state-funded ambitious rights-based programmes
guaranteeing rural employment and access to subsidized food grain. In China, on
the other hand, the thrust has been on greater investment in economically backward areas and on indigenous innovation efforts in SOEs. Unfortunately, leaderships in both countries have fallen short of balancing justified efforts on
addressing distribution-related concerns with greater productivity-enhancing
reforms in critical sectors of their economies like domestic service industries.

The latter, in both countries, have been on the downswing due to regressive political economies, as discussed in Chapter 5. More market-oriented reforms, without diluting the inclusive character of national economic policies, are required in both economies for reviving their growth trajectories and enabling them to acquire global competitive advantages in cutting-edge service sectors. Unless they do so, they will not be able to narrow their distance from the TPP and run the risk of falling behind in dominating future world trade.

It is easy to form superficially conclusive impressions about China and India being miles away from matching the exacting standards of the TPP in terms of the current states of their domestic regulations. These impressions fail to pay adequate attention to the fact that both countries have been trying to introduce regulatory changes in several 'difficult' areas, albeit with limited success at times, as discussed in Chapter 6. The gaps between the domestic regulations of China and India vis-à-vis those expected to be institutionalized by the TPP are not uniform across sectors and issues; nor are they exclusive to China and India. Many of these symbolize differences in perspectives that several TPP members have with the United States on subjects that have traditionally been divisive and contentious in international trade: exemptions on tariff cuts in agriculture, market access in state-dominated services like telecommunication and financial services, stronger investor–state dispute (ISD) mechanisms, opening up government procurement markets, making SOEs subject to competitive regulations, stricter IP protection provisions for safeguarding proprietary knowledge and subjecting potential damages on environment and labour inflicted by trade practices to enforceable dispute settlement provisions.

There are three factors contributing to the distances that China and India would have with the TPP on all the above. First, the continuing prevalence of some institutions and systemic practices with inward-looking and protective mindsets keen on preserving incentive structures that discourage competition in certain sectors of the economy; second, the reluctance and resultant inexperience of negotiating new generation issues in international trade talks; and third, the reservation on making most, if not all, commitments and obligations 'binding' and subjecting all deviations to enforceable dispute settlement processes similar to resolving commercial disputes. While the first two are intrinsic to the histories, structures and transformative struggles of the two economies, the third is a fundamental disagreement with the regulatory approach of the TPP, personifying the US approach to international trade negotiations.

Notwithstanding historical and structural roadblocks, the Chinese leadership under President Xi is displaying pragmatism and eagerness in moving closer to the TPP. Knowing full well the importance of engaging the United States and reducing the differences between the US and Chinese approaches to trade negotiations for reaching the TPP, China has embarked on bilateral investment negotiations with the United States. The negotiations are radical given the Chinese willingness to adopt the US approach and including all service sectors within the purview of talks. This and other measures, such as the pilot Shanghai Free Trade Zone (FTZ) for experimenting with deeper financial sector reforms, as discussed in Chapter 7, are part of China's strategies of developing institutional capabilities for joining the TPP. India is yet to form such responses and is expected to focus more on negotiating the RCEP. While the success of China's strategies would depend on the ability of the new leadership to steer market-oriented reforms through a domestic political community sharply divided on the subject, India's future strategies, other than overcoming similar domestic political constraints, would need to introduce greater policy clarity and institutional coordination in its external trade negotiations.

Much as China and India are trying to assess the implications of the TPP for identifying the consequences of their joining the group, or staying away from it, the lack of alternative options is becoming increasingly prominent. Despite the enthusiasm over BRICS (a coalition of the world's major emerging markets comprising Brazil, Russia, India, China and South Africa) providing an alternative emerging market economic architecture, the collective is yet to become cohesive enough for contemplating a plurilateral trade agreement. Over time, it could offer such a solution, though some BRICS members are likely to be wary of the possibility of China assuming leadership of the group and positing it as the second pole in the global trade order for rivalling the US influence in mega RTAs like the TPP and the TTIP. As of now, the possibility appears remote. Shying away from the TPP and investing proportionally greater negotiating resources at the WTO is again not an entirely sensible alternative given the WTO's inability to push ahead on the DDA and its limitations in handling new generation trade issues and complications.

While both the TPP, and China and India, would be distinctly better off with each other, the current TPP architecture, reflecting overt dominance of the US economic, regulatory and strategic priorities, would need to become more plurilateral in character for including China and India. Both countries would also aspire to the same. The most optimal solution for harmonious existence of China and India in the TPP would be to negotiate for rules that genuinely advance trade liberalization while taking note of the specific circumstances of emerging markets and acquire a more non-binding character. The United States needs to appreciate the importance of including China and India in the TPP, given their economic size and strategic significance. China and India on the other hand need to comprehend the importance of their playing a greater and constructive role in global trade governance by taking forward the trade liberalization agenda by incorporating new issues. Inflexibilities in their respective outlooks towards modern trade and trade regulations would only widen the gap between the US-led vision of global trade and that of the emerging markets. The TPP would in that case remain largely a US ambition without becoming a holistic integration framework for the Asia-Pacific; China and India would be left searching for new spaces in their home turf and remain as large emerging markets unprepared for playing the roles in global and regional trade commensurate with their economic sizes and strategic weights.

Notes

1 'Emerging economies have shifted the balance of power in world trade – Lamy', WTO News: Speeches – DG Pascal Lamy, 26 November 2012, online, available at: www.wto.org/english/news_e/ppl_e/sppl258_e.htm (accessed 18 November 2013).
2 The PTAs, FTAs and RTAs – either signed bilaterally by countries, or gathering countries into a common regional economic framework – aim to create preferential access into markets of contracting countries over and above what is available through the WTO. This book avoids using these terms interchangeably and sticks to FTAs and RTAs as generic terms for describing bilateral and regional agreements respectively, wherever referred.
3 Computed from the world GDP estimates of the IMF.
4 Ibid.

2 TPP

Structure, issues and contradictions

Negotiations at the TPP have continued for more than four years since the first round of talks at Melbourne in March 2010. Along with the progress in negotiations, more countries have joined talks, with the TPP now including 12 economies from the Asia-Pacific. It is becoming increasingly clear that achieving the ambitious goals of the TPP will be far more difficult than originally envisaged. The conclusion of negotiations has missed repeated deadlines, the latest being the APEC leaders' meeting in Bali in October 2013. The difficulties in concluding negotiations arise from a host of issues, including differences in negotiating priorities between members, the US decision to substantially discuss market access issues bilaterally with countries with whom it does not have FTAs, and the divergence in approaches for negotiating RTAs between the United States and Asian members of the TPP. All these issues will continue to influence future negotiations, as more countries, particularly large Asian economies like China, India and Thailand, aim to join the TPP.

This chapter examines the context and features of the TPP by studying its geographical features and historical origin, the structural characteristics of the bloc as reflected by its economic size and the external trades of the members, the key features of the TPP template, particularly the facility of 'docking' in more countries through an open annexation clause and the wide coverage of traditional and non-traditional trade issues, and the various contradictions in negotiating priorities and postures. Certain factors forcing the prolongation of negotiations are examined in detail, along with the possibility of their forcing the TPP to reconcile to less ambitious standards. If economically large and strategically significant countries like China and India join the TPP, the chapter argues, the United States' ability to decisively steer negotiations in a direction of its choice may decrease, given the greater balance of economic power within the group.

Geography and origin

The TPP is being negotiated by Australia, Brunei, Canada, Chile, Japan, Malaysia, Mexico, New Zealand, Peru, Singapore, Vietnam and the United States. Brunei, Chile, New Zealand and Singapore comprise the original P4, which came together to form the Trans-Pacific Strategic Economic Partnership

(TPSEP) Agreement in May 2006, which forms the basis of the current TPP. The P4 was expanded from 2008 onward with the joining of Australia, Malaysia, New Zealand, Peru, the United States and Vietnam at different points in time. Later entrants include Canada and Mexico, which have been formally participating in negotiations since December 2012. Japan is the latest to join the TPP and has been participating in the negotiations since August 2013. The TPP club is expected to enlarge further given the active interest expressed by various countries from the region. South Korea is interested in joining and is expected to do so once the TPP framework acquires greater clarity.[1] Similar interests have been expressed by Thailand and Taiwan. After initial hostile impressions, the new leadership in China is looking at the TPP objectively and taking measures, as will be discussed in the later chapters, for joining the TPP. While India is yet to formally take a position on the TPP, primarily since it is not a member of the APEC (Asia Pacific Economic Cooperation), discussions on the TPP and the imperatives for India in preparing for it, are becoming more intense in India's policy circles and government agencies.

As of now, the TPP is a sub-group of the APEC economies. The geographical sweep of the framework covers several segments of the Asia-Pacific and includes Southeast Asia (Brunei, Malaysia, Singapore, Vietnam), Northeast Asia (Japan), Oceania (Australia, New Zealand), South America (Chile, Peru) and North America (Canada, Mexico, United States). The APEC members not currently participating in TPP negotiations include China, Indonesia, Papua New Guinea, the Philippines, Russia, Taiwan, Thailand and South Korea. Many of the non-participating APEC countries are likely to join the TPP in future; the TPP's 'APEC' orientation is distinct. The maturing of the TPP, quite expectedly, has given rise to hopes of it paving the way for achieving a greater FTAAP.

The early seeds of the TPP were sown in 1998, when a group of APEC economies, including the United States, planned an FTA. While the idea did not make much progress, two of the consulting economies – New Zealand and Singapore – first negotiated a bilateral PTA, and then, with Chile, launched talks on the Pacific 3 Closer Economic Partnership (P3) in 2002. All three economies, and Brunei, which joined the trio in April 2005, are relatively small open economies and rely substantively on foreign trade and investment for sustaining economic growth. The TPSEP, or the P4 agreement as it is more popularly referred to, was announced in June 2005 and came into force from 28 May 2006. This was the first major RTA among the Pacific-rim countries, cutting across three continents and regions – Southeast Asia, Oceania and Latin America. Interestingly, the agreement took off almost immediately after the Doha Round of talks was launched by the WTO in November 2001. The polarization of opinion among WTO members on the implementation of the DDA and the imminent possibility of multilateral trade talks and further trade liberalization getting stuck (which they indeed have), inspired many members to seek greater market access through smaller regional compacts with like-minded partners, which were arguably more effective forums than the humungous WTO.[2] The P4 agreement is one such example. It is also an example of the APEC economies attempting to put together a 'high quality' trade framework extendable to the rest of the region by including more like-minded economies through an open annexation clause, as it is now noticed in the TPP and the RCEP.

The economic and strategic significance of the P4 agreement changed vastly with the United States' decision to join it. Initially, the United States decided to participate only in the financial services and investment negotiations at the TPSEP, but subsequently it committed itself fully to expanded negotiations. The US decision was largely influenced by the stalemate at the WTO over the DDA, which heightened in July 2008 over irreconcilable differences between the United States and developed countries, particularly China, India and other emerging markets (Wen 2012). President Bush formally notified the Congress about the administration's plans to join the P4 in September 2008. For the United States, joining the P4 and expanding the group was an effective way of expanding its commercial presence and business links with the Asia-Pacific, at a time when the fast-track Trade Promotion Authority (TPA) for securing new FTAs had expired and the Congress was unwilling to renew it (Tibung 2012).[3] The TPSEP's structural framework and approach to trade liberalization was also in sync with the US vision of a 'gold standard' trade agreement.

Australia, Vietnam and Peru followed soon, expanding the P4 club. The new US administration under President Obama reaffirmed the US commitment to the TPP by formally notifying the Congress in December 2009 about its plans to negotiate with the TPP member countries. A few weeks before notifying the Congress, President Obama reiterated the American intention to participate in the TPP negotiations for shaping a regional agreement with 'broad-based membership and the high standards worthy of a twenty-first-century trade agreement'.[4] The most pressing factors behind the decision included reviving economic growth through higher exports and creating new jobs at a time when the world economy was experiencing a major economic contraction and the United States its worst economic downturn since the 1930s. Engaging in the TPP marked the 'cornerstone of the Obama Administration's economic policy towards the Asia-Pacific' for deepening links with the robust markets of the Asia-Pacific.[5]

Negotiations on creating a framework for the expanded TPP from the P4 agreement began in March 2010 in Melbourne. Malaysia joined the talks from the third round in Brunei in October 2010. The frequency of negotiations gradually increased and the negotiations themselves became more intense as the members worked towards wrapping up the talks by the APEC leaders' meeting in Hawaii in November 2011. But the talks remained inconclusive, underlining the complexity of issues being discussed and the difficulties in resolving them. The TPP leaders reiterated their commitment to the agreement and announced its broad outlines. The official statement released on the occasion also underpinned the challenges involved in speedy conclusion of the negotiations:

we recognize that there are sensitive issues that vary for each country yet to be negotiated, and have agreed that together, we must find appropriate ways to address those issues in the context of a comprehensive and balanced package, taking into account the diversity of our levels of development.[6]

By December 2013, 19 rounds of talks had taken place with the negotiators working to conclude the agreement as soon as possible, after missing another deadline in Bali in October 2013. Stakes are high in reaching an early conclusion, particularly for the United States, as more delays will cast doubts upon its ability to provide effective leadership in getting a diverse group of countries to agree on a common set of rules. It might also mean greater traction for parallel and upcoming regional economic integration agreements like the RCEP that do not involve the United States (Barfield 2013).

Economics and trade

The current membership of the TPP represents 37.8 per cent and 31.9 per cent of the world GDP respectively, measured in nominal and PPP terms (Table 2.1). This is a huge leap forward compared with the P4, which barely added up to 1.0 per cent of the global GDP. Between them, the current TPP members represent almost two-fifths of the global output measured in nominal terms, which when Korea, Thailand, China and India are included becomes more than half. At present, the TPP is a bigger economic entity than the EU (23.3 per cent and 19.6 per cent of global GDP in nominal and PPP terms) and the NAFTA (25.8 per cent and 22.9 per cent of global GDP, nominally and in PPP). Only the TTIP being negotiated by the United States and the EU has a larger economic size

Table 2.1 TPP members' shares in world GDP (%)

Country	World GDP (nominal)	World GDP (PPP)
Australia	2.0	1.1
Brunei*	0.0	0.0
Canada	2.5	1.7
Chile	0.4	0.4
Japan	8.4	5.6
Malaysia	0.4	0.6
Mexico	1.7	2.2
New Zealand	0.2	0.2
Peru	0.3	0.4
Singapore	0.3	0.4
United States	21.6	19.0
Vietnam	0.2	0.4
Total	37.8	31.9

Source: World Bank; computed on the basis of the latest year GDP estimates available for individual countries.

Note
* Brunei's shares are 0.02 per cent (nominal GDP) and 0.03 per cent (PPP GDP) respectively and have been rounded to one decimal place.

than the TPP. The latter also accounts for more than 60 per cent of the APEC's economic size.

The TPP's significant share in the world economic output is largely due to the presence of the world's largest and third largest economies – those of the United States and Japan. With the two economies accounting for a third of the world GDP (around a quarter if measured in PPP, Table 2.1), they are responsible for expanding its economic size and enhancing its strategic influence. Indeed, Japan's entry in the TPP considerably balances the overwhelming economic dominance of the United States. Such balancing has also been partially contributed by the other two NAFTA economies – Canada and Mexico – with a combined share of more than 4.0 per cent in world GDP. South Korea's impending entry will also contribute to the balancing, as will eventually the entries of China and India, whenever they happen.

The United States has been able to exert considerable influence in the TPP negotiations right from the beginning as a result of its economic size. It is hardly surprising that market access negotiations in goods and services at the TPP, as well as those on the WTO plus and WTO extra issues are resembling US bilateral FTA negotiations, with the core talks taking place between the United States and the TPP members with whom it does not have FTAs. Japan's entry might partly change the scenario by making the economic power within the group more balanced; but at the same time, it is also going to make consultations between the United States and Japan the key to the resolution of several issues. Until China joins the TPP, Japan can leverage its economic weight and strategic proximity to the United States by contributing substantially to the 'high quality twenty-first century' rule-making process of the TPP trade agreement by assuming leadership with the United States (Mulgan 2013). There is little doubt that among various bilateral dynamics, the US–Japan talks will be the most critical in shaping the future framework of the TPP. Japan and the United States have had major differences over Japan's restrictive policies in agriculture, automobiles and insurance. Failure to resolve these issues can adversely affect the long-term prospects of the TPP along with their bilateral relationship (Cooper and Manyin 2013).

Apart from some of the world's largest economies, the TPP also has some of the most populous countries and an overall share of 11.3 per cent in global population (Table 2.2). The four most populous countries – United States, Japan, Mexico and Vietnam, which are the world's third, tenth, eleventh and thirteenth populous countries, with a combined share of 9.3 per cent of the global population – contribute significantly to the current TPP population, exceeding 800 million. The population shares, like economic size, again point to the significance of the United States and Japan in the TPP collective. It also points to the influence that Vietnam commands as a country with a large and growing population coupled with an impressive growth performance, which makes it an attractive market for other TPP members; this would explain why an economy like Vietnam with a pronounced state-owned sector and underdeveloped trade facilitation institutions – given its entry in the WTO in as late as 2007 – was still allowed entry in the TPP (Lim *et al.* 2012).[7]

Table 2.2 TPP members' shares in global population (%)

Country	Share
Australia	0.3
Brunei	0.0*
Canada	0.5
Chile	0.2
Japan	1.8
Malaysia	0.4
Mexico	1.7
New Zealand	0.1*
Peru	0.4
Singapore	0.1*
United States	4.5
Vietnam	1.3
Total	11.3

Source: online, available at: http://en.wikipedia.org/wiki/List_of_countries_by_population (accessed 29 September 2013).

Note
* Singapore, New Zealand and Brunei's actual shares in world population are 0.076 per cent, 0.063 per cent and 0.0055 per cent and have been rounded to one decimal place.

It is not easy to dispel notions about the TPP being a collective of rich and wealthy economies from the Asia-Pacific region. Half of its current members – Australia, Canada, Chile, Japan, Mexico and the United States – are OECD countries with better income and living standards than those elsewhere in the world. Most of the OECD members in the TPP have per capita incomes not only higher than the world average (US$10,172), but also higher than that of the APEC (US$14,031) (Table 2.3 and Figure 2.1). Chile and Mexico are two

Table 2.3 Per capita incomes of TPP members (US$)

Country	Nominal	PPP
Australia	67,036.0	44,598.0
Brunei	41,127.0	53,348.0
Canada	52,219.0	42,533.0
Chile	15,363.0	22,363.0
Japan	46,720.0	35,178.0
Malaysia	10,381.0	17,143.0
Mexico	9,742.0	16,731.0
New Zealand	32,000.0	32,219.0
Peru	6,573.0	10,940.0
Singapore	51,709.0	61,803.0
United States	49,965.0	49,965.0
Vietnam	1,596.0	3,635.0
Average	32,036.0	32,538.0

Source: World Bank.

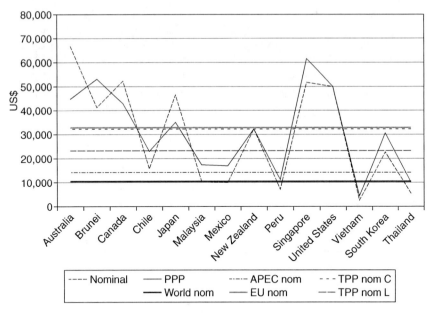

Figure 2.1 TPP, world and EU per capita incomes (source: compiled from World Bank
Statistics).

Note
TPP nom C is the TPP12; TPP nom L includes South Korea and Thailand.

exceptions in this regard. They introduce some degree of heterogeneity in income
levels among the TPP members, which is enhanced by Peru and Vietnam, the two
lowest per capita income members in the group. It is noticeable that two of the
non-OECD TPP members – Singapore and Brunei – are among the world's highest
per capita income countries in PPP terms, strengthening the notion of the TPP
being a conglomerate of wealthy nations. The TPP's current per capita incomes –
US$32,036 (nominal) and US$32,538 (PPP) – are almost as much as the EU's –
US$32,672 (nominal) and US$33,014 (PPP) – and could have been larger than it
had it not been for Vietnam. Even Vietnam has a higher per capita income in PPP
terms. This is true of the other relatively lower per capita income TPP members
like Chile, Mexico, Malaysia and Peru, reinforcing the economic strength of the
bloc given the relatively high purchasing powers of even the lower income
members. Indeed, the APEC itself is a collection of relatively higher income economies with only Thailand, Vietnam and Papua New Guinea having per capita
incomes lower than the world average. It is hardly surprising that the United States
is keen on integrating its economy and producers closer with the region through the
TPP, given the Asia-Pacific economies' potential of absorbing greater American
exports on account of their high purchasing powers.

The economic heterogeneity within the TPP is pronounced in terms of the differences in living standards of its members. This is evident from the dispersion

in per capita incomes, both in nominal and PPP terms (Table 2.3). The hetero-geneity helps the TPP in countering notions of being a club of rich economies. But it also complicates ongoing negotiations by bringing varied perspectives and offensive and defensive interests on different issues. The differences in eco-nomic structures and levels of economic progress and development among members are responsible for generating distinct comparative advantages and varied specializations, and divergent perspectives on market access. The US strategy of fashioning market access negotiations through bilateral consultations with members with whom it does not have PTAs is facing obstacles arising from sharp differences in degree of development and economic structures; particularly with countries like Vietnam and Malaysia. The difficulties in agreeing to the US demands and conforming to the TPP's regulations are particularly high for Vietnam, which is required to commit deeper liberalization for agricultural tariffs and in domestic regulations governing SOEs, government procurement and IP, fairly soon after implementing the liberalization requirements for joining the WTO in 2007.

The TPP currently accounts for 25.3 per cent of global merchandise trade and 24.7 per cent of global commercial services trade (Table 2.4). These shares make it a bigger entity than the EU in world trade, with the latter's shares being 15.5 per cent share in global merchandise trade and 22.9 per cent share in services trade.[8] The United States, Japan, Canada, Singapore and Mexico are the major TPP members, with significant shares in global merchandise trade; barring Mexico, and along with Australia, these economies, have significant shares in global services trade as well.[9] An interesting point to note in this regard is the bloc's having a greater share in global commercial service exports (25.5 per cent) than merchandise exports (23.5 per cent). This is primarily on account of the United States and Singapore, the two TPP members with relatively greater shares in commercial service exports than service imports (Table 2.4). On the other hand, the greater share of the TPP in world merchandise imports is also primarily due to the United States' greater share in these imports vis-à-vis exports (Table 2.4). As a whole, the US prominence in services trade has made the TPP bloc a net exporter of services, while it is a net importer of merchandise. This is structurally similar to the characteristics of the EU, which is also a net exporter of services and a net importer of merchandise. It is also noteworthy that the inclusion of China in the TPP may alter its structural characteristic given China's large share in global merchandise trade.

One of the implications of being a net exporter of commercial services is the importance being attached by the TPP to issues involving trade in services. Unlike trade in goods, where market access is often a function of tariffs, trade in services entails determination of market access by domestic regulations in spe-cific sectors on various occasions. Regulations governing the establishment of foreign banks and entry of foreign workers are pertinent examples. The thrust on market access in services has led to the TPP's strong focus on addressing 'behind the border' handicaps to trade in addition to border measures like tariffs and technical barriers. The thrust, again, reflects the United States' offensive export

Table 2.4 TPP members in world merchandise and commercial services trade

Member	Merchandise trade (%)			Commercial services trade (%)		
	Export	*Import*	*Trade*	*Export*	*Import*	*Trade*
Australia	1.5	1.3	1.4	1.2	1.5	1.4
Brunei	0.1	0.0	0.0	0.0	0.0	0.0
Canada	2.5	2.5	2.5	1.8	2.5	2.2
Chile	0.5	0.4	0.4	0.3	0.4	0.3
Japan	4.5	4.6	4.6	3.4	4.2	3.8
Malaysia	1.2	1.0	1.1	0.8	1.0	0.9
Mexico	1.9	2.0	1.9	0.4	0.6	0.5
New Zealand	0.2	0.2	0.2	0.2	0.3	0.3
Peru	0.3	0.2	0.2	0.1	0.2	0.1
Singapore	2.2	2.0	2.1	3.1	2.9	3.0
United States	8.1	12.3	10.2	13.9	10.0	12.0
Vietnam	0.5	0.6	0.6	0.2	0.3	0.3
Total	23.5	27.1	25.3	25.5	23.8	24.7

Source: WTO.

interests given its strong comparative advantages in global commercial service exports. Several other members in the TPP, including Japan, have either greater comparative advantages or relatively greater shares in merchandise trade, and are therefore likely to have offensive interests in market access in goods. The United States and Singapore are the only TPP members that are net exporters of services, while all the rest are net importers. Other major TPP economies including the United States, Canada, Japan and Mexico, are net importers of goods as well, though the United States is a far bigger importer and has a larger trade deficit in goods than the rest. Despite some being net importers, the shares in global merchandise exports and trade for almost all the TPP members excluding the United States and Singapore, are larger than in services trade. It is therefore natural that the United States' offensive interests in obtaining greater market access in services in other TPP member economies is being traded off vis-à-vis similar demands for goods in the US market from other economies (e.g. New Zealand's demand for greater access in the US dairy market might be secured in return for its complying with stronger IP rules in drug pricing and patenting software[10]).

A closer look at the structural features of the merchandise and services trades of the TPP members reveals more on the natures of individual comparative advantages, their influences on negotiations and the evolving framework of the TPP agreement. Some of the members – New Zealand, Chile, Australia, Malaysia, Canada and Vietnam – are significant exporters of agricultural products (Table 2.5). Obtaining greater access in agricultural markets of other members, as expected, has been a key focus of these countries, with almost all of them eyeing greater access particularly in the US market in sugar, nuts, fruits, seafood and dairy. Similar demands for greater access are being raised for the protected

Table 2.5 TPP members – structural features of merchandise and commercial services trade (Shares in %)

Member	Export merchandise trade			Import merchandise trade		
	Agriculture	Fuel and mining	Manufacture	Agriculture	Fuel and mining	Manufacture
Australia	12.6	59.0	10.5	5.8	18.9	69.1
Brunei	0.1	96.4	3.3	17.2	3.0	79.3
Canada	13.3	34.1	45.1	8.1	15.2	72.2
Chile	23.4	61.8	13.0	8.0	26.5	65.5
Japan	1.3	4.6	88.2	11.2	40.1	47.0
Malaysia	17.1	20.2	62.0	11.3	17.4	69.2
Mexico	6.6	19.8	70.7	8.3	13.0	76.5
New Zealand	63.9	9.0	22.0	11.1	19.2	66.0
Peru	17.0	49.5	10.6	11.8	16.7	70.7
Singapore	2.5	21.0	68.3	3.8	34.4	60.1
United States	11.4	12.5	65.3	6.1	23.1	67.2
Vietnam	22.9	11.6	64.0	12.3	15.9	68.9

Member	Export commercial services trade			Import commercial services trade		
	Transport	Travel	Other services	Transport	Travel	Other services
Australia	10.7	61.8	27.5	26.1	45.2	28.7
Brunei	49.4	27.8	22.8	36.6	39.3	24.2
Canada	18.1	22.4	59.5	23.5	33.2	43.3
Chile	59.7	15.1	25.2	58.4	16.9	24.7
Japan	26.9	7.7	65.4	29.9	16.5	53.7
Malaysia	13.9	52.3	33.8	34.9	27.5	37.6
Mexico	5.6	77.6	16.9	48.3	31.2	20.6
New Zealand	20.0	55.3	24.7	28.1	31.9	40.0
Peru	22.2	59.1	18.7	42.2	21.2	36.6
Singapore	28.8	14.8	56.4	29.3	17.8	52.9
United States	13.6	25.8	60.7	21.6	21.9	56.5
Vietnam	28.6	64.1	7.3	70.3	14.6	15.1

Source: WTO.

Japanese market in agriculture. While Malaysia and Vietnam have some major agricultural exports, they also maintain tariffs for protecting domestic producers and are facing demands for lowering these tariffs. Agriculture negotiations have been consuming considerable time and energy in the TPP, with most contested decisions on tariff cuts and exemptions pertaining to agriculture products. On the other hand, economies with greater reliance on natural resource exports such as Australia, Chile, Canada and Peru are bargaining for greater tariff cuts on fuel and mining imports. Mexico's offensive interest in manufacturing exports would urge it to seek greater access over and above what is available through the NAFTA in the US and Canadian markets, and new access in the Asian markets. Japan, Malaysia, Vietnam and Singapore – the Asian economies – are predominantly manufacturing exporters and would look forward to preferential access in the US and NAFTA markets, wherever they do not have bilateral FTAs. The market accesses eventually sanctioned and exemptions accommodated by the TPP would depend significantly upon the extent by which countries are able to persuade domestic constituencies opposed to tariff cuts, such as the Japanese agriculture and automobile lobbies and sugar and textile manufacturers in the United States.

Structural aspects of commercial services trade also play decisive roles in determining country positions on market access. As mentioned earlier, the United States' offensive interests urge it to seek greater access in various services, of which telecommunication and financial services are its particular interests, given the globally prominent positions it enjoys in their exports. The United States, as well as Japan, Canada and Singapore, given their proficiencies in other commercial service exports, demand greater access to member country markets in financial and telecom services (Table 2.5). These, however, may not be easy for other members to concede, particularly those having large SOEs. There could also be sharp differences of opinion on opening up domestic transport sectors including shipping and maritime services. The United States' efforts to secure greater access for its innovation and knowledge-intensive service exports, such as software and entertainment products, and safeguarding their comparative advantages, has also resulted in IP rules occupying a prominent part of the negotiating agenda. IP provisions, more on which are discussed later in this chapter, have been among the most controversial issues at the TPP.

The heterogeneity among the TPP members is also driven home by the differences in human development levels. As expected from a collective comprising diverse economies – high-income OECD countries including some from the rich G8 club (United States, Japan, Canada; Australia and New Zealand are OECD but not in the G8); high-income non-OECD nations (Singapore, Brunei); middle-income countries (Chile, Malaysia, Mexico); and relatively lower-income economies (Peru, Vietnam) – the human development indicators vary widely, ranging from countries ranking among the top ten in human development (Australia, United States, New Zealand, Japan) to those among the top 60 and 70 (Mexico, Malaysia, Peru) and beyond the top 100 (Vietnam).[11] Like the structural characteristics of an individual member country's external trades, human development levels also influence postures in TPP negotiations, given the protection demanded by local industries and producers for preserving economic prospects and supporting jobs – demands that lower human development economies can hardly overlook due to lack of adequate social security coverage and safety nets for vulnerable populations.

Structural features and issues

Outline

The TPP is being negotiated as 'a landmark, 21st-century trade agreement, setting a new standard for global trade and incorporating next-generation issues that will boost the competitiveness of TPP countries in the global economy'.[12] Following the failure to meet the deadline at the APEC leaders meeting in Hawaii in November 2011, the leaders of nine countries negotiating the TPP announced the broad outlines of the framework on the sidelines of the APEC meeting on 12 November 2011.[13] Canada, Mexico and Japan have since joined the TPP negotiations. While their entries will influence the substantive negotiations, the overall framework is unlikely to change. The agreement aims to achieve the following:

1   Comprehensive market access by removing tariffs and other barriers to trade in goods and services and also in investments.
2   Facilitate the development of supply chains among TPP members.
3   Build on the existing work of the APEC and other forums by incorporating in the TPP specific cross-cutting issues like regulatory coherence across members, competitiveness and business facilitation, addressing the concerns of small and medium enterprises (SMEs) in using trade agreements effectively and strengthening institutional capacities for meeting development priorities in member countries.
4   Promote trade and investment in innovative products and services, including those related to the digital economy and green technologies.
5   Equipping and updating the agreement for addressing future issues as well as new issues emerging out of expanding the agreement to new countries.

The TPP aims to expand and develop on the P4 framework agreement. The United States and other negotiating members take the P4 framework as broadly representative of a 'twenty-first century trade agreement'. There is little doubt that the P4 agreement is far more exhaustive than other FTAs in the region, particularly the ASEAN FTAs, given its comprehensive coverage of goods including agriculture and the commitment to negotiate financial services and investment. The TPP negotiations though have gone well beyond the scope of the P4 deal by taking on several 'next-generation issues', as will be discussed later, and also by pushing for a more 'binding' deal with stricter dispute settlement and enforcement measures. Both in terms of the new issues, as well as the binding approach, the United States' FTA with South Korea (KORUS), in force from 15 March 2012, is being taken as the benchmark for negotiations. As the USTR notes: 'As the first US FTA with a North Asian partner, the KORUS FTA is a model for trade agreements for the rest of the region, and underscores the US commitment to, and engagement in, the Asia-Pacific region'.[14]

Open annexation

The original P4 agreement was keen on expanding its membership, and accordingly had an accession clause enabling 'any APEC economy or other state' to join the framework on mutually agreeable terms.[15] The clause further specified that accession would proceed after considering the circumstances of the 'new' economy, particularly with respect to the schedule of its liberalization. To an extent, the ambition for expanding the TPP club, albeit with the eventual objective of creating a FTAAP, is implicit in the broad framework of the TPP outlined on 12 November 2011 through its 'Living Agreement' feature: 'to enable the updating of the agreement as appropriate to address trade issues that emerge in the future as well as new issues that arise with the expansion of the agreement to include new countries'.[16] Expansion of the TPP is also a distinct US priority: 'The United States and its negotiating partners share a vision for the TPP based on the long-term objective of expanding the group to additional countries across the Asia-Pacific', as emphasized in the US trade policy agenda.[17]

Including accession clauses in RTAs can be tricky. Some members might feel that such a clause facilitates 'back door' entry of other 'like-minded' parties into the group on non-economic strategic grounds; otherwise too, leaving open the option of taking on more members is usually not a preferred choice among parties to an RTA, as the addition of new members spreads the preferential access benefits wider over a group of countries, diluting the 'exclusivity' in the process. It is not clear yet whether the final version of the TPP agreement will contain exactly the same accession clause as in the P4. But an accession clause is expected enabling other countries to join if they satisfy the eligibility criteria; indeed retention of the 'other state' category in the accession clause in addition to APEC states, as in the P4 agreement, will enable non-APEC countries to become part of what is till now a pure APEC sub-group. While this might encourage non-APEC countries like India, notwithstanding the open accession clause, entry of new members and the scope of expanding membership might be limited given the high entry prices of exhaustive trade liberalization and 'WTO plus' commitments that would be demanded from new members (Schott *et al.* 2013). Nonetheless, the clause is expected to remain in the TPP given the commitment of key stakeholders like the United States to make it a broader regional pact and a 'Living Agreement'.

Coverage

The TPP is unprecedented in its ambitious sweep and coverage of issues. The ambitious sweep is consistent with the US effort to arrive at a 'high quality twenty-first century' trade agreement with a group of like-minded trade partners as committed as itself to trade liberalization. The TPP is not only far wider than the WTO framework in scope and coverage, but also, in several respects, more ambitious than several bilateral FTAs signed by the United States, including with some of the TPP members. As evident from the framework outlined earlier, the TPP has gone well beyond the usual coverage of traditional FTAs in the degree of comprehensive market access it aims to achieve in trade in goods, services and cross-border investment, along with the focus on cross-cutting trade issues and new challenges for global trade. The agreement discusses 29 chapters and has more than 20 negotiating groups finalizing legal texts on competition policy, capacity-building, cross-border services, customs laws and procedures, e-commerce, environment, financial services, government procurement, IP, investment, labour, rules of origin (ROOs), legal administration of the framework, sanitary and phytosanitary standards (SPS), technical barriers to trade (TBT), telecommunications, temporary entry provisions, trade remedies for addressing member rights and obligations, textiles and apparel and market access in goods.

At the core of market access negotiations are the TPP's attempts to streamline and eliminate tariffs on around 11,000 tariff lines for improving market access in goods. Along with tariffs, the TPP is focusing on the removal of non-tariff measures (NTMs) obstructing market access. Most of the NTMs comprise SPS and TBT. While the former are regulations by host countries for enhancing food safety and animal and plant health, the latter pertain to domestic regulations involving standards and procedures for protecting the health and safety of consumers and the environment. For SPS and TBT, the TPP wants to build upon and enforce the rights provided under the WTO, implement them uniformly and coherently across the TPP countries and induct appropriate scientific knowledge and advancements in framing the quality standards. SPS measures are often the subject of disputes between countries due to their adverse effects on trade, and the TPP aims to minimize such possibilities. The negotiations have also focused on framing common ROOs for enabling efficient determination of the 'origin' of the product for availing preferential tariffs by member country producers and enhancing efficiencies of supply chains across the bloc.

Services comprise an important part of the TPP negotiations. The core objective is to eradicate various barriers affecting trade in services, irrespective of the mode of service provision,[18] and to institute laws governing foreign investments in the member countries in ways that ensure non-discriminatory treatment for foreign investors. The TPP also aims to maximize the security of foreign investments and to protect investors by proposing effective dispute mechanisms. These aims, however, – as discussed later – have become controversial as they result in allowing foreign investors greater scope for arbitrating against host country governments. For cross-border services, the goal is to secure 'fair, open and transparent' markets, with negotiations proceeding on the basis of the 'negative list' approach. A 'negative list' approach is a more liberal framework than the conventional 'positive list' method: the former assumes a series of rules to be applicable for all services and the same degree of market access in all, unless some services are specifically mentioned in a negative list. The latter assumes the application of specific rules and market access commitments in only those services that are specifically mentioned in schedules of commitments by countries. Specific attention is being devoted to market access in telecommunications and financial services, which, as mentioned earlier, are sectors of offensive interest for the United States and other major service exporters in the TPP. Talks on financial services are aiming to create new market opportunities and are also emphasizing on protecting the rights of financial regulators for safeguarding efficient functioning of financial markets. Telecom talks are focusing on increasing access of telecom service providers across the TPP countries for enhancing the choices for consumers and the competitiveness of businesses.

Among the ambitious and controversial aspects of the TPP negotiations are the IP issues, more on which is discussed later. While agreeing to develop and enforce the IP obligations under the WTO, the specifics of patent, copyright, trademark and geographical indications (GIs) are being discussed by the TPP for implementing a common set of IP rules across member countries for safeguarding inventions and knowledge. Negotiations are also focusing on traditional knowledge, generic resources and enforcement. IP is one of the areas where negotiations are likely to be prolonged, with members having radically different postures on several issues.

All the issues mentioned so far are 'WTO plus' issues: these are issues that figure in the multilateral rule-based system administered by the WTO, but have continued to evolve, primarily due to the complexities surrounding them and the difficulty of achieving consensus among members. The TPP's objectives on these 'WTO plus' issues – cutting tariffs on goods, removing NTMs and streamlining SPS and TBT, creating greater market access in cross-border services, determining new IP rules, fixing common ROOs and value addition norms, and trade remedies for addressing the rights and obligations of members – involve scaling-up on the existing commitments of the members at the WTO. In addition, the TPP is also considering 'WTO extra' issues, which are currently beyond the WTO's mandate.[19] These include financial services, SOEs, competition policy, environment, labour standards, government procurement, customs laws and e-commerce (Palit 2013b). As mentioned earlier, the KORUS FTA is serving as a benchmark for TPP negotiations on the WTO plus and extra issues. The FTA has provisions for addressing market access commitments in several services, including financial services, and also has significant provisions on competition policy, labour, environment and government procurement.

An important part of the 'WTO plus' issues being discussed by the TPP is competition policy. Though competition policy was originally a part of the WTO, it was subsequently dropped, making it, more appropriately, a 'WTO extra' issue.

The focus of competition policy negotiations is on arriving at a common framework for business laws and regulations among members that will correct the competition-distorting impact of extant corporate laws. Competitiveness and business facilitation, as mentioned before, is a critical component of the TPP, as outlined in the framework announced on 12 November 2011; the thrust of the competition text in the agreement is also on establishing and maintaining laws and authorities adequately qualified and equipped for achieving competitiveness objectives. Competition policies, again, are controversial as they have significant impacts on roles of SOEs in TPP member countries. These are discussed at length in Chapters 5 and 6 with respect to the complex political economy they create in China and India and the gaps that both countries have, right now, in their current regulations compared with the expected TPP standards.

Environment talks – another specific 'WTO extra' issue being discussed threadbare – are directed at extracting prohibitive commitments from members in flouting environment and pollution norms citing trade and investment grounds, defraying from illegal logging and trade in endangered species and incorporating binding dispute settlement provisions enabling producers to challenge member states roles in preserving environment norms; the latter provision, as expected, has generated considerable controversy (Schott *et al.* 2013; Fergusson *et al.* 2013). The chapter on labour, similar to environment, emphasizes on the protection of rights, by getting members to agree on appropriate workplace practices and employability concerns. Similar to environment, differences in opinion among negotiating members and concerns of various stakeholders including civil society have been aroused over the proposed enforcement of rights. The main concerns in this respect are over whether deviations from complying with environment and labour standards should be subject to the same dispute settlement provisions as commercial matters.

Along with labour and environment, another WTO extra issue being widely debated and discussed is government procurement. Procurement markets of states in different countries are not only large, but are also characterized by discriminatory preferences towards various business and interest groups. As discussed in Chapters 5 and 6, discriminatory preferences in procurement are prevalent in China and India, making this a difficult issue for both countries to tackle in their RTA negotiations. Breaking into these 'reserved' markets in the TPP member countries is an important objective of the TPP; the 12 November 2011 outline also specifies: 'Government procurement packages are being negotiated with each country seeking to broaden coverage to ensure the maximum access to each other's government procurement markets, while recognizing each other's sensitivities'.[20] The objective is easier stated than implemented. Finally, with respect to e-commerce, another new generation trade issue, the TPP's aim is to reduce customs duties on digital products and services and expedite electronic transactions across member countries by authenticating them. The customs procedures, on the other hand, are focusing on simplification and harmonization for the effective growth and coordination of supply chains across members.

One of the biggest challenges for the TPP pertains to the cross-cutting issue of achieving regulatory convergence among members. This follows from the TPP's urge to address 'behind the border' issues impeding market access – again a fallout of the emphasis on enhancing market access in services. Minimizing obstructions created by differences among domestic regulations in member countries, arguably 'behind the border' factors augmenting trade costs and affecting the competitiveness of exporters, is expected to facilitate the seamless movement of goods and services among members. Achieving regulatory convergence across the enormously wide range of issues being discussed by the TPP is indeed a phenomenal challenge, not only in terms of harmonization and the alignment of rules, but also in overcoming conflicts between various interest groups and domestic constituencies. The next section focuses on some of these conflicts, which might eventually result in the TPP settling for more modest standards than what it aspires to.

Will ambitions materialize?

Prolonged and difficult negotiations highlight the problems in achieving the 'gold standard' the TPP is aspiring to. Most of the problems arise from the widely divergent views of members on various issues and the pressures being exerted by domestic interest groups on country negotiators for both offensive and defensive interests. While the eventual TPP template will indicate to what extent host country negotiators and governments have achieved issue-based convergence by resisting (or yielding to) domestic influences, the possibility of the TPP being far more 'accommodative' than it had set out to be is distinct. This section discusses some of the aspects of the ongoing negotiations that are likely to stunt the TPP's ambitions.

Suboptimal negotiating structure

The TPP emphasized on 'no exceptions', and the exhaustive elimination of barriers to market access as a necessary condition for achieving gold standard (Elms 2012). With respect to trade in goods, the emphasis implies minimizing special and differential (S&D) treatment by discouraging countries from exempting 'sensitive' products from tariff cuts, and the maintenance of long phase-out periods for tariff reduction on specific items. Minimizing S&D provisions would have been conceptually and operationally easier to implement had the TPP decided to develop a composite tariff schedule, dictating tariff phase-outs for all members. This, however, appears unlikely, with key tariff negotiations taking place between the United States and the five countries with whom it does not have bilateral FTAs (Brunei, New Zealand, Malaysia and Vietnam and now Japan); for the rest, the United States has decided to take the tariff commitments in its existing FTAs as the benchmark market access. By deciding not to re-open the earlier FTAs, the United States has deviated from the holistic negotiating approach proposed by other members such as Australia, New Zealand and

Singapore, who preferred negotiating a unified market access deal (Lewis 2011): the reluctance to revisit exemptions in existing FTAs is largely due to defensive concerns.

The rather odd negotiating structure permitting parallel bilateral FTA-style negotiations within a broader multi-country framework immediately encourages drift from the desired gold standard of a common schedule with zero tariffs across a wide range of goods for all members (Elms 2012). By accepting market access in existing US FTAs as sacrosanct, the TPP is legitimizing the exceptions therein, such as for sugar in the US–Australia FTA. The success of domestic protectionist interests in the United States (discussed in more detail later) in stalling re-negotiations has cast serious doubts on the ability of the TPP to minimize exemptions as such (Solis 2012).

Sensitivities on agriculture

The negotiations have been experiencing strong pressure to expand the scope of S&D treatment, particularly in agriculture. As mentioned earlier, several TPP members – Australia, New Zealand, Canada, Chile, Malaysia, Vietnam and even some of the US agribusinesses and processed food manufacturers – have interests in bringing down agricultural tariffs in TPP markets. Countries like Canada, Mexico and Vietnam also maintain high tariffs on agriculture imports and have product-specific defensive interests. Contrasting interests have complicated negotiations in market access on agriculture, which have compounded after Japan's entry. Japan has traditionally maintained high tariffs on agriculture imports (applied average MFN tariff of 23.3 per cent) and allows duty-free access to only 46.3 per cent of its total agricultural imports (WTO 2012). Domestic farmer lobbies in Japan are virulently opposed to its entry in the TPP and lowering tariffs on farm imports. The influential Central Union of Agricultural Cooperatives (JA-Zenchu) has urged for maintaining protection on agriculture by insisting on higher import tariffs and excluding sensitive items from tariff cuts.[21] The unhappiness of key domestic constituencies indicates the Japanese government's inability to achieve consensus over Japan's joining the TPP; discontent over the decision remains even after Japan's formal entry, pointing to the challenges that Japan and other members including the United States will encounter in limiting S&D treatment for agriculture. Indeed, S&D treatment delayed Canada's entry at the TPP, given the protection it extends to domestic dairy and poultry products and Canada's initial efforts to seek exemption from cutting tariffs on these products (Elms and Lim 2012).

Agriculture symbolizes both offensive and defensive interests of the United States in market access negotiations, which is evident from its refusal to grant concessions on several farm products in its bilateral FTAs, while demanding greater access from partners (Lewis 2011). From well before Japan's entry in the TPP, agriculture negotiations became complicated over New Zealand's demand for greater access to the US dairy market and the resistance of the US dairy industry to such access, due to its perception of the monopolistic advantage enjoyed by the New Zealand dairy giant Fonterra on account of its command over the domestic milk procurement market in New Zealand. These defensive interests of the US dairy industry are in contrast to its offensive interests in prying open the Japanese and Canadian dairy markets. Further complications are created by sugar, where domestic producers in Australia are demanding the re-opening of negotiations for obtaining greater access in the US domestic market, as such access was not allowed in the US–Australia FTA. The United States also has offensive interests in lowering tariffs on rice imports in TPP members such as Vietnam, Malaysia and Japan, who would prefer rice to be exempted from tariff cuts. The conflicting interests produced by contrasting positions might constrain far-reaching liberalization in agriculture.

Bilateral trade-offs

Complications on achieving exhaustive liberalization in market access in goods extend beyond agriculture to textiles, apparel and footwear. The latter symbolize the significance of specific bilateral negotiations within the larger multilateral framework of the TPP and the imbalance created by a clash of offensive and defensive interests. Vietnam's strongest offensive interest in the TPP negoti-ations is getting preferential access in the textiles, apparel and footwear market in the United States, for which, it is demanding lower tariffs and simpler ROOs. Peak tariffs in the US market on textiles and footwear are currently more than 30 per cent; furthermore, the US insistence on 'yarn forward' ROOs makes it imperative for textile and footwear manufacturers to procure all their raw material and intermediate imports from within the preference zone (TPP in this case) for availing the benefits of cheap tariffs (Elms 2012; Schott *et al.* 2013). Vietnam is opposed to the proposal and is demanding preferential tariff benefits on textile materials obtained from outside the TPP as otherwise it might lose its competitiveness, which is partly due to its access to cheaper raw material. The US domestic textile and footwear firms are opposed to Vietnam's demands as they apprehend a loss of market share from cheaper Vietnamese exports. The eventual compromise by the United States on textile tariffs and more liberal ROOs will probably depend on the extent by which Vietnam lowers its own tariffs on agriculture imports, as well as its commitments in services, investment and SOEs.

While Japan's entry in the TPP has reduced its internal economic imbalance, it has also added new dynamics to the negotiations. Earlier the bulk of market access talks took place between the United States and its four non-FTA partners (Brunei, Malaysia, New Zealand and Vietnam). Japan is the fifth non-FTA partner and the most significant in economic size. Japan's relatively late entry in the negotiations might result in the re-negotiation of earlier issues. It can also initiate discussions on outstanding issues in the US–Japan bilateral trade, such as automobiles. Producers on both sides are unhappy over the restricted access they have in each other's automobile markets. While Japanese car imports face high tariffs in the US market, American cars encounter various NTMs, such as quotas under the Preferential Handling Procedure (PHP) programme, standards, certification and 'green' technology norms. Both countries have agreed to resolve these issues bilaterally parallel to the TPP negotiations. The United States is also keen on obtaining greater access in Japan's postal delivery and insurance market and the removal of barriers caused by SPS measures, competition policy, government procurement and IP, all of which, again, are being addressed bilaterally.[22] Automobiles have featured in market access talks between the United States and Malaysia too, particularly Malaysia's preferential policies towards local producers. Other issues dominating the US–Malaysia bilateral talks in the TPP include Malaysia's high tariffs on sensitive agricultural imports, food certification requirements and entry barriers in the government procurement market. With sizeable parts of the TPP negotiations dictated by bilateral contentions between the United States and its non-FTA partners, the final agreement is likely to end up with specific bilateral commitment schedules on various issues; the latter would most likely have exemptions and varying liberalization commitments inducing deviation from the high base set by the TPP.

IP irreconcilabilities

Agreeing on uniform IP rules is proving to be tough, given the deep divide between the United States and several other members on the subject. Many TPP countries (including Canada, Chile, Mexico, Peru and Vietnam) have been on the USTR's Watch List reflecting US concerns over weaknesses in their national IP regulations and enforcement.[23] Two Asian TPP Members – Brunei and Malaysia – have been removed from the USTR's Watch List since the TPP negotiations began, on account of their efforts to increase IP protection and enforcement. Canada, which was earlier on the Priority Watch List, has been brought down to the less sensitive Watch List. Chile is the only TPP member to figure on the Priority Watch List now: the list also includes Thailand, a potential entrant, and China and India. There is hardly any member in the current TPP bloc with whom the United States has not had issues over IP, except possibly Australia and Singapore. Vietnam has been identified for counterfeiting and piracy issues, particularly Internet piracy; such concerns have been flagged for Peru too. Both Peru and Chile remain on the USTR Watch List, despite being FTA partners of the United States, indicating the divide that continues to exist between the United States and countries with which it has formal bilateral agreements.

As a net exporter of IP and with offensive interests in services, the United States is keen on implementing IP rules in the TPP that not only guarantee greater protection than the Trade-Related Intellectual Property Rights (TRIPS) agreement of the WTO, but also than some of the US FTAs. Several US industries, whose comparative advantages are significantly determined by the degree of protection on their IP, are pressurizing for the TPP to achieve 'gold standard' by making it take on IP rules that are significantly TRIPs plus.[24] Introducing such rules is exceedingly difficult given the differences in perspectives between members on what should be the rational and optimal degree of IP protection in a RTA framework, as well as on the necessary regulatory changes that such protection shall ordain, particularly in enforcement.

The IP proposals of the TPP, as gleaned through various leaked texts, and the flavour and content of IP provisions in some of the recent US FTAs, like the KORUS, have strong implications for the global pharmaceutical industry, digital and entertainment products and Internet management. They also have implications for innovation efforts in developing countries. Many of the proposed rules such as longer patent terms for compensating delays in obtaining patents, long data exclusivity periods for new products and rights to 'evergreen', patent registration linkage enabling holders to act against introduction of similar products, disallowing pre-grant opposition for patents, patentability rights to holders on new uses and forms of existing products, limited flexibilities for regulating medicine prices and empowering customs authorities to act hard against suspected infringements are measures difficult to accept and implement for various countries (Flynn *et al.* 2011). Similar problems exist with the TPP's copyright proposals given their implications on trade in digital and entertainment products. These rules also have consequences for Internet governance, particularly the use of Internet and cyberspace. The proposals are not only stronger than those in the TRIPS, but also in some respects stronger than the plurilateral Anti-Counterfeit Trade Agreement (ACTA) that includes the United States and some other TPP members.[25] Restricting the reproduction of all copyrighted material, including the temporary storage of electronic data, allowing copyright owners the right to block parallel trade, extending copyright life terms, acting on the circumvention of technologies regardless of intent to infringe, and empowering customs to act on suspected counterfeits without formal complaints, are strong measures with considerable repercussions for several national regulations and users of IP-intensive products and services.

With the US views over the 'twenty-first century' content of IP rules being rather different from the corresponding views held by the other TPP members, including OECD countries like Canada and New Zealand, the divergence over IP in TPP is not just symbolic of different perceptions between the developed and developing countries, or the more colloquial 'North–South' gulf; it is reflective of a tussle between the American and non-American postures, with the former significantly shaped and influenced by domestic business interests, particularly the digital and entertainment product lobbies, pursuing large market access opportunities through the TPP. These interests are ingrained as top priorities in the United States' current international trade negotiations, such as the KORUS FTA following the executive directions provided by the Congress on the negotiating contents for WTO plus and WTO extra issues in the 10 May 2007 agreement (discussed in later chapters). While the eventual IP rules adopted by the TPP will reveal to what extent varying postures and views have been accommodated, excessive IP protection can be counterproductive by not being trade-enhancing and by discouraging innovation and creativity (Frankel

2012); as of now, several non-US TPP members appear to be subscribing, at least partially, to this cynical view.

Divide over new generation issues

The quest for accommodating new generation issues – competition policy, treatment of SOEs, government procurement, labour and environment – have, expectedly, created hurdles in taking forward negotiations. Like IP and services, these issues pertain to substantive changes that negotiating members need to implement in their domestic regulations. They also impinge on the discriminatory preferences that many countries have maintained for specific interest groups due to social, political and economic reasons. Furthermore, as discussed with respect to China and India later, these issues hardly figure in the FTA negotiations of most Asian countries; Asian TPP members like Malaysia and Vietnam, and also Japan in some respect, are not comfortable in negotiating these issues due to their lack of experiences.

Competition policy negotiations are intricately linked to the treatment of SOEs. In Malaysia and Vietnam, as well as Singapore, government-linked companies (GLCs) play prominent roles in the national economies. These are investment companies controlled by the federal government. At the same time, SOEs, directly owned by the state are often major producers and consumers in host country economies like Vietnam. For economies like the latter, as much as for China, and partly India, it is difficult to agree to reforming competition laws for diluting the prominence of these enterprises, given their key roles in supplying public goods, developing and maintaining strategic industries critical for national security like defence and energy, the employments they provide and the political influence they wield in determining national economic policies. Closely connected to the treatment of SOEs and competition policy are reforms proposed in government procurement. Again, in TPP economies with large state sectors, procurements by SOEs and government agencies and departments are substantive. Governments often employ procurements for extending discriminatory incentives to preferred groups, like the 'Bumiputra's in Malaysia.[26] Even if Malaysia eventually agrees to open up government procurement, it will be reluctant to withdraw selective preferences; for SOEs too, it has sought flexibilities.[27] Vietnam is also likely to seek exemptions in government procurement and treatment of SOEs. In this respect, the divergence between the US perspective and those of several other TPP members is evident from the fact that the United States, Japan and Singapore are the only TPP members that have acceded to the Government Procurement Agreement (GPA) of the WTO, with New Zealand planning to do so soon. Some US FTAs with TPP members do have provisions on competition policy, procurement and SOEs. But exporting the same content and flavour to the TPP is not easy, and the structural and institutional characteristics of some members might act as significant constraints.

On labour and environment again, the US insistence on the TPP members agreeing to ratify and uphold various multilateral agreements on both issues that the members are signatories to, and ensuring commitments through binding dispute settlement mechanisms, have caused considerable discomfort. There are concerns that failures to enforce commitments on protecting labour and environment rights might be construed as trade barriers and invite retaliatory action. The United States though is unlikely to soften its emphasis given the sensitivity of labour and environment issues for the Congressional Democrats (Capling and Ravenhill 2011). Recent US FTAs such as those with Peru and South Korea make the failure to enforce labour and environment standards subject to generic dispute settlement mechanisms, as applicable for commercial matters. The US insistence on imparting identical 'binding' characteristics to labour and environment rules in the TPP would amount to substantive 'meddling' in national regulations and widen the perspective gap between the United States and other countries on these subjects.

Dispute over settling disputes

Groups within the United States itself have been debating the virtues of including a strong ISD settlement provision, which allows investors from a member country to raise claims against other member governments. The controversy has been intense, with even an OECD member such as Australia asking for exemption from the provision. Australian companies have invoked ISD provisions in bilateral investment treaties (BITs) to initiate arbitration against developing countries,[28] but the country's reservations on the provisions have been significantly accentuated after the tobacco manufacturer Phillip Morris, under the Australia–Hong Kong BIT, challenged the Australian government's tobacco regulation of 2011. While quasi-nationalist concerns over investor biases in ISD provisions empowering foreign investors to impinge on sovereign decisions, albeit partially, have been agitating several members, there are also worries over strong ISD rules making national regulators overtly cautious in pronouncing new laws apprehending legal action on what might be deemed expropriation (Schott *et al.* 2013). Indeed, the ISD is another example of the 'binding' thrust of the TPP on tough dispute settlement measures in investment, competition policy, labour and environment. The proposed measures are radical enough to not only produce intense debates, but also fears among members over becoming part of an agreement that might involve giving up far too much sovereign regulatory and policy space.

Final thoughts

The American entry in the P4 radically changed its economic weight and strategic significance. With the United States, the TPP, as an expanded edition of the P4, was no longer a barely noticeable sub-group of APEC countries attempting WTO plus trade liberalization.; it was a major forum for pursuing a plurilateral free trade agenda in the Asia-Pacific. With a range of exhaustive issues and membership expanding over time, the TPP, under US leadership, is 'perhaps the most ambitious trade negotiation underway in the world'[29] and 'a growing platform for regional economic integration'[30] in the Asia-Pacific. As more countries express interest in joining the TPP, the possibility of it creating a pan-regional template for integrating Asia-Pacific economies through the FTAAP is becoming more distinct.

The United States' sheer economic size compared with the rest of the TPP members has exerted considerable influence upon the issues being discussed and the nature of negotiations. The TPP's strong emphasis on removing market access barriers in services is primarily due to the United States' preeminent position in global services trade and as the world's largest exporter of commercial services. The comparative advantages of the United States in service production and exports have motivated it to seek greater market access in member country service sectors at a time when the US economy is desperately seeking solutions for long-term economic recovery. The urge for greater access has compounded the emphasis on removing 'behind the border' barriers to trade, making the TPP move into the sensitive turfs of domestic policies and regulations in contentious WTO plus and WTO extra areas like IP, government procurement, competition policies and SOEs. Indeed, for the United States and some other TPP members, the negotiations provide an opportunity for frontloading the agenda for global trade liberalization with WTO plus and extra issues. The United States has been unsuccessful in pushing these through at the WTO and has preferred inserting them in its bilateral FTAs, which are mostly with partners of much smaller economic size and significance in global trade. The United States' overarching influence on the TPP negotiations and their structuring are also evident from most critical negotiations on market access being conducted bilaterally between the United States and its non-FTA partners.

Entry of more members, particularly major economies from Asia like China and India will complicate negotiations due to greater divergence in perspectives on various issues. Japan's entry at a relatively advanced stage and its implications on negotiations is an example of the complications that can be expected. Apart from more divergent perspectives, the influence of specific bilateral talks on overall negotiations will increase as economies with larger sizes and strategic weights join the talks with the United States being forced to negotiate (or even re-negotiate) several issues. The problems being experienced over a clash of conflicting offensive and defensive interests produced by contrasting comparative advantages of member countries in specific areas will become even greater. The eventual outcome is likely to be a more 'sober' and moderate TPP, with toned down ambitions.

Larger membership and economic heterogeneity among members are therefore likely to be the deterrents to the TPP's ambition. Indeed, economic heterogeneity has been the most fundamental roadblock in taking forward the trade liberalization agenda in the Asia-Pacific, initially through voluntary liberalization consistent with open regionalism, and more recently in moving towards the FTAAP. The United States has little experience of negotiating FTAs with countries from Southeast and Northeast Asia, except Korea and Singapore.

Negotiating priorities are different for countries like Malaysia and Vietnam, which have large state sectors and relatively inward-looking domestic policies, compared with Korea and Singapore, which are among the most 'open' countries in the region and the world. Even Japan maintains far greater market access restrictions than Singapore and Korea. Japan, Malaysia, Vietnam and prospective TPP members like Thailand, China and India, are more accustomed to negotiating 'Asian' style FTAs and RTAs, largely influenced by the ASEAN FTAs. The latter, as discussed in greater detail later, focuses more on market access in goods and traditional trade issues (e.g. ROOs, disputes, NTMs), allows S&D treatment and maintenance of exceptions, and hardly covers WTO plus issues. Even Australia and New Zealand have fewer WTO plus and WTO extra issues in their FTAs and RTAs than the TPP. These issues are prominent in the US FTAs. As a result, gaps in the negotiating approach and issue-based perspectives between the United States and several TPP members are becoming increasingly wider. Countries with little experience in dealing with WTO plus issues are unable to convince and carry along domestic constituencies on many of these issues; they also tend to focus more on market access in goods. A larger TPP membership with more Asian countries will widen the negotiating gaps as many of the latter will be preoccupied with market access in goods and will have defensive interests in most WTO plus issues.

China and India's entries in the TPP will correct its economic imbalance, which, despite Japan's entry, is still biased towards the United States. This, though, has implications for the US strategy towards the TPP. Expanding the TPP to an FTAAP and probably an even bigger trans-regional trade compact has certain downsides that the United States is beginning to realize. First, as more powerful Asian economies come on board, the US dominance in steering the negotiations will ebb. Second, the inclusion of more countries will precipitate the divergence of core interests from those of the United States and might take the TPP in a direction that is sub-optimal from an US perspective and only partly reflective of what the United States would have wanted it to be. And finally, more countries and more intense parallel bilateral discussions would entail greater deployment of negotiating resources and energy. With the TTIP making progress and looming large on the US negotiating priorities, there would be difficult choices in distributing negotiating resources between the TTIP and TPP, an undesirable outcome of which, for the United States, would be the prospect of both attaining suboptimal outcomes.

Notes

1 'South Korea warms to idea of joining TPP trade group', *Financial Times*, 27 October 2013, online, available at: www.ft.com/intl/cms/s/0/e675c4d8–3c85–11e3-a8c4–00144feab7de.html#axzz2kUQCODKZ (accessed 13 November 2013).
2 'The New Zealand–Singapore–Chile–Brunei Darussalam Trans-Pacific Strategic Economic Partnership', New Zealand Ministry of Foreign Affairs and Trade, Wellington, New Zealand, October 2005, online, available at: www.mfat.govt.nz/downloads/trade-agreement/transpacific/trans-pacificbooklet.pdf (accessed 28 September 2013).

3 Under the TPA, the US president is authorized by the Congress to enter into bilateral trade agreements. Bills on these agreements pass through simpler legislative procedures under the TPA. The TPA expired in July 2007. See Tibung (2012) and Fergusson *et al.* (2013) for more details.
4 President Obama's comments at Suntory Hall, Tokyo, Japan on 14 November 2011. See Fergusson *et al.* (2013).
5 'The United States in the Trans-Pacific Partnership', Office of the United States Trade Representative; *Fact Sheets*, November 2011, online, available at: www.ustr.gov/about-us/press-office/fact-sheets/2011/november/united-states-trans-pacific-partnership (accessed 28 September 2013).
6 'Trans-Pacific Partnership Leaders Statement', Office of the United States Trade Representative; November 2011, online, available at: www.ustr.gov/about-us/press-office/press-releases/2011/november/trans-pacific-partnership-leaders-statement (accessed 28 September 2013).
7 Analysts regarding the TPP as an attempt to cultivate an 'anti-China' alliance would interpret Vietnam's entry as vindication of their stance.
8 Computed from WTO (2012).
9 Australia, Canada, Japan, Mexico, Singapore and the United States are ranked 21 and 19, 13 and 11, 4 and 4, 16 and 16, 14 and 15, 2 and 1 in global merchandise exports and imports, and 23 and 18, 18 and 12, 6 and 5, 43 and 34, 10 and 11, 1 and 1 in global commercial services exports and imports, respectively (WTO 2012). The estimates are inclusive of intra-EU trade and reflect ranks for 2011.
10 See Fergusson *et al.* (2013) for detailed discussion on the trade-off involved in market access talks for dairy.
11 Human Development Index (HDI), 2013, UNDP, online, available at: http://hdr.undp.org/en/media/HDR2013_EN_Summary.pdf (accessed 2 October 2013).
12 'Enhancing trade and investment, supporting jobs, economic growth and development: outlines of the Trans-Pacific Partnership Agreement', Office of the United States Trade Representative, online, available at: www.ustr.gov/about-us/press-office/fact-sheets/2011/november/outlines-trans-pacific-partnership-agreement.
13 Ibid.
14 'US–Korea Free Trade Agreement', Office of the United States Trade Representative (USTR), online, available at: www.ustr.gov/trade-agreements/free-trade-agreements/korus-fta (accessed 3 October 2013).
15 *Trans-Pacific Strategic Economic Partnership Agreement*, Chapter 20, Article 20.6, pp. 20–22, online, available at: www.mfat.govt.nz/downloads/trade-agreement/trans-pacific/main-agreement.pdf (accessed 1 October 2013).
16 As in Note 12 above.
17 'Bilateral and regional negotiations and agreements', ch. 3, p. 151; 2013 Trade Policy Agenda and 2012 Annual Report, Office of the United States Trade Representative (USTR) online, available at: www.ustr.gov/sites/default/files/Chapter%20III%20-%20Bilateral%20and%20Regional%20Negotiations%20and%20Agreements.pdf(accessed 2 October 2013).
18 The GATS of the WTO specifies four modes of service supply: cross-border (mode 1), consumption abroad (mode 2), commercial presence (mode 3) and presence of a natural person (mode 4).
19 See Horn *et al.* (2009) for distinction between 'WTO plus' and 'WTO extra' issues in the context of US and EU FTAs. Overlaps occur between the two categories in some issues such as IP and government procurement.
20 As in Note 12 above.
21 'Japanese agricultural group head submits comment to USTR, urging TPP members to treat agriculture as an exception', *Japan Agri News*, 6 June 2013; http://english.agrinews.co.jp/?p=387 (accessed 28 September 2013).
22 'Fact sheet: Non tariff measures: US consultations with Japan', Office of the United

States Trade Representative (USTR), online, available at: www.ustr.gov/about-us/press-office/fact-sheets/2013/april/non-tariff-measures-consultations-japan (accessed 3 October 2013).

23 The USTR Special 301 Report has a 'Priority Watch List' and a 'Watch List'. While both include countries that according to the USTR have specific problems with respect to IP protection, enforcement and market access for users and holders of IP, the Priority Watch List countries are the 'focus of increased bilateral attention concerning the problem areas'. '2013 Special 301 Report', Annex 1, p. 57, Acting United States Trade Representative Demetrios Marantis, Office of the United States Trade Representative, May 2013, online, available at: www.ustr.gov/sites/default/files/05012013%202013%20Special%20301%20Report.pdf (accessed 3 October 2013).

24 The Information Technology and Innovation Foundation (ITIF) for example is insisting that the US negotiators should keep on negotiating till the TPP achieves a 'gold standard' on core issues and should not agree on lower standards in their hurry to finish negotiations. 'US negotiators told TPP should be 'gold-standard' trade treaty', 29 August 2012, online, available at: www.tax-news.com/news/US_Negotiators_Told_TPP_Should_Be_GoldStandard_Trade_Treaty____57074.html (accessed 3 October 2013).

25 The ACTA was signed by the United States, Australia, Canada, South Korea, Japan, Morocco, New Zealand and Singapore on 1 October 2011. Mexico, Switzerland and the EU are also expected to sign the agreement. Details about the ACTA proposals and their implications are discussed in Yu (2012).

26 The term means 'son of the soil' and refers to the ethnic indigenous community in Malaysia. Discriminatory treatment for certain ethnic communities has also been a priority for New Zealand, and its FTAs, including the TPSEP, enables it to do so for the indigenous Maori community (Lewis 2009).

27 'Brief on the Trans-Pacific Partnership', Ministry of Trade and Industry (MITI), Government of Malaysia, online, available at: www.miti.gov.my/cms/storage/documents/1ed/com.tms.cms.document.Document_c5ada311-c0a8156f-72160910–3ecfcd41/1/TPP%20-%20Briefing%20Notes%20-%20Website%20%28FINALrev1%29.pdf (accessed 4 October 2013).

28 Australia's White Industries have used BIT provisions to move against India's Coal India Limited. More on this has been discussed in Chapter 6.

29 Asserted by US vice president, Joe Biden (Fergusson *et al.* 2013; p. 4).

30 Attributed to US national security adviser, Thomas Donilon (Fergusson *et al.* 2013; p. 9).

3 Economic implications

Trade diversion is always a worry for excluded countries when they see other countries and trade partners forging preferential trade alliances. The diversion possibilities in this regard are various. The most common is from preferential tariffs encouraging greater intra-bloc trade at the expense of trade with excluded members. The TPP is a worry for China and India in this regard as their exports to TPP members would be subject to higher tariffs than those from members inside. Furthermore, convergence of domestic regulations within the TPP might lead to new NTMs restricting market access for exports from outside the bloc. Trade diversion can also take place if bloc members have restrictive access to markets of excluded countries in specific sectors, but do not face similar restrictions within the bloc. For example, some TPP members currently encounter high tariffs on several agricultural exports to the Chinese and Indian markets (e.g. rice, wheat, sugar, fruits, vegetables, pulses, dairy, tea, coffee, edible oils, tobacco, liquor), as well as on motor vehicles, paper and wood products, specific industrial machinery, plastic and rubber items. These products might also encounter non-tariff barriers (NTBs) like special safeguards that are triggered when imports increase, or complex domestic regulations. The removal of tariffs and NTBs within the TPP might divert exports of these items from TPP members to China and India, to countries within the bloc.

It is difficult to quantify the net economic effects of new trade frameworks by measuring their trade 'creation' (i.e. new trade opportunities created among bloc members through fresh market access produced by preferential tariffs and other trade facilitation measures) and 'diversion' effects. Nonetheless, there are studies attempting to do so for various frameworks, and the TPP is not an exception. Empirical estimation of the projected gains from the TPP (Petri *et al.* 2012) under various scenarios identify Vietnam and Malaysia as the largest gainers, followed by Mexico, Canada, Singapore, Japan and South Korea. Most gains are expected for countries with the least bilateral FTAs with other TPP members like Vietnam and Malaysia who do not have bilateral FTAs with the United States, and Mexico and Canada who do not have bilateral FTAs with Asian members of the TPP such as Japan and South Korea. Japan is also expected to gain significantly as it currently does not have preferential access to the US market. The studies also project significant losses for China and India, both in income and exports, with the quantum of losses being more sizeable for China, primarily from trade diversion (Petri *et al.* 2012). Indeed, while the TPP is found to generate welfare gains for its member countries and overall global production (under the strong assumption of it eliminating tariffs and other trade costs arising from transport and policy factors) non-TPP large economies like China are likely to suffer losses (Li and Whalley 2012).

This chapter examines the trade diversion possibilities for China and India from the TPP. The analysis proceeds on the basis of the linkages that both countries have with the TPP members in their current trade structures and takes note of the preferential accesses that they have with some members through FTAs. The emphasis is on identifying the potential for trade diversion from the large-scale elimination of tariffs within the TPP bloc as well as the growth of new regulations and frameworks, which might have trade-restricting impacts.

China: trade diversion from tariff liberalization

China's trade with the current TPP members is 33.6 per cent of its total trade (Table 3.1). The TPP can be viewed as an RTA knitting together trade partners accounting for more than one-third of China's merchandise trade into a preferential trade bloc.

There is considerable difference among the TPP members in their relative significances as trade partners of China. Brunei, Peru and New Zealand, between them, account for barely 0.5 per cent of China's total trade. Australia, Canada, Chile, Malaysia, Mexico, Singapore and Vietnam are the more important trade partners for China; nonetheless, the sizes of their trades with China are far smaller than those of the United States and Japan with China. The latter account

Table 3.1 China's trade with TPP members

	Export (%)	Import (%)	Trade (%)
Australia	1.8	4.7	3.2
Brunei*	0.0	0.0	0.0
Canada	1.3	1.3	1.3
Chile	0.5	1.3	0.9
Japan	7.8	11.2	9.4
Malaysia	1.5	3.6	2.5
Mexico	1.3	0.5	0.9
New Zealand*	0.0	0.0	0.0
Peru	0.2	0.5	0.4
Singapore	1.9	1.6	1.7
United States	17.1	7.0	12.3
Vietnam	1.5	0.6	1.1
Total	34.9	32.3	33.6

Source: *China Statistical Yearbook 2012.*

Notes
* Figures are for 2011; Brunei and New Zealand's shares are 0.0 due to rounding of decimals.

for 21.7 per cent of China's total trade, and 24.3 per cent and 18.2 per cent of its total exports and imports, which is sizeable enough to worry China about the implications of trade diversion caused by the more preferential market access regime of the TPP for its members, which may reduce access space for Chinese producers. The degree of tariff-induced trade diversion is a function of the difference between MFN and preferential tariffs specific to RTAs and FTAs; export prospects in the American and Japanese markets, which are China's second and fourth top destinations for exports,[1] may be adversely affected if the TPP fixes tariffs that are either zero or much lower than the MFN tariffs that Chinese exports currently encounter in these markets. Conversely, China's imports from these countries, particularly Japan (and Korea in the future) might be diverted to members within the bloc by lower intra-bloc tariffs. These import diversion prospects also exist for imports from Australia, Chile, Malaysia and Peru. China is a net importer of merchandise for all these countries, as it is for Japan.

Diversion possibilities for countries with bilateral FTAs

The differentials between tariffs faced by Chinese exports in TPP member markets can be grouped in two categories: those with respect to members with whom China has bilateral FTAs, and those with whom it does not. The differentials are expected to be less for the former since Chinese exports would already be experiencing preferential tariffs in these markets. Hence the diversion possibilities are expected to be less for these markets. The eventual diversion prospects, apart from the differentials between China's FTA tariffs and the TPP tariffs, would depend significantly upon the coverage of tariffs. If TPP tariff cuts extend to products that are exempted from similar cuts in China's FTAs, then China's diversion losses would be greater.

As Table 3.2 reveals, China's current FTAs with TPP members include Chile and Peru, which account for 0.9 per cent and 0.4 per cent of China's merchandise trade. It also has an FTA with New Zealand, which was the first country to support China's inclusion in the multilateral trade framework of the WTO and confer it the status of a 'market economy'.[2] Other TPP members with whom China is linked through bilateral RTAs are the ASEAN members of the TPP – Brunei, Malaysia, Singapore and Vietnam. These countries are part of the preferential market access framework of the China–ASEAN FTA.

The China–Chile bilateral FTA has been operational since October 2006. It includes trade in goods and has a supplementary section on trade in services. Both countries had agreed to eliminate tariffs on 97 per cent of goods traded bilaterally over a ten-year period beginning from the commencement of the FTA. Chile's final offer list for tariff cuts includes almost 8,000 items (eight-digit level of tariff classification) while China's similar offer includes more than 7,000 items.[3] From a Chinese perspective, the FTA offers incremental market access over a period in time given that the tariffs are to be brought down to zero from a base rate of 6 per cent, which is the applied MFN tariff in the Chilean market for agricultural and non-agricultural products (WTO 2012). The

Table 3.2 China's trade agreements with TPP members

Countries	Nature of agreement
Australia	Being negotiated
Brunei	Part of ASEAN FTA
Canada	No agreement
Chile	Bilateral agreement
Japan	Being considered
Malaysia	Part of ASEAN FTA
Mexico	No agreement
New Zealand	Bilateral agreement
Peru	Bilateral agreement
Singapore	Bilateral agreement; Part of ASEAN FTA
United States	No agreement
Vietnam	Part of ASEAN FTA

Source: China FTA Network, online, available at: http://fta.mofcom.gov.cn/english/index.shtml (accessed 13 June 2013).

Note
Agreements being negotiated are those being discussed between the two countries, while agreements being considered are the ones at more preliminary stages, where feasibility studies have been completed or are going on.

preferential tariffs have helped China in becoming the second largest source of imports for Chile after the United States. The China–Chile trade balance though is in favour of Chile because of China's large imports of minerals like copper. Even if the TPP slashes tariffs to zero on all items that are being treated similarly under the China–Chile FTA, tariff-induced trade diversion will not be significant for China given that the FTA is expected to make 97 per cent of goods trade tariff-free by 2016. The only possibility of diversion is if the TPP includes the excluded products in its tariff elimination programme.

The bilateral agreement between China and Peru came into effect from March 2010. This FTA has almost as extensive coverage for eliminating tariffs as the one with Chile, and also includes provisions on trade in services, investment, TBT and IP. Though Peru currently accounts for only 0.4 per cent of China's total trade, China, over time, has become Peru's largest trading partner and a major market for its exports, particularly copper and other metals. As with Chile, the China–Peru trade balance is skewed towards Peru. The pattern and structures of Chile and Peru's trades with China reflects the benefits that natural resource-rich exporting countries from Latin America have reaped following the economic boom in China and the high demand for copper, iron ore, wheat and soybean (Herreros 2012). From a trade diversion perspective, Peru's average MFN tariffs on agriculture and non-agriculture goods are 4.1 per cent and 3.6 per cent (WTO 2012), which are even lower than Chile's. With several products having already become zero tariff on commencement of the FTA, China already has preferential access to Peru's market, and might expect marginal diversion if the products experiencing phased reduction, or exempted, are liberalized faster under the TPP. With respect to both Chile and Peru though, while direct diversion prospects are limited, Chinese exports are likely to face greater competition from TPP member countries that currently do not have preferential access to these markets through FTAs.

China's FTA with New Zealand again has a wide coverage of items for preferential tariff treatment. Indeed, Chile and New Zealand, along with Singapore, are part of the P4, which provides the base for the TPP. These have been traditionally open economies with low tariffs and these characteristics are reflected in their bilateral FTAs also. The China–New Zealand FTA also includes detailed provisions on trade in services, the bilateral movement of people, IP and TBT. China's biggest benefit from the agreement was avoiding the imposition of anti-dumping duties on its exports (Article 62 of the FTA), which has been a major barrier for Chinese exports in several markets due to the lack of a 'market economy' status at the WTO. New Zealand's dairy exports, on the other hand, obtained preferential access into China's domestic market, though the agreement has provisions for triggering safeguards if imports exceed thresholds (Article 13).[4] China's trade deficit with New Zealand is reducing over time, with the latter now enjoying a surplus with China having become a major market for dairy, logs and wood product exports from New Zealand (McNicol 2013). Given the small size of its trade with New Zealand, the preferential access through the FTA and deep penetration of Chinese exports in the domestic market, China will not be worrying too much over trade diversion. With New Zealand's average MFN tariffs on agricultural and non-agricultural goods being only 1.4 per cent and 2.1 per cent (WTO 2012), the differential between MFN and preferential tariffs will be small and hardly trade distorting. China might have some concerns about import diversion though. For example, if TPP members do not impose special safeguards on dairy imports from New Zealand, such restrictions by China on some dairy imports like milk, cheese and yoghurt might induce diversion within the TPP. China's reliance on milk imports from New Zealand and Australia is rather heavy due to quality issues surrounding its indigenous dairy brands. Import supply distortions have repercussions for domestic consumers, particularly infants, as was seen recently when China banned the import of milk powder from New Zealand after reports of contamination (Tajitsu 2013). Access to bigger markets in the TPP, particularly the United States, can create some diversion of imports from New Zealand, in addition to safeguard barriers.

China is formally integrated with five TPP negotiating members – Brunei, Malaysia, Singapore, Thailand and Vietnam – through its Framework Agreement on Comprehensive Economic Cooperation with ASEAN. China also has a bilateral FTA with Singapore. The China–ASEAN economic cooperation framework includes both an FTA in goods and an economic integration agreement in services. The goods FTA specifies 'sensitive' items (Article 3), where tariffs are brought down more gradually. While on 'normal' items tariffs are to be reduced to zero over the period 2005–2012, tariffs on sensitive items are to be reduced to 20 per cent by 2012, and further to 0–5 per cent by 2018. Within sensitive items, tariffs on 'highly sensitive' products are to be reduced to 50 per cent by 2015.[5]

The agreement also specifies safeguard measures that can be used by members during transition periods for reducing imports (Article 9).

The sensitive items and their tariff treatment in the TPP will be an important determinant of the prospects of China's trade diversion from the markets of the ASEAN members of the TPP with whom it has FTAs. Sensitive items represent a restricted space in access to the Chinese and ASEAN markets for exporters from both sides. They are also a feature of the ASEAN+1 FTAs, which are discussed in Chapter 4. While the China–ASEAN goods FTA extends preferential tariffs to almost 98 per cent of the traded goods, sensitive items, including highly sensitive products, accommodate a slower pace of tariff reduction and retention of high tariffs in several cases. Malaysia, for example, has more than 600 such tariff lines, including both sensitive and highly sensitive products (Table 3.3). These stretch across a wide variety of products including chemicals, plastics, rubber, steel, industrial machineries, readymade garments, motor cars and motor cycles. Steel, garments, textile, electronic items, motor vehicles, chicken eggs and sugar are among Vietnam's sensitive items (Table 3.3). Sensitive items reflect sectors where Malaysia and Vietnam have responded to the defensive interests of domestic industries. These are particularly strong in highly sensitive items, which include several agricultural items for Malaysia (e.g. fowls and fowl eggs, milk and cream, rice, tobacco), steel products and a large number of motor vehicles and transports with varying engine capacities. As mentioned earlier in Chapter 2, Malaysia's reservations regarding opening up the agricultural sector

Table 3.3 Sensitive items in the China–ASEAN FTA

Country	Sensitive list	Highly sensitive list
Brunei	47 six-digit items specifying 180 tariffs and another 19 tariff lines	27 six-digit item specifying 630 tariff lines and another seven disaggregated tariff lines
Malaysia	272 six-digit items specifying 398 tariffs, out of which eight specify none	96 six-digit items covering 267 disaggregated tariff lines, out of which 10 six-digit items do not specify tariff lines
Singapore	One six-digit item specifying four disaggregated tariffs	One six-digit item specifying two disaggregated tariffs
Vietnam	388 six-digit items	140 six-digit items

Source: 'Modality for Tariff Reduction/Elimination of Tariff Lines Placed in the Sensitive Track' Annex 2, ASEAN–China FTA, online, available at: www.mofat.gov.bn/download/cn/02–01–03.pdf (accessed 27 August 2013); 'Vietnam to Implement Commitments to Slash Taxes Within ACFTA', online, available at: www.mof.gov.vn/portal/pls/portal/SHARED_APP.UTILS.print_preview?p_page_url=http%3A%2F%2Fwww.mof.gov.vn%2Fportal%2Fpage%2Fportal%2Fmof_en%2Fdn&p_itemid=2736576&p_siteid=53&p_persid=0&p_language=en (accessed 27 August 2013).

Note
While the modalities for reducing tariffs in the sensitive and highly sensitive lists are specified at the six-digit level of HS classification in Annex 2, the further disaggregated tariff lines are at different levels of disaggregation such as eight-digit (Brunei, Singapore, Vietnam) and nine-digit (Malaysia).

are evident in the TPP negotiations. But if it eventually does, then the TPP members will get preferential access to a sector of the Malaysian market, where China does not enjoy such access through the ASEAN FTA.

The China–ASEAN FTA has different rules for tariff liberalization for different ASEAN countries. These rules also specify different modalities for sensitive and highly sensitive items. For the former, applied tariffs are to be cut to 0–5 per cent by 2018 for the ASEAN-6 (Brunei, Indonesia, Malaysia, Philippines, Singapore and Thailand) and by 2020 for the remaining four (Cambodia, Lao, Myanmar and Vietnam). The latter group also does not need to reduce tariffs on sensitive items to 20 per cent before January 2015, while the rest were to do so by January 2012.[6] If the TPP becomes operational before 2015, which is likely, and eliminates tariffs on 'sensitive' items on which Vietnam can continue to hold high tariffs under the China–ASEAN FTA (388 six-digit items (Table 3.1)), then Chinese exports of these products may become cramped for access in Vietnam's domestic market. Similarly, if the TPP's immediate tariff elimination programme includes the 'highly sensitive' items, then Chinese exports of these items too will face access disadvantages, as under the China–ASEAN FTA Vietnam does not need to bring down tariffs on its highly sensitive items before 2018, and even by then, not below 50 per cent. Similar disadvantages would be encountered by Chinese exports for sensitive and highly sensitive items in the domestic markets of Brunei and Malaysia. Till 2018, that is the time by when they need to reduce tariffs on sensitive products to 0–5 per cent, both can maintain higher tariffs on Chinese exports. For highly sensitive items, they are allowed to maintain even higher tariffs, which need not be reduced below 50 per cent till 2015.

High tariffs on specific items have implications if they are in areas pertaining to the major export interests of other countries. For China, high tariffs in the Malaysian market, for example, will be a matter of concern if they are in areas of its specific export interest, and if those tariffs are taken off for TPP members. China's specific sectors of concerns in this regard will be where it has strong comparative advantages, such as chemicals, plastic, rubber, garments, steel and machineries. Many of these attract high tariffs as sensitive items under the China–ASEAN FTA. Brunei, under the P4 agreement, has lower preferential tariffs than the China–ASEAN FTA: such as HS401691 and HS854449, which under the FTA with China, attract average tariffs of 5 per cent and 11.4 per cent, and lower rates of 2.5 per cent and 10 per cent respectively in the P4's TPSEP.[7] Furthermore, under the China–ASEAN FTA, Brunei has the flexibility of maintaining tariffs of up to 50 per cent on the import of several vehicles and their parts till 2015, as these are highly sensitive items. Under the P4 agreement though, it is committed to withdraw tariffs on most vehicle and parts imports by 2015.[8] The P4 example could be an indicator of the relative degree of disadvantageous tariff differential that might face China's exports in some sectors in terms of tariffs in the ASEAN FTA vis-à-vis the TPP. Exhaustive tariff liberalization under the TPP therefore can produce trade diversion possibilities for China if it covers sensitive items under the China–ASEAN FTA, particularly from the outset, as well as items of China's offensive export interest.

Diversion possibilities for countries without bilateral FTAs

China does not have bilateral trade or economic collaboration agreements with five of the TPP negotiating members (Table 3.4). It is negotiating a bilateral FTA with Australia. The negotiations began on 18 April 2005 and have since been through 19 rounds of official talks. Prolongation of talks for more than eight years indicates the complexity of issues involved. Australia is China's seventh largest trade partner, with a share of 3.2 per cent in its total trade (Table 3.4); China is Australia's largest trade partner, accounting for 23 per cent of its merchandise trade. Though both countries are keen on finalizing the agreement given their strong bilateral trade ties, contentious issues, particularly a higher threshold limit on Chinese investments into Australia without prior approval from the Foreign Investment Review Board, and easier access of Australian industries in China's financial services sectors, have lengthened discussions (Murdoch 2013). The new leaderships in both countries are keen on finalizing the FTA at the earliest, with Australia's Prime Minister Abbott setting a year's deadline after his meeting with President Xi in October 2013.[9]

China is also discussing a trilateral FTA with Japan and South Korea. The CJK (China, Japan, Korea) FTA negotiations were launched in November 2012 and two rounds of talks were held in March and August 2013 respectively, reporting progress, which has been limited largely because of uneasy strategic relations between China and Japan, given outstanding territorial disputes.[10] While the FTA can bring significant economic benefits for all three[11] and may also facilitate progress on the RCEP and the TPP, the three countries need to overcome several strategic complications impeding movement: Korea's concerns over the FTA aggravating trade imbalance with Japan, Japan's concern over losing market share in China to Korea, and the concerns of both Korea and Japan over the FTA symbolizing China-led economic integration in the region and its downsides (Chiang 2013). Japan's participation in the TPP negotiations and the involvement of all three countries in the RCEP talks might hasten progress on the FTA, but could also impede it if priorities are different. While China is involved in trade talks with Australia and Japan in other regional forums, it is not involved in similar consultations with the NAFTA members of the TPP – Canada, Mexico and the United States. China, however, is negotiating a BIT with the United States, as a preparatory step towards the TPP, more on which is discussed later.

Overall MFN tariffs currently faced by Chinese exports in TPP members' markets with which China does not have FTAs are the highest in Mexico (Table 3.4). Mexico accounts for roughly 1 per cent of China's total trade (Table 3.1). Notwithstanding high tariffs, China's trade relations with Mexico have deepened over the years and China is now a major trade partner of Mexico, accounting for 8.3 per cent of its merchandise trade. While China is the fourth largest market for Mexican exports, with a share of 1.7 per cent in total exports, it is the second largest source of Mexico's imports, accounting for 14.9 per cent of its total imports (WTO 2012). The United States remains the largest source of Mexico's

Table 3.4 MFN tariffs in TPP members without bilateral FTAs with China

Country	Final bound			Applied			Duty-free imports	
	Overall	Agriculture	Non-agriculture	Overall	Agriculture	Non-agriculture	Agriculture	Non-agriculture
Australia	10	3.5	11	2.8	1.4	3.1	49.5	49.9
Canada	7	18	5.3	4.5	18	2.5	52.3	67.4
Japan	5.3	22.8	2.6	5.3	23.3	2.6	46.3	82.6
Mexico	36.1	44.5	34.8	8.3	21.4	6.3	36.2	67.3
United States	3.5	4.9	3.3	3.5	5	3.3	40.4	50.3

Source: WTO.

imports and accounts for almost half of these. US exports enjoy preferential access to the Mexican market through the North American Free Trade Agreement (NAFTA). The preferential access is mutual as is evident from the United States absorbing 78.7 of Mexican exports (WTO 2012). The quantum of preferential access enjoyed by the NAFTA members between themselves might increase from greater tariff liberalization in the TPP. Such a possibility may be detrimental for Chinese exports prospects, which will continue to face the higher MFN tariffs. China will hope that the differential between the MFN and preferential NAFTA tariffs does not widen any further given that the United States, as mentioned in Chapter 2, is likely to take the market access commitments in its current FTAs as the given benchmarks for the TPP. Among all the NAFTA markets, greater preferential access will produce the greatest disadvantages for the Mexican market given its higher tariffs, compared with the United States and Canada. The preferential access obtained by Mexican textile exports in the US market under NAFTA has led to considerable displacement of Chinese textile exports despite them being cheaper. The TPP might enhance the diversion given that textiles is one of the sectors, along with apparel and footwear, where the United States maintains high tariffs, and which it might lower in the TPP (Jie 2012).

An implication of lower tariffs among TPP members is their getting deeper access into each other's markets. China's worries in this regard will be particularly high for the greater access that other TPP members are likely to get into the US and Japanese markets. After China and the EU, Canada, Mexico and Japan are the largest sources of imports for the United States and all three are in the TPP. For Japan, the United States and Australia are among its largest sources of imports. The United States and Japan are China's major sources of imports too. The TPP will increase the access of its members in the US and Japan markets, which might come into conflict with China's export strengths and comparative advantages in some cases, particularly with Mexico, Malaysia and Vietnam in manufacturing exports like transport and telecom equipment, auto components, machineries and textiles. Malaysia and Vietnam do not have bilateral FTAs with the United States, and neither does Japan. They all currently face MFN tariffs in the US market, as does China. The TPP will change the dynamic, with all these countries getting greater preferential access in the US market compared with China. Indeed, these concerns reverberate in the empirical analyses forecasting the effects of the TPP (Chunding and Whalley 2012; Petri *et al.* 2012), where Japan and South Korea's entry in the TPP imply significant gains for both countries but indicate greater losses for China. There are also concerns over the TPP producing FDI-distorting effects: as long as China is not in the TPP, labour-intensive export-oriented FDI currently based in the mainland has incentives to relocate to other TPP members in the region for taking advantage of preferential tariffs in textiles and apparel and other low-cost volume-based exports.

India: trade diversion from tariff liberalization

India's trade with the TPP bloc is less than that of China's. While China's trade with the bloc accounts for 33.6 per cent of its total trade, India's is a smaller proportion of 20.3 per cent (Table 3.5). Like China, there are some TPP members with whom it has stronger trade links than the rest. The United States, Singapore and Japan are among India's top ten merchandise trade partners. Together, these three TPP members account for 14 per cent of India's trade. Australia and Malaysia are also among India's major trade partners. None of the other TPP members are as significant in India's trade and occupy less than 1 per cent shares (Table 3.5).

India's relatively lesser trade integration with the TPP bloc compared with China, apart from the obvious factor of China having a far greater share in global trade than India (almost 10 per cent, compared with just above 2 per cent for India; WTO 2012), underlines the structural characteristics of merchandise trades of both countries and the concomitant significance of their trade partners. Seven Organization of Petroleum Exporting Countries (OPEC) members (United Arab Emirates, Saudi Arabia, Iraq, Kuwait, Qatar, Iran and Nigeria)[12] are among India's top 20 trade partners, highlighting the importance of crude oil and refined petroleum products in India's foreign trade. Crude oil is India's largest import while petroleum products are its largest exports. Some of the OPEC members mentioned above, who are major sources of India's crude oil imports, are also major destinations for petroleum product exports from India. These include the UAE and Saudi Arabia, which absorb more than 18 per cent of India's petroleum product exports. Given that petroleum products account for more than 20 per cent of India's total exports, its trade links would expectedly be high with

Table 3.5 India's trade with TPP members

	Export (%)	Import (%)	Trade (%)
Australia	0.8	3.0	1.9
Brunei	0.3	0.1	0.2
Canada	0.7	0.6	0.6
Chile	0.2	0.4	0.3
Japan	2.1	2.5	2.3
Malaysia	1.3	1.9	1.6
Mexico	0.5	0.5	0.5
New Zealand	0.1	0.2	0.1
Peru	0.2	0.1	0.1
Singapore	5.5	1.8	3.6
United States	11.3	5.0	8.1
Vietnam	1.2	0.4	0.8
Total	24.2	16.5	20.3

Source: Export–Import Data Bank, Ministry of Commerce, Government of India.

Note
Figures are for 2011–2012; totals of columns might not add due to rounding.

those countries, which are its major partners in oil trade. Among the TPP members, such links exist with Singapore, Japan, United States, Malaysia and Vietnam. While none of these countries are India's major sources of crude oil imports, they absorb India's petroleum exports, with Singapore being the largest with a 12.8 per cent share in petroleum exports, followed by Japan (4.0 per cent), United States (2.9 per cent), Malaysia (1.2 per cent) and Vietnam (0.04 per cent).[13] With several of India's major trade partners being OPEC members and non-Asia-Pacific economies, its trade links with the TPP are that much less.

This particular structural characteristic of an overt dominance of petroleum products in foreign trade is less noticeable for China. Fuel and mining products comprise only 3.1 per cent of China's exports, compared with 23.7 per cent of India's exports, while both are major importers of fuel (29.6 per cent for China and 39.6 per cent for India; WTO 2012). Within fuel and mining, oil trade (both exports and imports) is particularly significant for India. India is also a large exporter of ores and mineral products, unlike China. China is primarily a consumer of fuel and mineral products in its trade with the rest of the world, unlike India, which is both a consumer and a producer. In contrast to India, China's trade links are particularly strong with those countries with which it is integrated through the lower and upper ends of manufacturing value chains – both as suppliers of semi-processed and intermediate inputs as well as consumers of final products. Given such connections with Japan, the United States, Singapore, Malaysia, and Vietnam, all of whom are TPP members, China's trade links with the TPP bloc are much stronger. In this respect, its resultant trade diversion worries will also be greater than India's since the TPP bloc is less integral to India's current trade structure.

Diversion possibilities for countries with bilateral FTAs

Like China, India will be worried about the higher tariffs on its exports in TPP member markets compared with the preferential access available to members within the bloc. While China's trade diversion anxieties will be particularly high for the NAFTA and Japanese markets, India's apprehensions, in addition to the American and Japanese markets in particular, would also extend to the Singaporean and Malaysian markets. This is notwithstanding Indian exports enjoying preferential access in all these countries, except the United States, through bilateral FTAs. Both China and India are yet to have FTAs with any of the NAFTA members of the TPP, though Canada and India are negotiating one (Table 3.6). Compared with China, which has bilateral trade pacts with both Chile and Peru, India has an agreement only with Chile. On the other hand, like China, India is formally connected to ASEAN members of the TPP – Brunei, Malaysia, Singapore, Thailand and Vietnam – through its goods FTA with ASEAN. Negotiations on the bilateral trade in services agreement (TISA) between India and ASEAN have completed and the FTA is expected to be signed in December 2013. India has comprehensive economic cooperation agreements (CECAs) with Singapore, Malaysia and Japan.

Table 3.6 India's trade agreements with TPP members

Countries	Nature of agreement
Australia	Being negotiated
Brunei	Part of ASEAN FTA
Canada	Being negotiated
Chile	Bilateral agreement
Japan	Bilateral agreement
Malaysia	Bilateral agreement; part of ASEAN FTA
Mexico	No agreement
New Zealand	Being considered
Peru	No agreement
Singapore	Bilateral agreement; part of ASEAN FTA
United States	No agreement
Vietnam	Part of ASEAN FTA

Source: Ministry of Commerce and Industry, Government of India, online, available at: http://commerce.nic.in/trade/international_ta.asp?id=2&trade=i (accessed 13 June 2013).

Note
Agreements being negotiated are those being discussed between the two countries, while agreements being considered are the ones at more preliminary stages, where feasibility studies have been completed or are going on.

Chile is an important export destination for India in Latin America. While Brazil is its largest trade partner in the region, with whom India has more trade and enjoys a trade surplus, Chile has a positive trade balance with India given India's proportionally larger imports from the country.[14] India's major exports to Chile include pharmaceuticals, rubber and plastic products, garments, and iron and steel articles. Copper ore and concentrates overwhelmingly dominate India's imports from Chile. Chile is the biggest source of copper ore imports for India, much ahead of Australia, Indonesia and Peru, its other major sources of copper import. Structurally, the India–Chile bilateral trade is similar to the China–Chile trade, with Chile enjoying trade surpluses with both countries due to its substantive mineral exports, particularly copper. China and India's large demands for copper, motivated by their large infrastructure programmes and rapid growth in real estate, have made them reliant on supplies from Chile, the largest copper producer in the world. However, the FTAs of the two countries with Chile vary in their scope and coverage. The India–Chile FTA is much restricted, with India offering preferential tariffs on only 178 items at the eight-digit level of HS classification and Chile offering similar preferences on 296 items.[15] The degree of preferential access is miniscule compared with more than 7,000 items receiving such treatment under the China–Chile FTA. While there are talks of expanding the coverage of the FTA,[16] not much progress has been achieved to date. In this respect, the implementation of the TPP might create disadvantages for several of India's exports, given the tariff differential between MFN tariffs in Chile and the preferential tariffs in the TPP. Export prospects might suffer if these disadvantages manifest in products where Indian exports have been able to mark their presence in the Chilean market such as textiles and clothing, chemicals, rubber, plastic and pharmaceuticals. From a comparative perspective, access disadvantages in the Chilean market would be more for Indian products compared with China given the latter's far more exhaustive FTA.

The India–ASEAN goods FTA was implemented from January 2010 between India, Malaysia, Singapore and Thailand, and other ASEAN economies have subsequently joined the pact. As reflected in various other ASEAN FTAs, including the trade agreement between ASEAN members themselves, the India–ASEAN FTA has S&D provisions, allowing different signatories to liberalize tariffs according to their preferred time schedules. Furthermore, items are divided into distinct categories for phased tariff reductions, in a manner similar to that in the China–ASEAN FTA. Comparatively, however, the degree of market access permitted by the India–ASEAN FTA is more gradual than the China–ASEAN FTA, given that in the former even 'normal track' tariffs identified for reducing to zero are sub-divided in two groups, specifying different timelines for different countries. The remaining items are categorized into 'sensitive' and 'highly sensitive' groups, with tariffs for the former to be reduced to 5 per cent, and for the latter to a base level of 50 per cent, by 50 per cent and by 25 per cent respectively, for different sub-categories.[17] Finally, the FTA contains provisions for maintaining country-specific excluded lists where members can refrain from any tariff cut commitments (Table 3.7). This is again a feature of several of the ASEAN+1 FTAs: an aspect that may encourage the ASEAN members in the TPP to seek exemptions in TPP negotiations.

Prospects of trade diversion for Indian exports from the markets of the ASEAN members of the TPP need to be assessed in the dynamic context of the restrictions on market access built-in within the India–ASEAN FTA. The scope of restriction in terms of coverage of items under sensitive and excluded categories is more than that in the China–ASEAN FTA. Besides, the floor on tariffs for highly sensitive items is rather high, with several permitted to retain tariffs at 50 per cent. For sensitive items too, the floor is set at 5 per cent. For all these items therefore, Indian

Table 3.7 Tariff restrictions in India–ASEAN FTA

Country	Sensitive list	Excluded list
Brunei	706 eight-digit items	1,419 eight-digit items
Malaysia	689 eight-digit items	361 eight-digit items
Vietnam	1,268 eight-digit items	1,549 eight-digit items

Source: 'Schedule of Tariff Commitments, Brunei Darussalam', online, available at: www.mofat.gov.bn/download/in/07–01.pdf (accessed 18 September 2013); ASEAN–India FTA (AIFTA), Ministry of International Trade and Industry, Government of Malaysia, online, available at: www.miti.gov.my/cms/content.jsp?id=com.tm (accessed 18 September 2013); Schedule of Tariff Commitments Thailand and Vietnam Draft Indicative AIFTA Tariff Rate (HS2007), Ministry of Industry and Trade, Socialist Republic of Vietnam, online, available at: http://webtr.vecita.gov.vn/?Page=News_Detail&ChannelID=75&ArticleID=257 (accessed 18 September 2013).

Note
Items in sensitive category include those classified in the schedule of tariff commitments as highly sensitive. Brunei's tariff commitments do not include highly sensitive items.

exports to the ASEAN members of the TPP will encounter higher tariffs compared with the expected tariff-free market access for producers within the bloc. This anticipated disadvantage, and the consequent trade diversions, assumes that the TPP will not offer exemptions to its ASEAN members for items on which they can retain higher tariffs for Indian exports; if it does then some of the disadvantage may be negated. On the whole, diversion prospects from differentials between the ASEAN FTA tariffs and zero tariffs of the TPP exist for Indian exports across the ASEAN member markets for a wide range of products including beverages, food articles, chemicals, rubber and plastic products, textile and garments, leather products, iron and steel, wood and wooden products and a diverse range of mechanical and electrical machineries and instruments.

Diversion prospects will also be considerably influenced from the time when tariff reduction commitments under the TPP become operative. The India–ASEAN FTA offers fairly liberal tariff phase-out schedules to different countries in different product categories. For example, in the first set of normal track tariffs to be cut to zero, Vietnam is allowed time until 31 December 2018, while the rest of the ASEAN TPP members need to do so by 31 December 2013; the second set of normal tariffs extend the timelines further, to 31 December 2021 for Vietnam, and 31 December 2016 for the rest.[18] Assuming commencement of the TPP in the near future, Indian exports are likely to face higher tariffs in the Vietnamese market on some of its current major exports to the country, such as meat, fish, cereals and oil seeds, all of which, despite being in the normal track are not to be reduced to zero tariffs before December 2018. For some categories of cotton yarn, another of India's major exports to Vietnam, zero duty rates kick in only from December 2021. While diversion prospects in normal track products are relatively less in the Malaysian and Brunei markets, given that both countries are to set zero tariffs on these items by 2016, worries over loss of market access will remain over the sensitive track and excluded products. This is particularly because some of the latter include products of India's specific export interests such as garments, jewellery, machineries and also some categories of refined petroleum products.

The CECA implemented between India and Malaysia from July 2011 has a wider coverage of issues and includes trade in both goods and services. In terms of tariff commitments, however, the agreement is similar to the India–ASEAN FTA, with identical sub-categories in the normal track and sensitive list and with excluded items. From the perspective of obtaining additional access for Indian exports in the Malaysian market over and above what is available through the ASEAN FTA, the FTA with Malaysia has lower tariffs for Indian exports of basmati rice and motorcycles, and allows quota-based zero duty import of eggs from India.[19] India's bilateral economic cooperation agreement with Singapore allows all exports originating from India to enjoy duty-free access into Singapore,[20] making Singapore one TPP member with respect to which India does not have trade diversion worries.

India has signed comprehensive economic partnership agreements (CEPA) with two of its major Eastern neighbours – Japan and South Korea. Both are among India's major trade partners, ranked eleventh and thirteenth respectively, with shares of 2.3 per cent and 2.1 per cent in India's total merchandise trade. The S&D feature is noticed in the India–Japan FTA as well where items have been grouped into categories for which tariffs will be brought down phase-wise over 15, ten, seven and five years. Given that the agreement has come into force only from August 2011, for several items, the phasing out is still at a relatively early stage, introducing some concerns over the relative differential in the quantum of preferential market access vis-à-vis the TPP. In quite a few fish and meat products, as well as fruits (including the celebrated Indian mangoes) the tariffs have been removed with immediate effect; as have been tariffs on several of India's items of export interest such as petroleum products, garments, and gems and jewellery. India will have some concerns over the items excluded from tariff cuts in the FTA such as rice, wheat, milk and leather products.[21] As such, however, compared with the ASEAN FTA, India's worries regarding trade diversion from the Japanese market over differential tariffs following the TPP should be relatively less.

From a specific trade diversion perspective, India's bilateral FTAs with Japan and Korea put it at an advantage compared with China who does not have FTAs with either. A TPP coming into play in the immediate future with exhaustive tariff elimination and marginal S&D provisions might construe disadvantages for India for several years into the current decade. Thereafter, however, at least for the Japanese and Korean markets, India should not be worried over long-term trade diversions, with the tariff differentials largely levelling out except for a handful of sensitive items. Trade diversion worries from these two markets would be greater for China, which is therefore likely to push for a faster conclusion of the CJK FTA. On the other hand, the much wider coverage of China's FTAs with Chile and Peru and also with the ASEAN, indicate lesser diversion possibilities for China in these markets, compared with India.

Diversion possibilities for countries without bilateral FTAs

India is currently negotiating FTAs with Australia and Canada, two TPP members with whom it does not have FTAs. Beginning from 2011, five rounds of negotiations have taken place on the India–Australia CEPA. Given that the agreement aims to cover trade in goods, services and investment, negotiations are expected to take time. Bilateral trade has increased sharply in recent years, encouraging both countries to work towards the CEPA. Australia has an almost 2 per cent share in India's annual trade and enjoys a substantial trade surplus given India's large imports of minerals and ores from the country. Along with Australia, India is also negotiating a bilateral CEPA with Canada. A successful CEPA with Canada will enable India to obtain a toehold in the NAFTA market, which, till now, does not offer preferential access to Indian exports. There have been eight rounds of discussions on the CEPA, with both countries aiming to conclude the talks by 2013. The deadline, however, has been missed given the delays in finalizing tariff schedules and rules for trade in services and investments (Zilio 2013), as well as the impending general elections in India. Between

Australia and Canada, the former is also involved in the RCEP negotiations along with China and India.

Mexico and Peru are two TPP members with whom India does not have bilateral FTAs and where the bound and applied MFN tariffs are relatively high (Table 3.8). Both countries are relatively small trade partners for India, with shares of only 0.5 per cent and 0.1 per cent respectively in India's trade. As markets with further potential for increasing trade, prospects of India's trade diversion from the two markets will increase if TPP members facing the MFN tariffs in these markets obtain greater preferential access post-TPP. This particularly applies for Malaysia, Vietnam, Australia and New Zealand, who do not have bilateral trade deals with Mexico and Peru. Till the ongoing CEPAs are concluded, India will continue to face relatively high tariff barriers in Australia and Canada as well. Again, for these markets too, the TPP tariffs may create substantial differentials from the MFN tariffs and concomitant access limitations for Indian exports. It will therefore be to India's advantage to conclude negotiations with Australia and Canada at the earliest so that the preferential tariff advantages obtained from the bilateral CEPAs can offset the market access disadvantage created by the TPP.

India's primary trade diversion concern with the TPP will be over the US market. The TPP bloc's share of around a fifth of India's exports is largely due to the United States, which accounts for almost half of the share, accounting for 11.3 per cent of India's total exports. With other TPP member countries slated to obtain preferential access in the US market, there is reason for India to be anxious over trade diversion. Particular concerns are likely to be over readymade garments, cotton yarn and fabric and marine products – India's major exports to the United States – and their adverse prospects vis-à-vis similar exports from Southeast Asian economies enjoying preferential market access under the TPP. As mentioned in Chapter 2, lower textile tariffs in the US market are a major demand of Vietnam's in the TPP negotiations. If these tariffs were indeed lowered, then India and China will encounter considerable disadvantages in the US market. Indeed, preferential access to the US market through the TPP for economies like Vietnam that do not have such access right now appears to be a major determinant of the potential economic gains from the TPP (Petri *et al.* 2012). Unless such access is balanced through preferential access secured elsewhere, China and India, which neither have FTAs with the United States nor are in the TPP, will have to encounter some prospects of trade diversion.

Trade diversion from NTMs

NTMs comprise measures employed by countries for restricting imports, other than tariffs. These include import quotas, anti-dumping and countervailing duties, safeguards for reducing the physical volume of imports, SPS measures and TBT. Regional and multilateral trade agreements focus on removing NTMs and their incidence for facilitating trade. The TPP also attempts to do so by discouraging the imposition of anti-dumping and countervailing duties, and

Table 3.8 MFN tariffs in TPP members without bilateral FTAs with India

Country	Final bound			Applied			Duty-free imports	
	Overall	Agriculture	Non-agriculture	Overall	Agriculture	Non-agriculture	Agriculture	Non-agriculture
Australia	10.0	3.5	11.0	2.8	1.4	3.1	49.5	49.9
Canada	7.0	18.0	5.3	4.5	18.0	2.5	52.3	67.4
Mexico	36.1	44.5	34.8	8.3	21.4	6.3	36.2	67.3
New Zealand	10.1	6.0	10.7	2.0	1.4	2.1	51.0	67.9
Peru	29.3	30.8	29.1	3.7	4.1	3.6	60.8	73.9
United States	3.5	4.9	3.3	3.5	5.0	3.3	40.4	50.3

Source: WTO.

removing export-deterring SPS and TBT measures by emphasizing domestic regulatory coherence among the members.

Information available on five NTMs from the WTO – anti-dumping, counter-vailing, safeguard, SPS and TBT – during January 2003 to December 2012 reveals the nature and extent of such measures prevailing in TPP member markets and affecting Chinese and Indian exports. These measures can be divided into two categories: those that affect all exporting countries and those that specifically affect China and India. Tables 3.9 and 3.10 illustrate the two categories. Anti-dumping and countervailing duties are common to both Tables 3.9 and 3.10, since these are deployed specifically for blocking exports from China and India. Safeguards and TBTs are generic restrictions arising from the domestic regulations of the host countries and feature only in Table 3.9, since these affect exports from all countries. The SPS measures are occasionally spe-cific to exports from China and India, as documented in Table 3.10; but a host of these measures, imposed for maintaining food safety and the health of animals and plants in countries initiating these measures, can affect exports from any-where, including China and India, and are reflected in Table 3.9.

China has been a major target of the anti-dumping duties imposed by the TPP members. Out of the 163 anti-dumping actions initiated against Chinese and Indian exports during January 2003–December 2012 (Tables 3.9 and 3.10), only 13 were against Indian exports. The NAFTA economies have been particularly active in imposing anti-dumping duties on Chinese exports, followed by Australia. The NAFTA is collectively responsible for 102 anti-dumping duties against Chinese exports among the 130 such duties that remain effective across the TPP bloc. The

Table 3.9 NTMs in TPP members affecting exports

Country	Anti-dumping			Countervailing			Safeguard		SPS		TBT	
	I	F	W	I	F	W	I	F	I	F	I	F
Australia	20	14	15	7	3	2	1		141	18	60	13
Brunei											1	
Canada	20	17	16	16	14	5	2		477	15	323	26
Chile							4	3	253	32	183	1
Japan	1	1							208	19	339	19
Malaysia	2	1	1				1		9	5	29	2
Mexico	25	15	33	3	2	1	1		36	7	204	5
New Zealand	5	4	2						247	67	53	1
Peru	10	8	12				2		326	207	45	
Singapore									18	7	13	8
United States	80	70	32	42	29	9			1,759	377	741	31
Vietnam							2		36	11	22	2
Total	**163**	**130**	**111**	**68**	**48**	**17**	**13**	**3**	**3,510**	**765**	**2,013**	**108**

Source: WTO, Integrated Trade Intelligence Portal.

Notes
The measures are for the period 1 January 2003 to 31 December 2012; I, F and W represent 'initi-ated', 'in force' and 'withdrawn'.

Table 3.10 NTM in TPP countries specific to Chinese and Indian exports

Country	Anti-dumping			Countervailing			SPS	
	I	F	W	I	F	W	I	F
Australia	20	14	15	7	3	2	2	1
Brunei								
Canada	20	17	16	16	14	5		
Chile							3	
Japan	1	1						
Malaysia	2	1	1					
Mexico	25	15	33	3	2	1		
New Zealand	5	4	2				1	1
Peru	10	8	12				11	11
Singapore								
United States	80	70	32	42	29	9	2	
Vietnam								
Total	**163**	**130**	**111**	**68**	**48**	**17**	**19**	**13**

Source: WTO, Integrated Trade Intelligence Portal.

Notes
The measures are for the period 1.1.2003 to 31.12.2012; I, F and W represent 'initiated', 'in force' and 'withdrawn'.

United States leads other TPP members with a tally of 70 anti-dumping duties in force against China. China's 'non market economy' (NME) status as specified in its accession protocol to the WTO enables easy initiation of anti-dumping investigation against Chinese exports.[22] From 11 December 2016, 15 years after China's entry in the WTO, Chinese exports are to be treated as those originating from a market economy in anti-dumping investigations (Tietje and Nowrot 2011). Till then, it is vulnerable to such actions from all TPP members as well as WTO members. China has been able to reclassify its status to that of a market economy under other FTAs that it has signed, including those with New Zealand and ASEAN. But given that the TPP has little possibility of doing so (unless China is invited to join) and the fact that the NAFTA members have been active in taking anti-dumping measures against China, the prevalence of NTM market access handicaps through anti-dumping duties are likely to prevail in the TPP for China. The incidence of the imposition of countervailing duties has also been relatively high on China, with 60 out of the 68 actions (Tables 3.9 and 3.10) aimed at Chinese exports and only eight against India. Canada and the United States have been the largest imposers of these duties. Unlike the anti-dumping provisions in the WTO, which are expected to become congenial towards China from December 2016, countervailing measures and duties, imposed on suspected subsidized imports from other countries, are not expected to undergo changes.

Anti-dumping and countervailing duties have targeted a large range of Chinese exports varying from marine and agricultural products (e.g. shrimps and mushrooms), inorganic and organic chemicals, glass and metal products, steel products, household and kitchen appliances, and wooden and paper products (Annexure 1).

In contrast, while both duties have had fewer incidences on Indian exports, the affected among the latter include marine products, chemicals, textile fabrics and steel articles (Annexure 2). India's problems with anti-dumping and countervailing actions in curbing market access prospects appear to be less compared with China for the TPP bloc. For some more time in the foreseeable future, China will have to counter the disadvantages of being an NME and will be particularly vulnerable to anti-dumping actions initiated by the United States. The protectionist impulse of US domestic producers has been a major determinant of high anti-dumping actions against China (Tanczos 2008). If such impulse continues to galvanize domestic producers to resort to trade remedies post-TPP, even after 2016, then China will continue to encounter market access limitations.

Other than anti-dumping and countervailing measures, NTMs comprise SPSs, which, from the perspective of the Chinese and Indian exporters to the TPP markets, can adversely affect market access. There are 13 specific SPS measures in force currently affecting Chinese and Indian exports in the TPP member markets. These (Table 3.11) pertain to the export of table grapes, cotton seeds, rice seeds, lentil seeds and a large variety of plants suspected of containing harmful pests for China, and fresh mangoes, lychees, broad bean seeds, cotton seeds, cotton fibre and rice from India. SPS measures aiming to protect food safety, and plant and animal health are often deployed with a protectionist agenda for discouraging agricultural imports. Several TPP members such as the United States, Canada, Peru, Chile, New Zealand and Australia show strong tendencies to initiate SPS measures that not only affect agricultural exports from China and India but also from other countries. American agricultural exporters backed by lawmakers have been pressing for strong SPS rules in the TPP for ensuring deeper access of these exports in the TPP markets.[23] Other agricultural exporter members in the TPP also have similar offensive interests. While considerable energy in the TPP negotiations have been spent on arriving at an efficient mechanism for resolving SPS disputes between members, China and India's worries would be over the ramifications of 'stronger' SPS measures for their agricultural exports to TPP countries. In this regard, it is interesting to note that even bilateral FTAs are not deterrents for the imposition of SPS measures. China and India have FTAs with Peru and Chile: but that has not prevented the imposition of SPSs by them on Chinese and Indian exports (Table 3.11). Given that several agricultural products are important exports for China and India, and the MFN tariffs on these in the TPP countries are higher than those in manufactured items, stronger SPS norms in the TPP bloc are likely to create additional handicaps for agricultural exports.

Adverse effects on exports can also be created by a more discriminatory application of SPS and TBT measures. Several of the latter currently maintained by the TPP members are generic and influence specific exports from China and India in the same way as they do exports from other countries. In terms of SPS measures (in force), the largest incidences of the generic deployments are by the United States (377), followed by Peru (207), New Zealand (67) and Chile (32) (Table 3.9). For TBTs (namely, domestic regulations pertaining to standards,

Table 3.11 SPS measures in TPP member countries raised for China and India

Country	China	India
Australia	Risks in importing table grapes from China and measures for achieving appropriate level of bio-security.	
Chile		Phytosanitary requirements governing import of fresh mangoes and lychees from India.
New Zealand		Specific requirements for imports of fresh mangoes.
Peru	1. Mandatory phytosanitary requirements for import of cotton seeds, rice seeds, and lentil seeds, originating in and coming from China. 2. Removal of certain pests from the phytosanitary requirements governing import of various plants, plant products and other regulated items (other than China, the measure affects Argentina, Australia, Brazil, Chile, Colombia, Costa Rica, Ecuador, Germany, Honduras, Mexico, Netherlands, New Zealand, Paraguay, Philippines, Spain, Thailand, United Kingdom and the United States).	1. Mandatory phytosanitary requirements for import of broad bean seeds, cotton seeds, moringa seeds originating in and coming from India. 2. Temporary suspension of issue of phytosanitary import permits for cotton fibre, not carded or combed, originating in and coming from India.
United States	Federal Order for specific requirements of import of specific plants containing host material of the citrus long-horned beetle and the Asian long-horned beetle for preventing the entry of these plant pests to the United States (other than China, the countries affected are Afghanistan, Croatia, European Union, Indonesia, Japan, South Korea, Malaysia, Myanmar, Philippines, Taiwan and Vietnam.)	Federal Quarantine Order for commercial shipments of rice from countries with Khapra beetle for preventing the entry of the latter in the United States. Commercial shipments to be inspected and accompanied by phytosanitary certificates declaring such shipments to be free of the beetle. Furthermore, non-commercial shipments of rice from countries with Khapra beetle to be prohibited (other than India, the measure affects rice exports from Afghanistan, Algeria, Bangladesh, Burkina Faso, Cyprus, Egypt, Iran, Islamic Republic of, Iraq, Israel, Libya, Mali, Mauritania, Morocco, Myanmar, Niger, Nigeria, Pakistan, Saudi Arabia, Senegal, Sri Lanka, Sudan, Tunisia, Turkey, United Arab Emirates).

Source: WTO, Integrated Trade Intelligence Portal.

Note
The products covered are for the period 1 January 2003 to 31 December 2012.

testing and certification procedures for products), the United States again leads (31), followed by Canada (26), Japan (19) and Australia (13) (Table 3.9). China and India might be anxious over the possibility of some of these generic measures being withdrawn for TPP members, while remaining in force for those outside the bloc. For example, on TBTs, the TPP is expected to focus on a framework that will include obligations for developing and maintaining standards among members that will reduce market access barriers in specific industries such as alcoholic beverages (wines and spirits), pharmaceuticals, medical instruments, food products and cosmetics. Once TPP members shift to common standards in these industries, non-TPP countries like China and India will need to align their export practices for suiting these standards. They will also wonder whether the extant TBT standard requirements (e.g. watermark certification for lavatory equipment and tap showers in Australia, specifications for the distribution and use of bioethanol and meat items in Chile, conformity certification, quality control and labelling requirements for medical devices and pharmaceutical products in Japan) are retained for non-TPP members and whether they are in harmony with the new ones proposed or not; as all these have implications for exports.

Final thoughts

The TPP does have a trade diversion threat for China and India given the additional preferential market access it will offer to its members. China's potential losses in this regard are expected to be greater than those of India given its relatively deeper trade links with the bloc. While the existing FTAs with some TPP members can partially neutralize the disadvantage in some TPP member markets, China's major worries will be from the significant preferential access that countries like Malaysia and Vietnam, which are its competitors in several export segments, will receive in the United States and NAFTA markets (Guoyou and Wen 2012). The preferential access will reinforce the competitive advantages of exports from these countries in areas where Chinese producers are experiencing rising costs, particularly through higher wages. China will be keen on balancing the disadvantage through parallel preferential access in the CJK FTA and the RCEP. An even better alternative would be joining the TPP itself.

India's trade linkages with the TPP member countries are relatively less than China's. This is particularly true with respect to the Asian members of the TPP. While six TPP members from Asia figure among the top 15 trade partners of China, only Singapore and Japan occupy similarly prominent positions in India's trade. The significance of energy products in India's merchandise trade and West Asian countries as its trade partners is responsible for this contrast. At the same time, India obtains a certain degree of preferential access in the Japanese and Korean markets due to its bilateral CEPAs with both countries. While its overall trade diversion losses therefore are expected to be much less than China's, its main worry will be over lesser access in the US and NAFTA markets as well as in Latin American TPP members markets where its FTAs have narrow coverage. Prompt conclusion of bilateral CEPA negotiations with Canada will be one of India's priorities given the access it will provide to NAFTA. The concern over competitor countries obtaining greater advantages through the TPP are mostly limited to Vietnam's access to the NAFTA. On the whole, however, given the shallow depths of some of India's FTAs with the TPP partners compared with China, particularly the ASEAN members, in terms of coverage of items and schedules for liberalization, there can be some additional trade diversion depending on the extent of tariff cuts eventually proposed by the TPP, the timelines and the exceptions allowed.

Both China and India will be worried over the TPP's treatment of NTMs and the impact on their trade prospects. Chinese exports have been major targets of anti-dumping duties given China's status of NME in the WTO. While this is expected to change from December 2016, China will be hoping that the United States and other major economies in the TPP do not continue to visualize it as an economy where pricing decisions are largely administered rather than being market-determined, and thereby more suitable for anti-dumping actions. The possibility, however, remains strong given the prevalence of SOEs in the Chinese economy and its large state sector. Such mindsets might continue to influence the imposition of anti-dumping duties on Chinese exports, particularly from the NAFTA members, despite the cessation of its NME status in the WTO. While India is not bothered with a similar concern, like China, it will be concerned over the TPP's implementation of SPS measures, which will influence the prospects of agricultural exports. Different SPS and TBT rules for TPP and non-TPP members may construe difficulties for exporters from both countries.

Additional possibilities of trade diversion exist through the effect of the TPP on imports and trade in services. The effect through imports depends on the extent by which domestic producers and industries in China and India rely on critical imports from the TPP countries and the extent by which these imports are diverted substantively within the TPP bloc compared with their flows now. China's strong trade linkages with TPP members like the United States, and Japan which are the major sources of its manufacturing imports, as well as Chile, Australia and New Zealand for mineral and dairy products, will apprehend it over import diversions. China's relationship with the Asian economies in this regard is particularly critical given that it runs large trade deficits with these countries on account of its reliance on intermediate and semi-processed imports, which are further processed in the mainland for dispatch as hi-tech finished products. Supply constraints with respect to these fundamental imports might imply higher production costs up the value chains for several hi-tech exports from China, particularly computer and electronic products. To an extent, India will also be worried about such possibilities, particularly if its large mineral and fuel exports from Chile and Australia are partly diverted within the TPP leading to higher prices for these products for countries outside the bloc. Finally, services negotiations at the TPP may create new regulations for cross-border trade in several services, entailing greater difficulties for service exporters from China and India. On the whole, trade diversion possibilities exist across a wide range of goods and service exchanges, making producers primarily in China, and to a lesser extent in India, circumspect about the outcomes of the TPP.

Annexure 1 China: products affected by anti-dumping and countervailing duties

Country	Anti-dumping duty
Australia	Dichlorophenoxy-acetic acid, sodium hydrogen carbonate, preserved mushrooms, tubeless steel remountable rims, aluminium extrusion, clear float glass, hollow structural sections, aluminium road wheels.
Canada	Carbon steel pipe fitting, steel fasteners, copper pipe fittings, seamless carbon or alloy steel oil and gas well casings, carbon steel welded pipe, thermoelectric coolers and warmers, aluminium extrusions, mattress inner spring units, oil country tubular goods, steel grating, pup joints, stainless steel sinks, steel pilling pipe.
Japan	Electrolytic manganese dioxide.
Mexico	High carbon ferromanganese, steel chains with welded links, carbon steel connections for welding, sodium hexameta phosphate, carbon steel nails, hydraulic bottle jacks, mushrooms, plastic atomizers, carbon steel black or coated nuts, seamless steel tubing, graphite electrodes, radio-guide type coaxial cable.
New Zealand	Peaches in preserving liquid, diaries, wire nails.
Peru	Polyester/cotton poplin fabrics, woven fabrics of cotton and polyester cotton mixes.
United States	Carbon steel plate, ferrovanadium, non-malleable and malleable cast iron pipe fittings, saccharin, polyvinyl alcohol, barium carbonate, refined brown aluminium oxide, polyethylene retail carrier bags, tetrahydrofurfuryl alcohol, floor-standing, metal-top ironing tables and parts, hand trucks and parts, wooden bedroom furniture, carbazole violet pigment 23, frozen warm water shrimp, crepe, tissue and lined paper products, magnesium metal, chlorinated isocyanurates, artist canvas, diamond saw blades and parts, activated carbon, polyester staple fibre, sodium hexametaphosphate, circular welded carbon quality steel pipe, steel nails, light-walled rectangular pipe and tube, laminated woven sacks, pneumatic tires, electrolytic manganese dioxide, steel wire garment hangers, raw flexible magnets, polyethylene terephthalate film, lightweight thermal paper, sodium nitrite, uncovered inner springs, graphite electrodes, circular welded austenitic stainless pressure pipe, steel threaded rod, hydroxyethylidene, diphosphonic acid, front-seating service valves, citric acid and salts, tow behind lawn groomers and parts, kitchen appliance shelving and racks, oil country tubular goods, pre-stressed concrete steel wire strand, steel grating, woven electric blankets, narrow woven ribbons with selvedge, magnesia carbon bricks, seamless carbon and alloy steel standard, line, and pressure pipe, potassium phosphate salts, seamless refined copper pipe and tube, drill pipe, aluminium extrusions, multi-layered wood flooring, optical brightening agents, high pressure steel cylinders, crystalline silicon photovoltaic cells.
South Korea	Chlorine chloride, ceramic tile, polyester filament draw textured yarn and partially oriented yarn, float glass, PET film, ethyl acetate, craft paper.
Thailand	Citric acid, cotton and polyester woven fabrics, sodium tripolyphosphate, unglazed/glazed ceramic flags and paving, flat hot-rolled in coils, inner rubber tubes for motorcycles, flat cold rolled stainless steel.

Country	Countervailing duty.
Australia	Aluminium extrusions, hollow structural sections, aluminium road wheels.
Canada	Steel fasteners, copper pipe fittings, seamless carbon or alloy steel oil and gas well casings, Carbon steel welded pipe, Thermoelectric coolers and warmers, aluminium extrusions, oil country tubular goods, steel grating, pup joints, stainless steel sinks, steel piling pipe.
United States	Circular welded carbon quality steel pipe, light-walled rectangular pipe and tube, laminated woven sacks, pneumatic off-the-road tyres, raw flexible magnets, lightweight thermal paper, sodium nitrite, circular welded austenitic stainless pressure pipe, circular welded carbon quality steel line pipe, citric acid and salts, tow-behind lawn groomers and parts, kitchen appliance shelving and racks, oil country tubular goods, pre-stressed concrete steel wire strand, steel grating, narrow woven ribbons with woven selvedge, magnesia carbon bricks, seamless carbon and alloy steel standard, line and pressure pipe, coated paper suitable for high-quality print graphics, potassium phosphate salts, drill pipe, aluminium extrusions, multi-layered wood flooring, high pressure steel cylinders, crystalline silicon photovoltaic cells.

Source: WTO, Integrated Trade Intelligence Portal.

Note
The products covered are for the period 1 January 2003 to 31 December 2012 and relate to those on which the anti-dumping and countervailing duties continue to remain in force and excludes those that have been withdrawn.

Annexure 2 India: products affected by anti-dumping and countervailing duties

Country	Anti-dumping duties
Canada	Carbon steel welded pipe.
Peru	Woven fabrics of polyester staple fibres, mixed mainly or solely with viscose rayon staple fibres.
United States	Pre-stressed concrete steel wire strand, carbazole violet pigment 23, frozen warm water shrimp, lined paper products, hydroxyethylidene, diphosphonic acid, commodity matchbooks.
South Korea	Choline chloride, PET film.
Thailand	Flat hot rolled in coils and not in coils.
Country	Countervailing duties.
Canada	Carbon steel welded pipe.
Mexico	Dicloxacillin sodium, amoxicillin trihydrate.
USA	Pre-stressed concrete steel wire strand, carbazole violet pigment 23, lined paper products, commodity matchbooks.

Source: WTO, Integrated Trade Intelligence Portal.

Note
The products covered are for the period 1.1.2003 to 31.12.2012 and relate to those on which the anti-dumping and countervailing duties continue to remain in force and excludes those that have been withdrawn.

Notes

1 China Trade Profile, WTO, online, available at: http://stat.wto.org/CountryProfile/ WSDBCountryPFView.aspx?Language=E&Country=CN (accessed 18 June 2013).
2 'New Zealand gives China market economy status', *China Daily*, 16 April 2004, online, available at: www.china.org.cn/english/BAT/93136.htm (accessed 9 July 2013).
3 China–Chile Free Trade Agreement, China FTA Network, Ministry of Commerce, People's Republic of China, online, available at: http://fta.mofcom.gov.cn/topic/enchile. shtml (accessed 9 July 2013) and Chile Trade Profile, WTO, online, available at: http:// stat.wto.org/CountryProfile/WSDBCountryPFView.aspx?Language=E&Country=CL (accessed 9 July 2013).
4 Free Trade Agreement between the Government of the People's Republic of China and the Government of New Zealand, online, available at: http://fta.mofcom.gov.cn/ topic/ennewzealand.shtml (accessed 20 August 2013).
5 ASEAN–China Free Trade Agreement, Department of Trade and Industry, Philippines, online, available at: www.dti.gov.ph/dti/index.php?p=688 (accessed 22 August 2013).
6 For details on rules pertaining to tariff reduction for sensitive and highly-sensitive items, see 'Modality for tariff reduction/elimination of tariff lines placed in the sensitive track' Annex 2, ASEAN–China FTA, online, available at: www.mofat.gov.bn/ download/cn/02–01–03.pdf (accessed 27 August 2013).
7 HS 401691 represents floor coverings and mats, of vulcanized rubber (excluding hard rubber), with chamfered sides, rounded corners or shaped edges or otherwise worked (excluding those simply cut to rectangular or square shape and goods of cellular rubber); HS 854449 represents electric conductors, for a voltage $<=1.000\,V$, insulated, not fitted with connectors. Tariff data is obtained from the tariff download facility of the WTO, online, available at: http://tariffdata.wto.org/ReportersAndProducts.aspx.
8 'The New Zealand–Singapore–Chile–Brunei-Darussalam Trans Pacific Strategic Economic Partnership', Ministry of Foreign Affairs and Trade, New Zealand, October 2005, online, available at: www.mfat.govt.nz/downloads/trade-agreement/transpacific/trans-pacificbooklet.pdf (accessed 3 September 2013).
9 'Tony Abbott driving China trade deal', *Australian*, 8 October 2013, online, available at: www.theaustralian.com.au/national-affairs/policy/tony-abbott-driving-china-trade-deal/story-fn59nm2j-1226734384620# (accessed 12 October 2013).
10 'China, Japan, S Korea FTA talks constructive', *BRICS POST*, 2 August 2013, online, available at: http://thebricspost.com/china-japan-s-korea-fta-talks-constructive/#. Uiwvnb-jA6U (accessed 8 September 2013).
11 GDPs of China, Japan and South Korea are expected to increase by 0.4 per cent, 0.3 per cent and 2.8 per cent under a trilateral FTA according to econometric simulations of a research study carried out jointly by the Development Research Centre, China, National Institute for Research Advancement, Japan and the Korea Institute for International Economic Policy, Korea. See 'Joint report and policy recommendations on the possible roadmaps of a free trade agreement between China, Japan and Korea', online, available at: www.nira.or.jp/pdf/0805report-E.pdf (accessed 8 September 2013).
12 These countries were ranked first, fourth, eighth, twelfth, fourteenth, seventeenth and nineteenth among India's trade partners in the year 2012–2013. Venezuela, another OPEC member, was ranked twenty-first. Export Import Data Bank, Department of Commerce, Government of India, online, available at: http://commerce.nic.in/eidb/ iecnttopn.asp (accessed 16 September 2013).
13 'India's first 25 product groups and first 25 countries (25*25 matrix) matrix of export for the period Apr-2012 to Mar-2013', *System on Foreign Trade Performance Analysis (FTPA)*, Department of Commerce, Government of India, online, available at: http://commerce.nic.in/ftpa/matrix.asp (accessed 16 September 2013).

14 India had a trade surplus of US$3.1 billion with Brazil in 2012–2013 and a trade deficit of US$4.1 billion with Chile in the same year.

15 'Preferential trade agreement with Chile', Department of Commerce, Government of India, online, available at: www.commerce.nic.in/trade/international_ta_indchile.asp (accessed 17 September 2013).

16 See 'Chile seeks India trade pact expansion', Reuters, Santiago, 26 January 2013, online, available at: http://in.reuters.com/article/2013/01/26/chile-trade-agreement-india-idINDEE90P04M20130126 (accessed 17 September 2013) and 'Expansion of India–Chile preferential trade agreement (PTA)', Department of Commerce, Government of India, online, available at: http://commerce.nic.in/trade/international_ta_current_details.asp#b7 (accessed 18 September 2013).

17 'Agreement on trade in goods under the framework agreement on comprehensive economic cooperation between the Republic of India and the Association of Southeast Asian Nations', Annex 1, Schedules of Tariff Commitments, pp. 21–26, online, available at: http://commerce.gov.in/trade/ASEAN-India%20Trade%20in%20Goods%20Agreement.pdf (Accessed 18 September 2013).

18 Ibid.

19 Annex 2–1, Schedules of Tariff Commitments, Comprehensive Economic Cooperation Agreement between The Government of the Republic of India and the Government of Malaysia, online, available at: www.commerce.nic.in/trade/IMCECA/Annex%202–1%20Tariff%20reduction%20and%20Elimination.pdf (accessed 18 September 2013).

20 Annex 2B, Schedule of Singapore, Comprehensive Economic Cooperation Agreement between the Republic of India and the Republic of Singapore, online, available at: www.commerce.nic.in/ceca/toc.htm (accessed 18 September 2013).

21 See 'Comprehensive economic partnership agreement between the Republic of India and Japan', Department of Commerce, Government of India, online, available at: http://commerce.nic.in/trade/IJCEPA_Basic_Agreement.pdf (accessed 18 September 2013) and 'India Japan CEPA comes into force: commerce secretary calls it a major step for a larger East Asian partnership', Press Information Bureau, Government of India, 1 August 2011, online, available at: http://pib.nic.in/newsite/erelease.aspx?relid=73596 (accessed 18 September 2013).

22 An NME is perceived as one operating under significant government control with large presence of state enterprises. For imports from a WTO member with NME status, the other member initiating anti-dumping investigations has considerable flexibility in deciding 'normal value' – the price at which it is available in the country of its production. Dumping occurs when exports are priced at below their normal values. For NMEs, which are assumed to have state enterprises with monopoly control over pricing, such normal values are difficult to determine, making it easy for other members to arbitrarily fix normal values and initiative investigations.

23 Letter by Congress Members to the USTR Ron Kirk, 3 August 2012, online, available at: http://adriansmith.house.gov/sites/adriansmith.house.gov/files/documents/Final%20Letter.pdf (accessed 23 September 2013).

4   Implications for Asian regionalism

The Asia-Pacific has been trying to economically integrate for more than two decades now. The APEC was born with the idea of promoting regionalism on both sides of the Pacific by encouraging members to liberalize trade in a voluntary and non-discriminatory fashion for eventual deeper and effective integration in the multilateral trade system of the WTO. Over time, regionalism in the Asia-Pacific became distinct by intra-Asian and trans-Pacific efforts; the former including ASEAN-centric regional collectives like the ASEAN+3 and ASEAN+6, and the latter the TPSEP of the P4 group. The TPP, which grew out of the P4 as a US-led regional integration effort, aspires to gather the APEC economies in the overarching pan-regional free trade compact of the FTAAP, as emphasized by the TPP country leaders' in their latest joint statement issued in October 2013.[1] The TPP's emergence has also simultaneously enthused intra-Asian integration efforts, which had become moribund during the latter part of the last decade, and have now revived through the RCEP.

The TPP's impact on the regional dynamics of the Asia-Pacific has significant implications for China and India. Both countries are in the RCEP and are likely candidates for joining the TPP in the future, particularly China, as it is part of the APEC, and at a fairly advanced stage in evaluating prospects of joining the TPP. Both countries have been active in the Asian regional integration initiatives for several years and have contributed to these through their FTAs with ASEAN and regional economies including current TPP members. Through these though, they have also contributed to the dense proliferation of RTAs in the region and the growth of the 'noodle bowl'.

This chapter reviews the TPP's emergence as a contemporary trans-Pacific integration effort in the context of the earlier initiatives by the APEC. It examines the parallel intra-Asian integration initiatives and China and India's roles in these efforts. It probes the probability of the TPP 'multilateralizing' regionalism and decongesting the noodle bowl by harmonizing tariffs and ROOs across the region. Finally, the chapter analyses the prospects of two concurrent integration paths in the region – the TPP and the RCEP – converging, or staying apart in the medium term, in the light of the differences in their templates.

Open regionalism, FTAAP and TPP

Regionalism in the Asia-Pacific under APEC proceeded on the basis of 'open regionalism'[2] encouraging members to pursue trade and investment liberalization on a non-discriminatory basis. RTAs and regional economic frameworks are typically discriminatory towards those excluded as the benefits of lowering market access barriers to trade and investment remain confined within the bloc. The greater acceptance of a multilateral trade framework for generating virtuous trade creation impacts and higher economic welfare is precisely because of its non-discriminatory nature compared with RTAs. The APEC encouraged its members to pursue unilateral trade liberalization in a manner that would extend the benefits of liberalization to non-APEC members also in a non-discriminatory fashion. The principle was enunciated in the Bogor Declaration of the APEC countries announced on 15 November 1994 with 'the long-term goal of free and open trade and investment in the Asia-Pacific' to be achieved by the developed countries of the region by 2010 and the less developed ones by 2020.[3] The progress on the goals, however, has been rather slow and in the meantime the Asia-Pacific has witnessed explosive growth of FTAs and RTAs. The complications created by these numerous agreements in terms of their overlapping rules and enhancing trade costs has forced re-thinking on their harmonization and integration, and has consequently raised demands from within the region for an FTAAP (Kim *et al.* 2011). The idea of an FTAAP was initially proposed in the APEC meetings in Chile in 2004 and Hanoi in 2006, and has gained traction over time.

The evolution of the TPP adds a new dimension to the possibility of achieving the FTAAP. The US commitment to the TPP is based on the eventual premise of expanding it to the whole of the region by upgrading it to an FTAAP through a 'bottom up' approach to liberalizing market access barriers. Given the active programme of East Asia-driven regionalism in the Asia-Pacific since the Asian financial crisis of 1997 and where the United States has hardly been present, the TPP, and the possibility of its growing into the FTAAP is a welcome outcome for the United States as this will imply the original APEC vision of trans-Pacific integration superseding the Asian model of intra-Asian integration (Lewis 2011). The open annexation clause of the TPP enabling more countries to come on board on its terms is suggestive of its ambition to expand by including more partners from the region and outside. Indeed, proceeding towards the FTAAP by making the TPP its preferred framework of trade liberalization and economic integration for the region would have motivated the United States to latch on to the TPSEP of the P4, as the latter was a rare example of APEC countries converging to a trade liberalization agenda broader and more exhaustive than those in the numerous FTAs and RTAs being signed in the region. The trade vision of the P4 was consistent with that of the United States with its focus stretching well beyond traditional market access issues.

The TPP's emergence as a parallel regional integration effort distinct from other 'Asia-centric' approaches (Figure 4.1) reflects a deviation from the

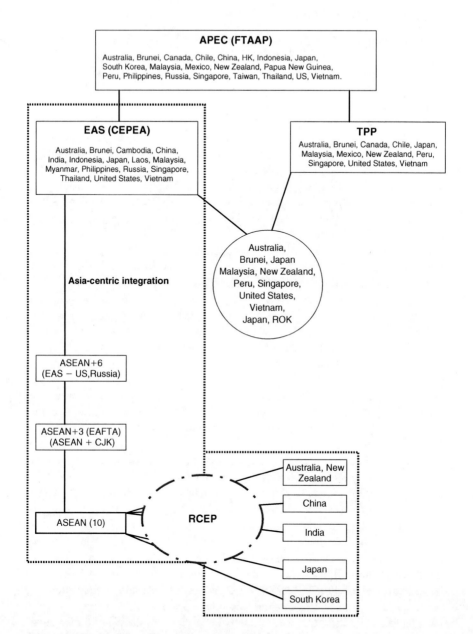

Figure 4.1 Regionalism efforts in the Asia Pacific.

APEC's pronounced goal of 'open regionalism'. As declared at the APEC economic leaders' meeting in November 2010 at Yokohama in Japan: 'An FTAAP should be pursued as a comprehensive free trade agreement by developing and building on ongoing regional undertakings, such as ASEAN+3, ASEAN+6, and the Trans-Pacific Partnership, among others'.[4] The emphasis on consolidating ongoing regional integration efforts into the FTAAP does reflect the desire, as mentioned earlier, to consolidate and harmonize existing RTAs and parallel efforts. Whether that is politically and economically feasible given the stark contrasts between the TPP's approach (reflecting largely the US FTA style and construct) and the ASEAN-centric FTA approaches, is examined later in this chapter, along with the possibility of the TPP congesting the 'noodle bowl' of FTAs further. What is otherwise noticeable is the APEC members' growing preference for mega-RTAs as the optimal construct for trade and investment liberalization in the region. Pursuing a discriminatory incentive-based framework, as a pan-regional RTA like the FTAAP is expected to resemble (more so given its growth out of a discriminatory framework like the TPP), is clearly a deviation from the non-discriminatory open regionalism strategy preached by the APEC for several years. While several factors would have contributed to the greater affection for large RTAs (e.g. slow progress on the DDA in the WTO, proliferation of RTAs, and most importantly, APEC's inability to push its own trade liberalization agenda with the early voluntary sectoral liberalization programme remaining a non-starter (Manzano and Bedano 2009; Kim *et al.* 2011)), adopting the anti-thesis of what it has long propounded might make the agenda for trade liberalization in the region a less participatory one.

Achieving the FTAAP will be difficult without sincere commitment of the regional economies to its economic agenda and active participation in its rule-making process. Reluctant participation and half-hearted commitments might result in the FTAAP's goals remaining unfulfilled due to the unwillingness of countries to reform domestic regulations. The TPP's effort to upgrade to the FTAAP by including more members needs to be tempered with a tolerant and accommodating spirit. The current US emphasis appears to be on making the cost of exclusion from the agreement high by making its template gold standard, if not platinum, and thereby 'force' others, particularly Asian economies, to agree to aggressive trade liberalization for enrolling in the TPP. It is difficult to say whether this strategy of pulling in more countries through the 'domino' effect will work effectively, particularly when it comes to large Asian economies like China and India. Domestic sensitivities across Asia might be too high in sectors preventing governments from latching on to the TPP even if they find it irresistible; and also, even after governments commit to negotiations, prolonging the latter with domestic constituencies crying foul. With the TPP following the strategy of adding more members only gradually, many countries might feel the cost of negotiations to be higher than what is entailed only through market access concessions and regulatory changes, as they will hardly be able to bargain for offensive and defensive trade interests in a trade framework that is considerably mature and advanced.

Several APEC countries would be distinctly uncomfortable with the high exclusion cost strategy given that they have been accustomed to dealing with more accommodating and non-binding frameworks. In this regard, the TPP runs the risk of being interpreted within large sections of the Asia-Pacific as not only discriminatory, but also an inward-looking bloc aiming to create high entry barriers for non-members and charging a high 'entry fee' for prospective entrants. This might turn out to be counterproductive in achieving the FTAAP. Making accession a less arduous process by encouraging others to join on in-principle commitments to liberalization and not insisting on market access commitments at pre-negotiation stage (Armstrong 2011; Solis 2012) might work better. This particularly applies for China and India whose entries would not only impart the TPP a more 'inclusive' character, but would also encourage more emerging markets to join.

Intra-Asian regionalism

The tendency towards carving out an Asian brand of regionalism has existed within the APEC since its inception. Right after the establishment of the APEC in 1989, Mahathir Mohammad, the Malaysian president, proposed an East Asian Economic Group (EAEG) for greater economic integration among countries in East Asia. The move reflected the spread of the 'bloc' psychology in Asia with the United States and Europe, notwithstanding the continuation of the Uruguay round of GATT talks, proceeding actively on regional arrangements like the NAFTA and the EU. The proposal, however, could not materialize due to stubborn resistance from the United States, which, due to its exclusion from the EAEG, feared strategic marginalization in the region and pushed for sustaining the APEC while preventing Japan from leading the EAEG (Khalifah 1992; Solis 2012).

Efforts among the Asian members of the APEC for achieving closer integration, nonetheless, continued, with the ASEAN FTA being the first RTA to come up in the region in January 1992. The fact that the ASEAN FTA became operational with six founding members of the WTO, and even before the latter itself became functional from January 1995, underscored the strategic value that regional economic agreements had acquired in the region, notwithstanding multilateral trade talks and the APEC's open regionalism. Six ASEAN countries – Brunei, Indonesia, Malaysia, Philippines, Singapore and Thailand – signed the agreement and were subsequently joined by the relatively economically backward group of Cambodia, Laos, Myanmar and Vietnam (CLMV) during various points of time in the 1990s. The ASEAN FTA institutionalized a system of common effective preferential tariff (CEPT) for its members with the target of slashing tariffs on almost all goods traded within the bloc to 0–5 per cent. At the same time, it allowed the CLMV countries longer tariff phase-out periods and exempted sensitive agricultural tariff products such as rice from tariff cuts.[5] This was an example of the S&D treatment, which subsequently became a key characteristic of the ASEAN FTAs. The ASEAN FTA was not a framework reflecting open regionalism and the extension of benefits of trade liberalization in a non-discriminatory fashion to countries outside the bloc, given that it allowed each member the liberty of imposing its own tariffs on countries excluded from the FTA. The AFTA was the precursor to a series of FTAs and RTAs that have since proliferated in the region with similar structures.

The Asian financial crisis of 1997 was a turning point in the history of regionalism in the region. The crisis highlighted the importance of countries in Southeast and Northeast Asia seeking regional solutions for integrating their financial and economic architectures, particularly in coordinating exchange rate movements and managing foreign exchange reserves. The urge led to the growth of the ASEAN+3 (China, Japan and South Korea) framework, which took shape in the aftermath of the crisis through coordinated regional surveillance efforts like the Chiang Mai initiative creating a common pool of contingent reserves and enabling bilateral currency swaps. Though the ASEAN+3 envisioned the creation of an East Asia Free Trade Area (EAFTA), it has not yet been able to do so largely due to strained strategic ties between China and Japan and the latter's apprehension of the framework being strategically dominated by China in the long run. In order to counterbalance the Chinese influence in the Asian integration space, Japan, and several ASEAN countries supported the formation of a broader grouping – the ASEAN+6, which has subsequently been christened the East Asian Summit (EAS) (Fergusson and Vaughn 2011). The EAS includes the ten-member ASEAN along with China, Japan, South Korea, India, Australia, New Zealand, Russia and the United States.[6] The EAS in terms of its current composition has expanded into an APEC+ grouping; apart from India, the other non-APEC members of the group are Cambodia, Laos and Myanmar. It is working towards a Comprehensive Economic Partnership for East Asia (CEPEA), which is an expanded edition of the EAFTA envisaged by the ASEAN+3.

Alongside the pan-regional integration efforts of the Asian members of the APEC, several FTAs and RTAs flourished in the region. The proliferation of RTAs has been rampant during the last decade. These agreements can be categorized into those that are 'ASEAN+1' frameworks and non-ASEAN bilateral FTAs, including those between individual ASEAN countries and non-ASEAN Asian countries. The ASEAN+1 agreements include ASEAN's FTAs with China, Japan, Korea, India, Australia and New Zealand. These agreements have fairly comprehensive coverage, including trade in both goods and services. The ASEAN and these six countries are now engaged in negotiating the RCEP (Figure 4.1), which is construed by many as an alternative, or a strategic 'Asian' response to the US-led TPP. More on the RCEP and its economic and strategic implications are discussed later. It is important to note that the RCEP follows the ASEAN+1 RTA negotiating structure assuming ASEAN centrality. In this respect, it is similar to the ASEAN+3, which also assumes ASEAN centrality with the latter being the 'hub' in the 'hub-and-spoke'[7] structure of regional integration in Asia.

Beyond the ASEAN+1 frameworks, several bilateral FTAs have been executed or are being negotiated by the Northeast and Southeast Asian countries. The FTA rush has been driven by the proactivity of major Northeast Asian economies – China, Japan and Korea. The proactivity of these economies again has been driven by a series of factors, including the slow or almost negligible progress in multilateral trade talks, the emergence of sizeable regional economic blocs like the NAFTA and the EU in the Western hemisphere, and, most importantly the urge to strengthen and consolidate regional production networks and supply chains for sustaining the significant intra-regional trade (Kawai and Wignaraja 2010).[8] Indeed, the desire on the part of these major Asian economies to create 'hub-and-spoke' formations through multiple bilateral FTAs with smaller regional economies, where the former are hubs and the latter spokes, is also motivated by efforts to strengthen production networks. It is interesting though that the key hubs themselves – China, Japan and Korea – are yet to organize themselves into a common economic framework, though they have been working on it for several years.

The noticeable feature of economic integration efforts among the Asian economies of the APEC has been the conspicuous absence of the United States. Indeed, the United States hardly features in the dense network of FTAs in the region. Except for FTAs with Australia and Singapore and the relatively recent KORUS FTA, the United States has no other bilateral agreements in Southeast and Northeast Asia. Its efforts to have FTAs with Malaysia and Thailand have not fructified. Its limited presence in the Asia-Pacific's FTA and RTA matrix is in sharp contrast to the region's economies, which are part of 23 bilateral FTAs within themselves and across each other, in addition to being part of the ASEAN+1 FTAs.[9] Major Asian economies have extensive bilateral FTA networks across Asia, with Japan having operational FTAs with individual Southeast Asian countries including Brunei, Malaysia, Indonesia, Philippines, Singapore, Thailand and Vietnam; India in South Asia; and negotiating with China and South Korea. China, in addition to the trilateral FTA being negotiated with Japan and Korea, has bilateral FTAs with Singapore, Thailand and Taiwan. Korea's operational bilateral FTAs are with India and Singapore, while it is negotiating with Japan, Indonesia, Malaysia, Thailand, Vietnam and China. Even Australia and New Zealand – the TPP members from Oceania – have multiple bilateral FTAs with Southeast and Northeast Asia. Apart from the operational FTAs with Malaysia, Singapore and Thailand, Australia is negotiating FTAs with China, India, Indonesia, Japan and Korea. New Zealand has functional FTAs with China, Hong Kong, Malaysia, Singapore and Thailand and is negotiating with Japan and Korea. The bilateral FTAs have stretched well beyond the domain initially specified by the core of Asian regionalism through ASEAN+3, with countries belonging to the ASEAN+3 not only striking deals with each other, but also with those beyond the ASEAN+3. Countries within the ASEAN+6 are doing so as well, with India negotiating FTAs with Australia and New Zealand.

Being a marginal contributor to Asian regionalism is not consistent with the traditional prominence that the United States has enjoyed in shaping the Asian regional architecture through strategic and security alliances (Fergusson and Vaughn 2011).[10] The US concern over being left out of the process of Asia-Pacific regionalism that was becoming increasingly dominated by Asia-centric integration efforts spawning a dense web of plurilateral and bilateral FTAs, has been a major motivation behind its involvement in the TPP (Du 2011; Fergusson and Vaughn 2011; Palit 2012b). This is also part of the larger US strategic commitment to the Asia-Pacific, which was evident from its agreeing to join the EAS. The question is whether the US-led TPP representing a regional architecture essentially trans-Pacific in nature and with US centrality, might come into conflict with the ASEAN-centric Asian integration efforts, as well as with FTAs between major Asian economies and other countries from the region, which assume centrality of the former. If the TPP framework eventually represents a collection of distinct US bilateral FTA-style market access arrangements with individual members, as discussed in Chapter 2, the American centrality in the framework will be undisputed. The possibility of contradiction between the TPP and ongoing Asian integration efforts will then narrow down to divergences between US-led FTAs and the Asian FTAs, with the latter including both the ASEAN agreements and the rest. With Japan having entered the TPP and Korea also likely to, much of the future contradictions between the TPP and Asian regionalism will depend on how China and India respond to the TPP, both through efforts to join the TPP as well as through the RCEP, which is now the most representative example of Asian integration. The next section will focus on China and India's views and efforts in Asian regionalism and their interests in the RCEP.

Asian regionalism, China and India

Both China and India have been actively pursuing FTAs for obtaining greater access in neighbourhood markets as well as in other parts of the world. They have been particularly active in signing FTAs during the last decade, again propelled by the disappointment over the lack of progress on implementing the DDA at the WTO and their failure to obtain substantial access in the WTO member country markets. The FTA drive has also been encouraged by factors influencing the growth of such agreements in Northeast and Southeast Asia as discussed earlier, particularly greater integration in regional production networks, and the persistence of protectionist barriers in major world markets (Wignaraja 2012).

Both countries have a fairly long history of participating in RTAs and are members of one of the earliest RTAs in the Asia-Pacific – the Asia-Pacific Trade Agreement (APTA) – covering countries from South Asia (Bangladesh, India and Sri Lanka), Southeast Asia (Laos) and Northeast Asia (China, Korea). Formerly known as the Bangkok Agreement, and having come into shape as a grouping of developing countries from the Asia-Pacific attempting trade liberalization, the APTA came into effect from June 1976. China joined the pact in November 2001 with the Bangkok Agreement getting re-named APTA at its first ministerial council in November 2005.[11] Though the APTA is hardly exhaustive in its coverage of issues with trade liberalization mostly confined to tariff cuts, it is politically and diplomatically symbolic given the inclusion of both China and India in a cross-regional framework connecting South and Northeast Asia (Palit 2012a). Some other features of this little discussed agreement often escape the attention of the analysts. The first is its historical relevance in predating all other major integration efforts in the region, including the ASEAN FTA. The second is its open annexation clause, similar to the TPP, allowing any developing country member of the Asia-Pacific to join the APTA.[12] And finally, it is the first example of China and India coming together in an RTA, the only other example being the currently negotiated RCEP.

A considerable chunk of the FTA activities of both countries is concentrated in Asia leading to the impression that the 'domino effect' or 'fear of exclusion' might have precipitated the rush (Jiangyu 2010), manifesting in competition for preferential market access with both aiming to avoid becoming cramped for market space in the economically robust Asian region (Palit 2012a). Apart from having bilateral agreements with ASEAN, both have comprehensive FTAs with Singapore, while India has a similar agreement with Malaysia and an FTA with Thailand. India is negotiating a bilateral FTA with Indonesia, and is ahead of China in securing formal comprehensive bilateral economic agreements with Japan and Korea. This is in contrast to China's FTAs in the region, which have focused on expanding links with economies on which it claims sovereignty, such as Hong Kong, Macau and Taiwan (Jiangyu 2011). China's bilateral FTAs with individual Southeast Asian countries are comparatively less than those of India, which is primarily explained by the difficult political relations it has with several members of the ASEAN. Similar strategic constraints are influencing the formation of the CJK FTA as mentioned earlier, in Chapter 3.

Both countries have FTAs with several TPP members, as mentioned earlier, in Chapter 3. Among the Latin American TPP members, which include Chile and Peru, China has FTAs with both while India has with Chile. In Oceania, China has an operational FTA with New Zealand and is in the advanced stages of negotiating an FTA with Australia. India is engaged in FTA talks with both countries. Till now, none of the countries have bilateral FTAs with the NAFTA members of the TPP. Both China and India, as mentioned earlier, are connected to Brunei, Malaysia, Singapore and Vietnam through their ASEAN FTAs.

China and India's rush for FTAs has often been accompanied by doubts over whether both countries in their haste to sign trade deals are entering into shallow agreements with limited coverage of market access and WTO plus issues (Wignaraja 2012). There has also been the criticism that many of the FTAs are intrinsically driven more by strategic intentions and less by commercial motives. As far as China is concerned, political and economic motives appear to have combined to encourage FTAs. While access to natural resources and new markets is the obvious economic rationale, creating a benign strategic environment, particularly in the neighbourhood, is often a compelling driver of FTAs

(Wen 2012).[13] Deals with relatively small trade partners like Chile, Peru, Costa Rica and Pakistan, have also been driven by a combination of strategic and economic factors, including deepening strategic ties with Latin American and South Asian countries,[14] getting preferential access into these markets and gaining access to natural resources and minerals. Similarly, China's FTAs with Macau, Hong Kong and Taiwan are also clearly dominated by both political and economic motives; not only has China been keen on connecting to its 'own' territories through formal institutional links, but has also tried to exploit the trade and investment synergies that exist between these countries and the mainland.[15] These FTAs have also helped in strengthening the 'hub-and-spoke' formations from the mainland's perspective. China's FTA with New Zealand, again a small trade partner, could have been influenced by the country's decision to recognize China as a 'market' economy, as the ASEAN also did in its FTA. The latter agreement has served dual strategic purposes – enabling China to gain preferential access into the large Southeast Asian market, particularly countries where it would have otherwise found difficult to strike bilateral deals (e.g. Malaysia, Indonesia, Philippines and Vietnam) – and also in establishing effective strategic communication with countries in a region where it has several territorial disputes.

Many of India's FTAs in its neighbourhood, such as with the South Asian countries – Afghanistan, Bhutan, Nepal and Sri Lanka, as well as with the MER-COSUR[16] – have been motivated by strategic factors, particularly India's long tradition of involvement in the Non-Aligned Movement (NAM) and encouragement of South–South trade (Wignaraja 2011). Similarly, its more recent FTAs with the Southeast and Northeast Asian countries have been part of its larger foreign policy agenda of looking east, which, of course, has strong economic motivations. Indeed, bilateral FTAs across the world, including the ones signed by the United States are often distinct for their political motives[17] as well as their economic benefits and it is difficult to segregate the political and economic determinants, since RTAs are not only important confidence building measures (CBMs) by themselves, but their economic benefits also have significant impacts on generating and maintaining cordial relations between countries (Martin *et al.* 2010, Palit 2012a). India's FTAs have not been exceptional in this regard, nor are those of China.

The issue of coverage of market access in the Chinese and Indian FTAs assumes particular importance in the context of these countries contemplating entry in the TPP in the future. An important point to note in this respect is the gradual transformation visible in the FTAs being signed by the two countries. As Wignaraja (2011, 2012) argues, there has been a perceptible change in the natures of Chinese and Indian FTAs, both in terms of the liberalization they envisage and the coverage of issues, including WTO plus issues. Most of China's recent FTAs have a wider range of products included under phased tariff cuts, and have shorter phase-out periods as well, compared with India's, which tend to have greater exemptions in terms of the exclusion of sensitive products and longer phase-out periods. The FTAs that both countries have with ASEAN are typical examples of such differences. On the other hand, both countries trod new grounds in their FTAs with Singapore, which not only has comprehensive coverage of goods, but also wider coverage of services and the inclusion of some WTO plus issues, like investment and trade facilitation. India appears to have struck a different chord from its earlier rather pervasively defensive stance in negotiating RTAs in its three recent CEPAs with Japan, Korea and Malaysia. All three agreements contain specific provisions on trade facilitation issues such as customs procedures and standards and performance for NTMS like the TBT and SPS measures, market access for services, investment, cooperation in government procurement, competition policy and IP.[18] Similarly, China's FTAs with ASEAN, Chile, Peru, and particularly the Cross-Strait Economic Cooperation Agreement signed with Taiwan, have specific provisions on market access liberalization in services and the inclusion of trade facilitation and investment issues. China also appears to be experimenting with alternative formats in its FTA negotiations: a sequential approach characterizing its FTAs with ASEAN, Chile and Taiwan, with goods being liberalized first and services later, appears to be gaining favour vis-à-vis the simultaneous liberalization approach in the FTA with New Zealand. For India, though, approaches appear to be FTA-specific, with a sequential approach in the ASEAN FTA co-existing with simultaneous approaches in the Japan and Korean FTAs.

An important point to note in terms of the transformations taking place in China and India's FTAs with respect to their coverage is that the FTAs with more economically advanced and 'open' economies appear to be more exhaustive than those with others. This is particularly true for India, with its FTAs with Japan, Korea and Singapore strikingly different from those with Sri Lanka and MERCOSUR, and even ASEAN. For China too, the Taiwan, New Zealand and Singapore agreements vindicate the hypothesis through their greater focus on policy and institutional aspects and WTO plus issues like IP and competition policy, though its FTA with ASEAN is more comprehensive in coverage of issues than the India–ASEAN FTA, and its latest agreement with Costa Rica being one of its most exhaustive ones. Clearly, the nature of FTAs are being significantly determined by the interests and comparative advantages of negotiating partners, which are more inclined to services and WTO plus issues for advanced, industrially mature and structurally modern economies like Japan, Korea, Singapore and Taiwan. Having said this, the treatment of WTO plus issues in China and India's FTAs, even with the latter partners, is still much less than what the TPP would demand. This is understandable since the market access commitments in services and investment, as discussed later in Chapter 6, are contingent upon such access permitted in domestic regulations. Once the latter change the commitments at the RTAs being negotiated as well are expected to become more liberal.

Regionalism in Asia and the Asia-Pacific region at large cannot afford to overlook the roles of China and India given the intricate and deep network of formal trade and economic linkages they have with the region through their FTAs. There are two discernible outcomes of the development. The first is the thickening of the 'noodle bowl' of trade agreements through rapid expansion of the 'hub-and-spoke' frameworks, where largely China, and partly India, has been aspiring to be regional production hubs. The emergence of the TPP might add another layer to the noodle bowl, or, might help to decongest it, as discussed later. The second outcome of the proactivity of China and India in Asian regionalism has been to demarcate distinct patterns of the process. China has been comfortable with the ASEAN+3 framework, which was initiated after the Asian financial crisis in 1997 for organizing a regional economic cooperation framework through currency swaps and simultaneously proposed moving on the EAFTA. China's active involvement in the regional integration process after the Asian financial crisis was in contrast to the indifference it had shown earlier. The activism, however, disturbed Japan (Park 2012). China's preference for the ASEAN+3 framework has been counterbalanced by the Japanese desire to match up to the Chinese strategic influence through the ASEAN+6 by including India, Australia and Japan. India has not been uncomfortable at the prospect since the ASEAN+6 offered it the opportunity of playing a proactive role in Asian regionalism. It appears now that the ASEAN+3 might be subsumed within the RCEP, which includes both China and India.

Irrespective of the strategic balance within the RCEP, it is clear that both China and India's efforts at regionalism, till now, have been more inclined towards an Intra-Asian integration framework, rather than the trans-Pacific integration that the TPP and FTAAP aim to achieve (Lewis 2011). Given the size and strategic importance of both countries in the region, they should attempt to consolidate the sub-regional intra-Asian integration within the Asia-Pacific by bridging South, Southeast and Northeast Asia. This has been happening at a fairly rapid pace given the large number of bilateral FTAs that both countries are party to in the region, as well as the ASEAN+ processes that they are involved in. Both should be working towards a pan-Asian FTA by motivating their FTA partners towards the objective, including an FTA between themselves (Jiangyu 2010). The RCEP might develop into this pan-Asian template with the active participation of China and India. The role of the two economies in RCEP, and their perspectives on the TPP, will be crucial in deciding whether the intra-Asian and trans-Pacific integration paths converge in future.

Noodle bowl: the TPP layer

Rapid growth of RTAs and FTAs in the Asia-Pacific has generated concern over their counterproductive outcomes in terms of higher trade costs manifesting through different ROOs, creating a complex set of parallel and overlapping rules and processes for exporters, and establishing multiple blocs and deals with discriminatory rules and varying levels of trade protection (Capling and Ravenhill 2011). The overwhelming determinant of the growth of the noodle bowl has been the sub-regional 'hub-and-spoke' pattern of the RTAs (Kim *et al.* 2011).

As mentioned earlier, large economic entities in Asia, primarily the ASEAN, China, Japan and Korea, and more recently India, have been actively carving out agreements with relatively smaller economies for benefitting as hubs. The situation has become complicated due to the emergence of overlapping hubs and their complex trade preferences and ROOs (Jiangyu 2011). It is becoming increasingly evident that the positive trade creation and welfare effects of new FTAs created through the hub-and-spoke form are being outweighed by the negative externalities they are generating. These externalities affect producers, particularly SMEs across the region, as they have to navigate between multiple tariff schedules and originating norms. An inevitable outcome of the difficulties is the relatively low use of FTAs and their preferential benefits. Several factors contribute to this, including the administrative costs of ROOs and other procedures for availing the FTA benefits, and a lack of information on specific preferences offered by different FTAs (Kawai and Wignaraja 2010, Zhang 2010).[19] Inadequate information is a critical handicap since it is difficult for users to keep note of mushrooming FTAs and the specific benefits they offer. There is little doubt that while the enormous growth of regional and bilateral agreements has made Asia a densely knitted region, it might have, in the process, significantly enhanced the opportunity costs of doing trade too.

Decongesting the noodle bowl in the Asia-Pacific by harmonizing multiple FTAs is the need of the hour, and the TPP was expected to play a significant role in doing so. Indeed, the aspiration of the TPP to grow into the FTAAP reflects the urge to make it stand out as a composite and coherent RTA that will induct more countries to acquire a pan-regional Asia-Pacific dimension. The question, as the TPP expands its membership is whether it will just be another RTA adding an additional layer to the noodle bowl? Or will it, through the structure it develops and the liberalization commitments it extracts from the members, subsume sizeable existing FTAs by 'multilateralizing' them and decongest the noodle bowl?

The challenge facing the TPP is sizeable. Nothing illustrates this better than the complex web of agreements between the TPP members. As Table 4.1 shows, there are 108 existing agreements between the TPP countries, with some countries connected through multiple agreements. New Zealand and Singapore are connected through three different agreements: the ASEAN–Australia and New Zealand FTA, the TPSEP of the P4, and the New Zealand–Singapore Closer Economic Partnership. Several other countries are part of two concurrent agreements. All the countries are also simultaneously negotiating various bilateral FTAs with other members, including between themselves. Australia is negotiating bilateral FTAs with Japan and Mexico; Japan, in addition to Australia, is negotiating with Canada and New Zealand; New Zealand is negotiating with Mexico, and Canada is negotiating with Singapore. The noodle bowl within the TPP itself will become even more dense if prospective entrants like Korea, Thailand, and China and India, at some stage join the group given their operational FTAs with other TPP members and those being negotiated.[20] Furthermore, seven TPP members, Australia, Brunei, Japan, Malaysia, New Zealand, Singapore and Vietnam, are negotiating the RCEP.

The TPP cannot multilateralize regionalism unless the participating countries and prospective entrants find it a decidedly superior alternative to the spate of

Table 4.1 FTAs between TPP members

	Aus	Bru	Can	Chl	Jap	Mal	Mex	NZ	Peru	Sing	USA	Viet	
Aus		✓		✓		✓✓		✓✓		✓✓	✓	✓	10
Bru	✓			✓✓	✓✓	✓		✓✓		✓✓		✓	10
Can				✓			✓		✓		✓		4
Chl	✓	✓✓	✓		✓	✓✓	✓	✓	✓	✓✓	✓	✓	11
Jap		✓✓		✓		✓✓		✓✓	✓	✓✓		✓✓	11
Mal	✓✓	✓		✓✓	✓✓			✓✓		✓✓		✓	10
Mex			✓	✓					✓		✓		5
NZ	✓✓	✓✓		✓	✓✓	✓✓				✓✓✓		✓	11
Peru		✓✓	✓	✓	✓	✓	✓			✓	✓✓		6
Sing	✓✓	✓✓		✓✓	✓✓	✓		✓✓✓	✓		✓	✓	14
USA	✓		✓	✓			✓		✓✓	✓			6
Viet	✓	✓		✓	✓✓	✓		✓		✓			8
	10	10	4	11	11	10	5	11	6	14	6	8	107

Source: FTA Database, Asia Regional Integration Center, Asian Development Bank, online, available at: www.aric.adb.org/fta (accessed 13 October 2013); Free Trade Agreements, Office of the United States Trade Representative, online, available at: www.ustr.gov/trade-agreements/free-trade-agreements (accessed 13 October 2013); Negotiations and Agreements, Foreign Affairs, Trade and Development Canada, Government of Canada, online, available at: www.international.gc.ca/trade-agreements-accords-commerciaux/agr-acc/fta-ale.aspx?lang=eng (accessed 13 October 2013); Australia's Trade Agreements, Department of Foreign Affairs and Trade, Australian Government, online, available at: www.dfat.gov.au/fta/ (accessed 13 October 2013); Villareal (2012); Elms and Low (2012).

Notes

Abbreviations: Aus-Australia, Bru-Brunei, Can-Canada, Chl-Chile, Jap-Japan, Mal-Malaysia, Mex-Mexico, NZ.-New Zealand, Sing-Singapore, Viet-Vietnam. Includes only plurilateral and bilateral FTAs that are in force and connecting the members.

agreements they are already a part of, and those they are negotiating. If the TPP does succeed in emerging superior, then the difficult and complicated task of harmonizing its structure with those of the existing FTAs and RTAs remains, as a precondition to the former superseding all the latter. A critical requirement in this regard is the integration of the various ROOs. Much of the TPP's success will depend on whether it is able to put in place simple and effective ROOs that encourage producers to use them.

The ROOs represent one of the various areas where the US-led trans-Pacific integration track of the TPP might be at considerable divergence from the Asian track approach of intra-Asian integration. The latter is inclined to using more liberal ROOs that usually pertain to having a fixed rule cutting across most products specifying a minimum percentage of the items to be produced locally (Capling and Ravenhill 2011). In a world where production is fragmented across locations and connected through various stages executed discretely in different countries, obtaining the benefits of low tariffs requires the product to 'originate' within the domain of parties specified by the RTA/FTA. This is decided on the basis of the proportion of local (or regional) value content. The lower the threshold of the local content, the more liberal the ROOs, and the greater the flexibility of the producers in sourcing larger content of cheaper raw material and intermediates from outside the bloc for processing and transform-ing final products internally and exporting them to other bloc members at the low tariffs. Also, for determining the final character of the product classifiable under different tariff lines for availing preferential tariffs, the product must display the transformation it has undergone at various stages. Liberal ROOs permit such transformation to be computed on a 'bottom up' basis within supply chains by allowing the final product manufacturers from a particular country within the RTA to aggregate or cumulate all specific transformations undergone in other countries within the bloc.

While Asian FTAs and RTAs show differences between themselves in the proportion of local content use in ROOs, they allow cumulation and are less restrictive than the ROOs in the US FTAs, which usually employ product-specific norms. The TPP is expected to adopt the latter given the United States' preferences and the fact that the TPSEP of the P4 also followed a similar approach. As discussed earlier in Chapter 2, a considerable part of the disagree-ment between the United States and Vietnam in the TPP negotiations arises from Vietnam's reluctance to follow the US proposed strict ROOs for textiles, which are likely to prevent it from using cheaper yarn from non-TPP countries for transformation into finished apparels in Vietnam and export to the TPP bloc at low tariffs. Unless the ROOs are carefully crafted in the TPP they may end up discouraging businesses from using the TPP, leaving the framework as another obtrusive layer in the regional noodle bowl.

The TPP, however, appears to have deviated from its multilateralizing goal right at the beginning, due to the US insistence on not re-opening market access negotiations with members with whom it has existing FTAs. The immediate repercussion of the decision prompted by defensive concerns on part of the US trade negotiators (Solis 2012), as discussed in Chapter 2, is to obliterate the possibility of having a common multilateral tariff schedule for all members. There are two obvious implications of the decision. First, the US action revealed the difficulty of enmeshing existing FTAs given the wide range of country sensitivities involved in doing so, particularly when it comes to minimizing exemptions from tariff cuts. Second, structurally, a tariff schedule indicating the common rates to be employed on different products for all members would have been a welcome measure for exporters given the simplistic appeal of such a schedule. That however, is unlikely and the TPP might end up with schedules indicating different rates to be employed by different members on the movement of the same product within the TPP. This is hardly different from the scenario created by multiple RTAs in the region right now.

The TPP covers an exhaustive range of issues and market access in goods and ROOs are only a part of these. But given that these are among the most 'basic' issues figuring in negotiations, and the ones that are the focus of the economies located in the 'factory' of the world (metaphorically Asia), resolving these is a key challenge to multilateralizing regionalism. If the TPP cannot harmonize and integrate liberalization programmes for market access in goods, it might find it almost impossible to achieve convergence in the more difficult WTO plus and extra issues. The noodle bowl appears destined to get thicker, notwithstanding the TPP.

TPP and RCEP: implications for regionalism

The announcement of the RCEP negotiations has ensured that both the TPP and the RCEP would become interlinked through their respective progresses. This has imparted a new dimension to regional integration efforts in the Asia-Pacific by bringing trans-Pacific and intra-Asian integration efforts head to head. Both represent sizeable economic blocs with considerable influence in global and regional economic and trade spaces. Given the presence of several common members, mutual influences on negotiations are inescapable. While the TPP has a head start and is at a far more advanced level with the end of talks in sight, delays surfacing from differences among members on various issues, as well as the expansion in membership following the entry of Japan, expands the scope for negotiations in the two forums influencing each other. The TPP's head start might get the common members to bring more TPP 'influence' on the RCEP than the other way around, which will increase, if more RCEP members like Korea and Thailand, and later China and India, join the TPP. The emergence of the RCEP as the prominent channel for Asia-centric integration efforts parallel to the TPP has dragged China and India – both of whom are negotiating at the RCEP – into the complex interplay between the two integration efforts.

The influence and inter-dependence between the TPP and RCEP frameworks can acquire two slants: they can hasten each other's progress leading to the two templates facilitating their eventual long-term convergence into a pan Asia-Pacific trade pact, possibly the FTAAP; alternatively, they might tread the path of confrontation and end up pursuing structurally different templates making the Asian and trans-Pacific integration tracks divergent and distant.

Both the frameworks, at least in terms of their stated objectives, are aiming to multilateralize regionalism by harmonizing the large number of RTAs and FTAs in the region by encouraging more and more countries to join their respective templates. The TPP describes its own template as 'a landmark, 21st-century trade agreement, setting a new standard for global trade and incorporating next-generation issues'.[21] The RCEP, on the other hand, defines itself as 'a modern, comprehensive, high-quality and mutually beneficial economic partnership agreement'.[22] Both are expected to have open annexation provisions allowing more countries to join the frameworks. In this respect, both are working towards the same end of a pan-regional Asia-Pacific free trade pact, arguably with different means symbolizing Australian prime minister Julia Gillard's view of their being 'paths to the same destination' (Hiebert and Hanlon 2012).

The similarity in end objectives between the TPP and the RCEP has encouraged analysts to argue their eventual long run convergence by stimulating mutual progress in trade liberalization across the Asian and Pacific economies.[23] This is also consistent with the APEC's vision of consolidating all regional integration efforts such as the TPP, ASEAN+3 and the ASEAN+6 (Kim *et al.* 2011). Endogenous regional integration efforts do often inspire larger compacts, particularly if the former begin generating external diseconomies, as the noodle bowl in the region does. The TPP is an example of such inspiration, although political economy and the strategic motivations discussed later in the book have probably played equally important roles in its growth. Steady progress in the TPP negotiations and its expansion by inducting large economies like Canada, Mexico and Japan, have recharged Asia-centric parallel integration efforts like the RCEP, led to movement on the stagnant CJK FTA, and quicker progress on several bilateral FTAs between negotiating members such as those between India–Australia and China–Australia. In their own specific ways, all these represent efforts to carve out distinct blocs within the Asia-Pacific, which could well be the stepping-stone to their eventual consolidation. The success of TPP and RCEP in superseding the existing FTAs and RTAs will be in the extent by which they can make the latter increasingly irrelevant and encourage members to switch loyalties to the multilateral TPP and RCEP compacts. While such a possibility exists theoretically, there are alternative views discounting the scope of such multilateralization, given the practical difficulties in consolidating multiple agreements with different rules and features.[24] Ultimately, however, the possibilities of the TPP and the RCEP templates converging for yielding an FTAAP-like framework in the distant future depends significantly upon the influence of common members in the two forums.

As of now, though, the templates of the two appear more diverging than converging. The divergence arises from the fundamental differences between structures of the trans-Pacific and Asian FTAs, which are again connected to the distinct focuses noticeable in the US and ASEAN FTAs. From an Asian integration perspective, the TPP is a separate arm's length 'non-Asian' track attempt for pooling in the region's economies. The RCEP and Asian regionalism fundamentally differs from the TPP construct in their ASEAN centrality. Though the TPP includes ASEAN economies like Brunei, Singapore, Malaysia and Vietnam, with the possibility of Thailand joining later on, it does not have Indonesia and the Philippines, and excludes the entire CLMV group with the exception of Vietnam. The inclusion of the CLMV group of relatively low income and backward economies considerably influences the nature of ASEAN's negotiations with different partners. This is evident from all the ASEAN+1 FTAs having longer tariff phase-out periods for the CLMV group, and also more exemptions and larger sensitive lists. Some of these characteristics have been discussed for the China–ASEAN and India–ASEAN FTAs in Chapter 3. More liberal treatment of negotiating members by taking note of their specific economic circumstances is a key feature of the ASEAN FTAs. The RCEP is committed to such S&D treatment and 'will include appropriate forms of flexibility including provision for special and differential treatment, plus additional flexibility to the least-developed ASEAN member states, consistent with the existing ASEAN+1 FTAs, as applicable'.[25] Though the TPP might eventually end up giving more exemptions than it originally aspired to, its declared aim is otherwise. The allowance of generous S&D creates an immediate difference between the two templates and marks a key disparity between the ASEAN and US approaches driving the RCEP and the TPP. Indeed, this also explains why the United States has been experiencing difficulties in persuading Malaysia and Vietnam to agree to less exemptions and deeper tariff cuts, as both countries are used to the ASEAN style trade compacts allowing considerable exemption space. China and India too are more accustomed to the ASEAN-style FTA frameworks and are unlikely to insist on lesser exemptions at the RCEP given that they are conscious about protecting key domestic constituencies.

Some other dissimilarities between the US and ASEAN FTAs may increase the distance between the TPP and RCEP. The ASEAN FTAs, reflecting the general flavour of the Asian track integration process, differ from the TPP in their non-binding and voluntary nature as opposed to the more binding thrust of the latter. In this regard, Asian regionalism reflects the initial spirit of the APEC's open regionalism. The RCEP is also not expected to be different. The second major difference between the TPP and RCEP is in their coverage of issues, which again resonates the characteristics distinguishing FTAs of the United States from those of the ASEAN. The coverage of the US FTAs is relatively larger in some specific aspects such as NTMs, e-commerce, government procurement, investment, services, labour and environment. ASEAN FTAs hardly reflect the WTO plus and extra issues and are instead more focused on traditional market access issues in goods as well as cooperation, dispute settlement and some trade facilitation measures like SPS and TBT. None of ASEAN's FTAs have specific provisions for labour standards. Moreover, US FTAs tend to have restrictive product-specific ROOs compared with the more liberal and general rules in the ASEAN FTAs. However, notwithstanding these differences, ASEAN FTAs are becoming more comprehensive in their product coverage and treatment of selective WTO plus issues, indicating the possibility of convergence between the US and ASEAN FTAs and similar congruence between the TPP and RCEP. It is particularly significant that Korea, a member of the RCEP, and a likely member of the TPP, has a comprehensive FTA with the United States, which is strikingly different from the usual ASEAN FTAs in coverage and issues, and which forms the base for the TPP. The roles of countries like Korea, Japan, Australia and Singapore, are particularly important in bridging the gap between the TPP and RCEP templates, given the more comprehensive FTAs they have with other Asian countries and the United States.

The possibility of the TPP and RCEP generating friction and mistrust is more on account of their geo-strategic perceptions colouring them as alliances vulnerable to strategic manoeuvring of the United States and China respectively (Palit 2013b). Such concerns exist among countries in Southeast Asia and also in the United States (Jianmin 2013). While the United States has been unabashed in its strategic prioritization of the Asia-Pacific and the importance it attaches to the TPP in this regard, China has been more muted on the RCEP. Nonetheless, it has fully committed and endorsed the RCEP and its ASEAN centrality (Xiaohui 2012). The likelihood of confrontation will increase if the United States and China fix the TPP and RCEP as frameworks of their respective strategic influence and try to develop them as templates accommodating their specific economic interests and comparative advantages (Palit 2013b). Such rivalry will create problems for regional integration and the ASEAN centrality of the RCEP (Pakpahan 2012).

RCEP, China and India

China has high stakes in regional integration in Asia given the traditionally significant role it has played in the process. Indeed, multilateralization efforts in the Asia-Pacific can be traced to the EAFTA initiative of the ASEAN+3 and China's active role in examining its feasibility by setting up an expert group in 2005 (Zhang and Shen 2011). The EAFTA, which was expected to go beyond the ASEAN+3 over time, was soon posited with the EAS and its alternative of the CEPEA in 2006. While the two frameworks were largely results of the strategic dynamics between China and Japan, the CEPEA planted India firmly into the Asian regional integration dynamics, along with Australia and New Zealand. However, neither the EAFTA, nor the CEPEA, took off substantively due to a variety of reasons, including the global financial crisis of 2008, the heavy engagement of major Asian economies in bilateral and regional agreements, and most importantly, the China–Japan strategic rivalry. The rest of the major economies in the region, including India, could hardly contribute to the regional initiatives given the China–Japan sensitivities. The onset of the TPP, however, acted as a wake-up call and pushed China and Japan into reviving the Asian multilateralization efforts. Both countries took the lead in jointly proposing faster implementation of the EAFTA and CEPEA in the fourteenth ASEAN+3 economic ministers' meeting in Bali in August 2011 (Rathus 2011). To a large extent, the initiative indicated a pragmatic reassessment of the regional scenario by China after the launch of the TPP. Given its exclusion from the grouping, China sensed the importance of speeding up parallel integration efforts in the Asian track where it clearly enjoyed a position of pre-eminence given its ability to stay largely unaffected by the global crisis. Its pragmatism was reflected in its lack of obstruction to the proposed RCEP initiative rolling out among the ASEAN+6, as opposed to its favoured ASEAN+3, and also in agreeing to work towards a regional trade framework to include WTO plus issues of services and investment. As the proposal matured to give birth to the RCEP in November 2012, China was again quick to allow ASEAN centrality in the initiative.

Given China's initiatives in shaping the process of Asian integration, it is expected to play a leading role in the RCEP negotiations. At the same time, its increasingly objective assessment of the TPP, particularly after Japan's entry, is also interesting to note. While it is firmly embedded in intra-Asian integration efforts, given its enormously powerful role in global trade and its strategic weight in the Asia-Pacific, it is unlikely to stay entirely excluded from the trans-Pacific integration process. How it does so is a matter of conjecture and will be revealed over time.

India, on the other hand, has increasingly become an important presence in the economic landscape of the Asia-Pacific due to its comprehensive FTAs with Malaysia, Singapore, Japan, Korea and ASEAN. Its shadow in the integration process will loom larger once it closes the FTA talks with Australia. As discussed in Chapter 3, its trade links with the TPP as a bloc are relatively less than those of China, since its major trade is in energy products, and most of its major energy trade partners are in its West, outside the Asia-Pacific and the TPP. Having said so, it has more bilateral FTAs with the TPP and RCEP countries than China largely due to its success in striking deals with Japan and Korea. The services FTA with ASEAN, to be signed in December 2013, the FTA with Canada, and the bilateral CECA with Indonesia[26] will connect it deeper to Southeast Asia and enable access to the NAFTA. Given these links, its increasing engagement with the ASEAN and Northeast Asia, and a steady but gradual change in the structure of its FTAs towards more comprehensive directions will encourage it to be proactive at the RCEP and watch closely the developments at the TPP. Like China, India has also been happy to accept the ASEAN centrality at the RCEP negotiations. It is noticeable that both China and India have become increasingly active in engaging the ASEAN with President Xi, Premier Li, and Prime Minister Singh visiting different countries of Southeast Asia within weeks of each other during September–October 2013. It is evident that both countries are happy to accept ASEAN as the core of Asia-centric integration and the RCEP.

Final thoughts

Regionalism in the Asia-Pacific has entered a new phase with the TPP. It has added a further layer to the on-going integration efforts in the Asia-Pacific and has characterized itself as the trans-Pacific track, distinct from the Asian track initiatives such as the ASEAN+3 and ASEAN+6. The TPP aims to extend to the entire region in the foreseeable future by drawing more economies in its fold. This is identical to the goal of the parallel Asian-track initiative of the RCEP. The TPP has succeeded in drawing more members as it has proceeded, while the RCEP has begun with a sizeable membership of 16 countries. While the TPP will aim to include more APEC economies, the RCEP will first focus on its core of ASEAN+6. The expansionist ambitions of both agreements have implications for the APEC economies that are not part of either, or both agreements, and also other Asian non-APEC economies having strong economic links with the Asia-Pacific. In this regard, the TPP and the RCEP have serious implications for China and India's perspectives and roles in regionalism given that both of them are currently excluded from the TPP but negotiating at the RCEP.

Whether the TPP can realize the US vision of enlarging into a pan-Asia-Pacific RTA, and whether it complements or conflicts with the RCEP in doing so, will be known over time. However, there is little doubt that as the latest trans-Pacific integration initiative aiming to gather APEC economies into a comprehensive modern high quality RTA under US leadership, the TPP deviates from the APEC's original stated goals of 'open regionalism' and non-discriminatory trade liberalization. As a binding rule-based framework insisting on prior trade liberalization commitments, the high entry fees for joining the TPP might make its journey towards the FTAAP an elusive goal. This is all the more a concern since many APEC economies still wedded to open regionalism and voluntary commitments might find the TPP approach stifling: the unhappy countries might brand the TPP a US trade template, rather than a representative and inclusive regional framework for the Asia-Pacific. The TPP might well fail to become an FTAAP then, in spite of being a gold (or even platinum) standard RTA. Indeed, an overwhelming US presence in the region has not been historically welcome, evident from Malaysia's President Mahathir's efforts to keep the United States at bay in his intra-Asian integration plan, as well as the distance maintained by the ASEAN+3 from the United States. Subscribing to a larger US FTA therefore might not make the TPP particularly popular in the region.

If the TPP shows signs of evolving into a model with strong characteristics of US FTAs, it might also turn into a hub-and-spoke formation for the region with the United States as the hub. This was a distinct possibility till the entry of Japan. Japan's prominence as a regional hub in several Asian FTAs has partially neutralized the possibility of the TPP's equilibrium shifting decisively towards a US hub. Entry of more prominent Asian economies currently functioning as cores of regional supply chains such as Korea, Thailand and China, as well as an emergent hub like India, will impart the TPP a more balanced regional flavour. Ideally, a pan-Asia-Pacific RTA should aspire to create a dense web of intraregional production networks that can be facilitated by several major economies with complementary structures. The entry of China and India can be critical in this regard.

The primary concern for China and India, as they negotiate at the RCEP, is to anticipate the TPP 'influence' on the RCEP negotiations. Such influences will manifest through common members. Given the pronounced 'non-Asian' flavour the TPP imparts to regional integration, common members are likely to encounter dilemmas over whether they should focus more on the Asian-track negotiating approach or the TPP style. All common members are Asian economies with ASEAN FTAs and would be split between negotiating styles and emphasis. As of now, the TPP and RCEP templates are different, primarily due to the TPP's thrust on greater WTO plus issues and regulatory coherence. These differences compound contrasting features of the US and ASEAN FTAs discussed earlier, characterizing the two frameworks. Notwithstanding the differences, common members might indeed succeed in making the distance between the two templates smaller than otherwise imagined. For China and India, it becomes imperative to engage in deeper dialogue and consultations with the common members for gauging evolving postures on various issues. Otherwise, they might well be caught unprepared on key negotiating points at the RCEP.

China and India belong to one of the earliest cross-regional integration efforts in the Asia-Pacific, the APTA. They have also been active in almost all other intra-Asian integration initiatives in the region. For pan-regional initiatives such as the ASEAN+3, ASEAN+6 and the current RCEP, they have accepted ASEAN centrality. The TPP poses a strategic dilemma for them in this regard, particularly China, which, as an APEC member, has begun considering the prospects of joining the TPP seriously. The TPP, for China (and India in the foreseeable future) not only entails getting accustomed to non-ASEAN style negotiations with new issues, but also a different bargaining space. Bargaining at Asian RTA negotiations is an entirely different ball game for China and India given their large economic weights in the region, particularly China's, putting them in relatively favourable positions for influencing negotiations. The TPP would be different given that their entries are likely to be not only conditional to significant market access commitments, but also bilaterally thrashed out with the United States on several matters. The economic weight of the United States is going to significantly influence the bargaining outcomes therein.

The progress on the TPP will not only influence the RCEP, but also various bilateral negotiations that China and India are having with TPP members. These include China's negotiations with Australia and the trilateral CJK FTA; for India, the relevant discussions are those ongoing with Australia and New Zealand. The TPP makes it important for both countries to review their ongoing FTA policies. If the TPP takes off with a defined set of rules and comprehensive coverage, and so does RCEP on several identical parameters and both show possibility of convergence, China and India will need re-think of the feasibility of pursuing bilateral 'hub-and-spoke' FTAs. Needless to say, like the rest of the TPP members and non-members with whom the former have FTAs, there will be concerns over the fate of the existing agreements. The latter have come into force after being ratified by national legislatures and governments might have to prepare for long and extensive debates for selling the new trade formats to their legislatures and constituencies. The TPP can set an example in harmonizing the existing FTAs by integrating their tariff schedules and by prescribing uniform ROOs. Unless it comes up with these innovations, it is likely to remain a 'stand-alone' structure adding another layer to the noodle bowl. Similar shortcomings imply an identical fate for the RCEP too.

From both the Chinese and Indian perspectives, the TPP is the proverbial 'Pandora's box'; capable of simultaneously accelerating the regional integration process towards an efficient direction, or causing it irreparable damage. Both countries have little option other than waiting and watching.

Notes

1 'We see the Trans-Pacific Partnership, with its high ambition and pioneering standards for new trade disciplines, as a model for future trade agreements and a promising pathway to our APEC goal of building a Free Trade Area of the Asia Pacific'. Trans-Pacific Partnership Leader's Statement, Office of the United States Trade Representative (USTR), online, available at: www.ustr.gov/about-us/press-office/press-releases/2013/october/tpp-leaders-statement (accessed 20 October 2013).
2 See Bergsten (1997) for a detailed conceptual exposition of 'open regionalism'.
3 '1994 Leader's Declaration' (Bogor Declaration – APEC Economic Leaders' Declaration of Common Resolve), Bogor, Indonesia, 15 November 1994, online, available at: www.apec.org/MeetingPapers/Leaders-Declarations/1994/1994_aelm.aspx (accessed 7 October 2013).
4 '2010 Leaders' Declaration Yokohama Declaration – *The Yokohama Vision – Bogor and beyond*', 13–14 November 2010, online, available at: www.apec.org/Meeting-Papers/Leaders-Declarations/2010/2010_aelm.aspx (accessed 8 October 2013).
5 'ASEAN Free Trade Area' (AFTA Council), Association of Southeast Asian Nations, online, available at: www.asean.org/communities/asean-economic-community/category/asean-free-trade-area-afta-council (accessed 9 October 2013).
6 The United States signed the Treaty of Amity and Cooperation (TAC) for joining the EAS in July 2009 and became a formal part of the EAS from October 2010. The Bush Administration was not keen on joining the EAS for a variety of reasons, including the no-intervention clause in the TAC that could have affected its human rights agenda for the region (Solis 2012). The Obama Administration, however, quickly decided to sign the TAC and enter the EAS for affirming its commitment to a bigger role in the region in line with its 'pivot to Asia' strategy.
7 Hub-and-spoke trade models reflect patterns where a partner in a bilateral trade agreement signs more and more bilateral FTAs with other countries enabling it to become a hub in a series of overlapping FTAs and enjoy simultaneous preferential access to markets of several partners. From an Asian perspective, ASEAN, and major economies like China, Japan and Korea have emerged as hubs given their large number of bilateral FTAs. This has, however, contributed significantly to the growth of the 'noodle bowl' in Asia.
8 The intra-regional trade, capturing trade between countries in sub-products figuring in different production layers of same industries, was estimated at more than half of the total trade of East Asia in 2008 (Kawai and Wignaraja 2010).
9 Free Trade Agreements, Asia Regional Integration Center, Asian Development Bank, online, available at: www.aric.adb.org/fta-country (accessed 10 October 2013).
10 Apart from promoting regional security alliances such as the Southeast Asia Treaty Organization, the United States has had bilateral strategic alliances and security relationships with several countries in the region, e.g. Australia, Japan, South Korea, Philippines, Thailand and Singapore, for several years (Fergusson and Vaughn 2011).

11 'Facts about the Asia-Pacific Trade Agreement (Bangkok Agreement)', *Informal Information Note*, Trade and Investment Division (TID), Economic and Social Commission for the Asia and the Pacific (ESCAP), Bangkok, Thailand, October 2006, online, available at: www.unescap.org/tid/BAfacts.pdf (accessed 11 October 2013).

12 Chapter VII, Accession and Withdrawal, Article 25, First Agreement on Trade Negotiations among Developing Member Countries of the Economic and Social Commission for Asia and the Pacific (Bangkok Agreement); Trade and Investment Division, United Nations, ESCAP, online, available at: www.unescap.org/tid/BKK.asp (accessed 11 October 2013).

13 Jianmin (2012) argues that China's FTA strategy combines strategic, economic, political and diplomatic objectives and are guided by economic development, access to resources, nullifying the 'China Threat' doctrine, marginalizing separate independence movements (e.g. Taiwan) and improving the international environment, particularly in the neighbourhood.

14 The FTA with Costa Rica also appears to have been motivated by the effort to switch diplomatic allegiance from Taiwan.

15 The Economic Cooperative Framework Agreement between China and Taiwan has balanced economic disadvantages for Taiwan, which it was facing vis-à-vis the ASEAN's FTA with China, where the former was getting preferential tariff access in the mainland. For China, more than economic gains, the objective has been to achieve stability in cross-strait relations and facilitate eventual re-unification (Huang 2012).

16 MERCOSUR is a trade and economic grouping from Latin America comprising Argentina, Brazil, Paraguay and Uruguay, with Chile and Bolivia as associate members. The group was formed in 1991 and is the fourth largest integrated market after the EU, NAFTA and ASEAN. The India–MERCOSUR PTA was signed in January 2004. Online, available at: http://commerce.nic.in/flac/india_mercosur_pta.htm (accessed 12 October 2013).

17 Most of the US FTAs are with its traditional military allies. They include relatively less significant trade partners (e.g. Bahrain, Costa Rica, El Salvador, Guatemala, Honduras, Panama, Peru, Israel), other than the NAFTA economies and Korea in Asia, underpinning the foreign policy and security objectives driving the FTAs, including cooperation on war on terror (Capling and Ravenhill 2011; Solis 2012).

18 The India–Japan and India–Malaysia CEPAs have additional provisions for the mutual recognition of product standards and SPS. The India–Malaysia CEPA does not have any provisions on IP, competition policy and government procurement.

19 ROOs in FTAs across Asia are classifiable into those that require change in tariff classification, value addition content and specific product. FTAs can involve all three, combinations among the three, or one of three. The most significant problem for exporters caused by the ROOs is reportedly the difficulty and cost of documentation (Zhang 2010).

20 Korea has operational FTAs with the ASEAN, Chile, Peru, Singapore and the United States, and is negotiating with Japan, Canada, Mexico, Vietnam and Malaysia. Thailand has: Trade deals with Japan, Australia, New Zealand and Peru; is part of the ASEAN FTA that connects it to Brunei, Malaysia, Singapore and Vietnam; is linked to Australia, Japan, New Zealand through the ASEAN+1 FTAs with these countries; and is negotiating FTAs with Canada, Chile and the United States. See FTA Database, Asia Regional Integration Center, Asian Development Bank (ADB), online, available at: www.aric.adb.org/fta-country (accessed 14 October 2013).

21 'Outlines of the Trans-Pacific Partnership Agreement', Office of the United States Trade Representative (USTR), online, available at: www.ustr.gov/about-us/press-office/fact-sheets/2011/november/outlines-trans-pacific-partnership-agreement (accessed 15 October 2013).

22 'Guiding Principles and Objectives for Negotiating the Regional Comprehensive Economic Partnership', online, available at: www.asean.org/images/2012/documents/Guiding%20Principles%20and%20Objectives%20for%20Negotiating%20the%20Regional%20Comprehensive%20Economic%20Partnership.pdf (accessed 15 October 2013).
23 See, for example, 'TPP, RCEP, APEC to Eventually Converge: Scholar', *Global Times*, online, available at: www.globaltimes.cn/content/815655.shtml#.Uly7yb-jCL0 (accessed 15 October 2013).
24 RCEP is likely to face this problem in consolidating existing ASEAN+1 FTAs (Menon 2013).
25 As in Note 18.
26 'India Indonesia to Strengthen Ties: Manmohan Singh', *ANI News*, 11 October, online, available at: www.aninews.in/newsdetail4/story135318/india-indonesia-to-strengthen-ties-manmohan-singh.html (accessed 15 October 2013).

5 The political economy

The TPP's evolution and geo-political significance is widely debated on its aim to 'contain' China, particularly if it is more a foreign policy and security agenda of the United States and its allies, rather than being just a virtuous trade agreement for the Asia-Pacific. These dilemmas and anxieties have also influenced opinions on the TPP in China. Over time, however, China's strategic perception of the agreement appears to have changed from a predominantly hostile impression to a more objective view, with the distinct possibility of China joining the TPP in the foreseeable future. While the shift represents a different evaluation of the strategic dynamics of the TPP by the new Chinese leadership, joining the TPP will require overcoming the factional divide in China's domestic politics and its effect on greater opening-up.

As a country with high strategic and economic stakes in the Asia-Pacific, India cannot afford to overlook the implications of the TPP: from both geo-political as well as trade and economic perspectives. Much like China, India too in a sense has been drawn closer to the TPP through the RCEP. But unlike China, it is not saddled with 'threat' perceptions over the TPP. India is far from being a regional hegemon in the Asia-Pacific, even from an aspirational sense. The threats that China, as the most significant entity in the region may encounter from aspirants of similar status within the region (e.g. Japan) and outside (e.g. United States) are non-existent for India. The political dynamics for India with respect to the future possibility of its joining the TPP is an outcome of the complexities surrounding its domestic politics, which, again like in China's case, are critical in deciding the course of its economic reforms and joining high quality trade agreements like the TPP.

This chapter examines the political economy of the TPP from the perspectives of China and India and in the context of their specific concerns. The emphasis in the examination of the Chinese perspective is on identifying factors leading to the TPP being labelled a US strategy for 'containing' China and their geo-political ramifications; the change in the Chinese views on the TPP following the change in the top leadership of the CPC; and the complex ideological positions and factions in China's domestic politics that may influence China's future reforms in its gradual move towards the TPP. Similarly, the analysis of the Indian perspective examines the geo-political context of India joining the

TPP and reviews in detail the complicated political dynamics in India and the role of different interest groups in influencing the country's future reforms and negotiation positions in major trade agreements.

Does the TPP try to 'contain' China?

Several Chinese experts consider the TPP as not only important, but also a desperate step by the United States to revive its flagging domestic economy (Guoyou and Wen 2012). These views echo identical US views in terms of the positive impact that a deeper connection to the Asia-Pacific may have on increasing American exports and creating local jobs.[1] The Asia-Pacific region and the TPP countries as a group are the United States' major goods and services trade markets and account for substantive exports by the US SMEs. It is also noteworthy that the Obama Administration's 'rebalancing' strategy towards Asia and commitment to the TPP occurred at a time when the US economy was anxiously searching for means for revival following the global economic downturn in 2008. Chinese experts following the TPP have opined it to be a key component in President Obama's ambitious target of doubling American exports in five years and creating two million jobs in the process (Wu 2010). Indeed, the announcement was followed with the unprecedented move of introducing a comprehensive strategy for boosting exports, reviving the President's Export Council and promoting new FTAs (Trumbull 2010). Given that Obama emphasized on the need to 'up our game' for reaching American exports to the world's fastest growing markets, the economic rationale of the TPP appears obvious.[2] Ironically, the US strategy of relying on exports for reviving growth as opposed to domestic consumption came at a time in history when China had begun attempting just the opposite. The switches in growth strategies and shift to new drivers was probably bound to cloud perceptions between the two countries, with the financial crisis of 2008 impairing the US ability to remain the undisputed global economic leader and leaving China well poised to close the already shrinking economic distance between the two.

The Chinese assessment of the United States' direct economic gains from joining the TPP, however, are distinctly marginal, forcing the impression of 'real' economic gains of the United States from the TPP to be more in enabling its enterprises to embed deeper in an Asia-Pacific trade compact upholding US trade interests (e.g. greater market access in services, government procurement, stronger IP rules, etc.) and regulatory characteristics of the US FTAs (Guoyou and Wen 2012). Typically, the emphasis on WTO plus issues and the export of US FTA regulations to a trade compact for the Asia-Pacific, has been viewed as sequential liberalization, with the US economic dominance in the TPP and resultant asymmetric negotiations giving it the shape of a pan-regional US FTA. These impressions also led to the growth of notions in China about the US intention to 'compete' with it in a region where China has enormous economic presence through well-established supply chains and production networks. Further anxieties have generated concerns over the purported impact of the TPP on

China's role in Asian regionalism, particularly the effect it might have on the ASEAN+3 and ASEAN+6 initiatives (Fan and Tong 2012). Indeed, for some Chinese experts, displacing China from its current proactive role in East Asian regionalism has arguably been a key motivation for the United States behind the TPP. This could be because notwithstanding entry at the EAS and the establishment of a summit mechanism with the ASEAN, the United States could hardly expect to balance the years of effort China has put into cultivating its strategic influence in the region through regional mechanisms like the ASEAN+3. Such a pre-emptive role by China in regional affairs, according to the United States, could well be part of its larger strategy to push the United States out of Asia (Du 2011).

The anxieties generated by the TPP and their role in speeding up China's proactivity in parallel integration efforts such as the CJK FTA and the RCEP have been discussed in Chapter 4. The 'containment' fears about the TPP, from a Chinese perspective, have been outgrowths of angst on the likelihood of greater economic competition in the Asia-Pacific and regionalism being imparted a decidedly US-driven flavour. The 'containment' argument visualizes the TPP from a geo-political perspective and interprets it as integral to the US efforts to return to the Asia-Pacific for increasing its strategic leverage, which is bound to have an adverse impact on China's rise and possibly prevent its anointment as the regional hegemon. Various pronouncements by the top officials of the Obama Administration, including the president himself, at different points in time on the importance that the United States attaches to the Asia-Pacific could have hardly avoided riling the Chinese; they indeed ended up doing so with the TPP getting identified as a regional strategic offensive in the garb of free trade. A variety of views on the purported strategic goals of the TPP have been expressed in China, most of which converge on the core objective of the TPP as limiting China's rise, with the United States taking over the East Asian integration process by weaning away its allies and other ASEAN members and gradually disengaging China from the latter (Wen 2012). The US entry in the EAS and reference to issues in the South China Sea, much to China's discomfort, was again, in the Chinese perspective, proof of the United States reaffirming its prominence in Asia-Pacific regionalism, which, through the TPP, would further squeeze out China given its focus on WTO plus issues and high regulatory obligations (Zheng *et al.* 2012). There have also been concerns over greater US presence in the region through the EAS and the TPP recharging the strategic divide between China and some countries in the region over territorial issues and weakening Chinese influence (Du 2011).

The Chinese anxiety over the TPP's geo-political intentions has also been strengthened by the TPP being branded a collective of US strategic allies from the Asia-Pacific. Perturbed impressions have identified the initiative reflecting the traditional US preference of choosing military allies as FTA partners (Wen 2012). A close look at the TPP club cannot negate the impression. Apart from Canada and Mexico, which are close North American allies of the United States, Asian members of the TPP like Australia, Japan, New Zealand and Singapore (and potential members like South Korea and Thailand) also have close defence and strategic alliances with the United States, as do the Latin American members Peru and Chile. China has also been irked over the inviting Vietnam to join the TPP, given its strategic discomfort with the country. It is indeed baffling that the United States and the other TPP members considered Vietnam more 'eligible' for joining the TPP and 'capable' of meeting its high standards than China given that Vietnam joined the WTO as late as in 2007 and has a one-party system and a large state sector (Jianmin 2012). If these features were responsible for casting doubts upon the ability of the world's second largest economy with 10 per cent and 5 per cent shares in global goods and services trades to implement necessary reforms for joining the TPP, then how could a country with similar features but an economy barely 3 per cent of the size of China (in PPP terms) and with 0.5 and 0.3 percentage point shares in world goods and services trades be deemed fit for doing so?

The shift in the US priority towards Asia took place at a time when the US preoccupation over West and South Asia gradually lessened with the perceived ebbing of terrorist activities in the regions (Du 2011). The eagerness to switch to Asia-Pacific by stitching together an alliance of what at least superficially appears to be a group of 'like minded' allies has been a source of consternation for China. Indeed, whether it be from the perspective of being squeezed out by the United States from the regional integration process, or the prospect of being strategically marginalized by a US-led collective of countries including its allies and those unhappy with China for various reasons, the geo-political threat perception of the TPP is not limited to Chinese scholars, but also other academic views analysing its political economy dimensions and interpreting it as a US foreign policy and security instrument for undermining Chinese influence (Capling and Ravenhill 2012). If the TPP does become driven more by foreign policy and security interests rather than trade and economic welfare-enhancing motives, it might not only prevent the agreement from achieving its high aspiration, but may also increase its strategic distance from China (Lim *et al.* 2012).

The views on the TPP aiming to strategically contain China, needless to say, have contradictory opinions, aired primarily by experts, who visualize the TPP as the stepping stone for the FTAAP, which cannot possibly materialize without China. The argument in this regard is to consider all ongoing integration efforts in the region as complementary, with trade liberalization achieved through the TPP and parallel efforts like the RCEP to eventually converge. The initial commitment to the expanded P4 talks in 2008 by the Bush Administration following the deadlock over the Doha round at the WTO was probably too early and immature to accommodate a geo-political containment aspect (Wen 2012). Thereafter, the growth of the TPP and its China containment objective – according to rebutters of the containment strategy – gained traction from the ceaseless and high-pitch US tirade against China in trade policy debates, particularly the alleged unfair trade practices by China and enforcement actions by the United States (Bergsten and Schott 2012; Schott *et al.* 2013). Noting that the United States and China need to work together for managing the complications of what is probably the most important bilateral commercial relationship in the world, the critics of the containment theory negate such motives on part of the United States. It is difficult to say how convincing such denials are for China given that economic and political motives are difficult to disentangle from FTA and RTA strategies pursued by the United States. It is amply clear though that the entry bar at the TPP is rather high for China, making it difficult for Chinese authorities to officially express their willingness to join the negotiations. While proponents of the non-containment view accept the progress that China has made in converging towards the TPP (Schott *et al.* 2013), the gap between the TPP's demands and China's preparedness remains noticeably large.

The Chinese government's official approach to the TPP was somewhat cautious and circumspect at the beginning. The leadership refrained from public posturing on the issue and instead adopted a 'wait and watch' policy. At the APEC meeting in Hawaii in November 2011, where the TPP leaders, led by President Obama, announced the broad outlines of the agreement, President Hu called upon businesses in the APEC to 'uphold the multilateral trading regime' and work towards making it 'balanced and inclusive'.[3] At the same time, he reiterated the importance of the APEC remaining committed to regional integration and China's commitment to all ongoing regional integration efforts (Fan and Tong 2012). The simultaneous endorsement of the multilateral trade regime and regional integration efforts by the Chinese president made China's posture rather ambiguous in terms of its preferred alignment. But its enthusiastic endorsement of the RCEP as a parallel integration effort in the region upholding the Asian-style integration initiatives with ASEAN centrality was clearly a signal that China refused to withdraw from its position of prominence in integrating Asia.

As an alternative to the TPP, the RCEP probably helped China in securing multiple strategic objectives such as assuring ASEAN about China's commitment to preserving ASEAN-centrality in Asia-centric regional integration efforts, preserving its own importance in regional integration without coming into direct conflict with the United States and entering a multilateral agreement including countries like Japan and India with whom it would have otherwise found difficult to have bilateral FTAs due to strategic reasons (Jianmin 2013). Given the efforts China has made in economically integrating Asia since the commencement of the EAFTA initiative through the ASEAN+3 as discussed in Chapter 4, it was important for it to stay committed to the RCEP. The latter was also expected to be a less demanding agreement than the TPP and one where China could exert considerable influence given its strategic weight in the region.

During 2009–2012 – the first four years of TPP negotiations – China's views on the TPP displayed a mixture of concern and caution. The concerns were more from a geo-political perspective and less on economics. On the latter again there have been contrasting views, including positive notions suggesting China's joining the TPP offering it an important opportunity for introducing critical reforms in the economy, as it was able to do by joining the WTO (Fan and Tong

2012). But fears of trade diversion from exclusion from the TPP, some of which have been discussed in Chapter 3, have also been highlighted. These include alarmist postures apprehending greater export competition between China and TPP members like Malaysia and Vietnam producing several similar products, as well as relatively unruffled impressions citing the contrasting comparative advantages and economic characteristics between the more industrialized TPP economies and China that are unlikely to generate export competition (Wen 2012). China's FTAs with several TPP members, including the ASEAN, provides it with a degree of comfort in minimizing trade diversion losses except for a few years during which the scheduled tariff cuts in China's FTAs might proceed at slower paces than those in the TPP, as discussed in Chapter 3. Such degree of comfort, though, was noticeably absent in analysing the geopolitical repercussions of the TPP, till the change in Chinese leadership.

As mentioned earlier, US experts rebutting the China containment objective of the TPP point to the shrill rhetoric against China by US trade officials as one of the factors responsible for shrouding the TPP with its allegedly sinister geopolitical motives. The US angst against China since the outbreak of the financial crisis in 2008 has indeed been conspicuous, highlighting the growing complexities between the two economies in their trade ties. The asymmetric bilateral trade relationship and the high trade surplus enjoyed by China has been one of the core irritants in the Sino-US relationship, with the United States accusing China's artificial manipulation of currency for increasing export competitiveness as the key factor behind the unsustainable deficit (Prasad 2010, Palit 2012a, Isidore 2012). Trade disputes have also been on the rise, with the United States bringing several litigations alleging unfair trade practices by China at the WTO and China also retaliating occasionally.[4] The perceived intention to come down heavily on China's trade practices was evident from the establishment of a new trade enforcement unit by President Obama in early 2012 for specifically 'investigating unfair trade practices in countries like China' (Morrison 2013).

In addition to the disputes, the United States has been unhappy over some domestic economic policies in China, particularly those favouring products incorporating home-grown innovations in government procurement, extracting commercial secrets of foreign companies for allowing greater access in the domestic market, persistent restrictions on the entry of foreign films and other audio-visual materials and maintaining caps on foreign investment in critical sectors like banking and insurance. More on these policies have been discussed in Chapter 6 in the specific context of the regulatory reforms being proposed by the TPP. In the present context, however, it is important to note that the frustrations produced by the economic crisis of 2008 and the desperation of the Obama Administration to increase exports and gain access to new markets for reviving the domestic economy, made it particularly critical of policies in China that were inimical to US business interests. Such views compounded the angst over China's currency policies, leading to sharp vitiation of the bilateral environment and an increase in diplomatic spats. China obviously did not take too kindly to the ceaseless tirade of the US administration against its policies, particularly when policies such as encouraging domestic innovation were aimed at steering China onto a different economic course and making it a global leader in innovation. It is hardly surprising that the shrill US trade rhetoric contributed to the impression of the TPP being a ploy to marginalize China.

The first four years of President Obama in office, which coincided with the last four years of the Chinese leadership under President Hu and Premier Wen was also noticeable for other grey spots in the relationship. In addition to bickering over currency and trade practices, these grey spots clouded perceptions on both sides and made China wary about the TPP. One of these was the concern raised by the United States over cyber espionage by Chinese firms (Morrison 2013). Though the US continues to raise the issue time and again with China, the sharp pitch of the allegations has moderated after the embarrassment suffered by the US administration following disclosures of American surveillance of computer and information networks of various countries by former CIA employee Edward Snowden. The United States also repeatedly voiced its concerns over continued Chinese support to North Korea. The Chinese civil rights activist Chen Guangcheng's seeking asylum at the US embassy in Beijing and eventual passage to the United States refocused international scrutiny on China's human rights record, increasing China's unhappiness over the US efforts to strategically marginalize it.

The changing regional dynamics in Northeast Asia was a further source of uneasiness for China and may have increased its discomfort with the TPP. China's relations with Japan and Korea have been traditionally fraught with historical controversies and territorial problems.[5] Nonetheless, it has had deep and extensive economic relations with both countries, which are among its largest trade partners. Since the establishment of diplomatic relations with China in 1992, South Korea has upped the ante in engaging China economically and diplomatically, despite its alliance with the United States, which is in contrast to Japan, another US ally in Northeast Asia, which has been uneasy with China's rise and keen on balancing China for maintaining its strategic influence in Asia (Park 2012). Nonetheless, the Liberal Democratic Party (LDP) in Japan and its key leaders, including Prime Minister Koizumi and Prime Minister Abe, took care in maintaining pragmatic postures towards China. However, the Democratic Party of Japan (DPJ), which assumed office in 2009 and had a rocky ride for the next three years with three prime ministers, adopted a hard line towards China with its tough stand on the Senkaku islands and emphasized the primacy of relations with the United States for Japan. On the other hand, South Korea also displayed what in the Chinese perception could be construed as a slant towards the United States as opposed to China, by taking a tougher stand towards North Korea (Park 2012). All these developments in Northeast Asia were worrisome for China, particularly the rising tensions with Japan. The TPP dawned on the region close on the heels of these tensions. The hardening of 'anti-China' postures on part of two of its closest neighbours and economic partners, both traditional allies of the United States and likely to join the TPP (Japan eventually has), could have hardly created a benign impression of the TPP for China.

Coupled with the fact that neither country, particularly Japan, was showing much interest in the trilateral CJK FTA,[6] commencement of the KORUS FTA, and the bilateral FTAs signed by both countries with India – another country perceived as strategically close to the United States – the impression of the TPP being part of a strategic game plan to marginalize China in the region naturally gained traction with the Chinese experts and the establishment.

China's new leadership and TPP

It would be erroneous to suggest that China's concerns over the TPP have reduced to nothing after the new leadership assuming office. But there is little doubt over a perceptible shift in the stance towards the TPP. Several developments combine to point to the shift, the foremost being the new leadership's eagerness to maintain good economic and commercial ties with the United States and its willingness to initiate regulatory changes and economic reforms for doing so. China's agreeing to negotiate a BIT with the United States is a major step in preparing for the TPP. Similarly its request for joining negotiations on the TISA – a plurilateral agreement for liberalizing global trade in services being negotiated outside the WTO – is another notable example, as is the launching of the Shanghai FTZ for introducing experimental reforms in critical service industries.

The United States took the lead in sending out the signal about its intention of not distancing China from the TPP by inviting it and other Asian countries to join the agreement late last year.[7] China refrained from making any official comments at the time, which could have been due to the ongoing process of leadership transition. Soon after Japan formally expressed its willingness to join the TPP in March 2013, encouraging feelers were again sent out by the United States, with the acting trade representative Demetrios Marantis commenting the TPP was open to China and other economies provided they convinced the rest of the group about their abilities to meet its standards.[8] The most significant bilateral communication between the United States and China on the possibility of the latter joining the TPP was witnessed in May 2013. Following the US undersecretary of commerce Francisco Sanchez's assertion that it would welcome China's joining the TPP, China's Ministry of Commerce responded positively suggesting it was studying the 'pros and cons' of joining the agreement on the principles of equality and mutual benefit.[9] The emphasis on 'equality' is significant, underlining China's desire to join the negotiations on its own terms; and also probably a veiled criticism of the talks not proceeding in an entirely 'equal' fashion among all participants. Earlier, in March 2013, commerce minister Chen Deming declared China's willingness to participate in all regional cooperation efforts that were 'transparent' and working on the principle of non-exclusion,[10] in what was again a pointed reference to the opaque and closed-door negotiations at the TPP, and China's disapproval of the same.

The rather radical shift in China's official posture towards the TPP since the new leadership assumed office, as well as the United States' increasingly positive overtures to get China on board, marks the reaching of a broad consensus by China on the subject and the greater receptivity of the United States to work closely with the world's second largest economy on trade and Asia-Pacific integration. President Obama's second term in office could well signal a fresh beginning in the US–China trade and commercial relations, with the new Chinese leadership also inclined to play ball. The latest developments have been accompanied by several positive opinions from experts on either side arguing for China's entry to the TPP. The views from China are supportive of the move as it provides a new opportunity to the Chinese economy for opening up further and introducing far-reaching domestic reforms.[11] On the other hand, opinions from the United States advocating China's entry to the TPP highlight the obvious benefits of the US businesses in gaining deeper and wider access to the Chinese domestic market and also, strategically, to achieving the significant objective of making China work in a multilateral institutional framework like the TPP imbibing US regulations and rule-based characteristics (Gross 2013). These positive impressions on both sides, however, co-exist with scepticism; while there are doubts over the United States' seriousness in inviting China to the ongoing negotiations given the repercussions that this might have on the American influence on the talks, there are reservations over whether China too, notwithstanding its willingness to join, might actually do so at a stage when negotiations are considerably advanced.[12] Similarly, influential opinions in China continue to worry over whether the US interest in including China in the TPP is indeed genuine given the heavy weight China will bring to the negotiating table and the difficulties it will have in meeting the entry requirements.[13]

The United States' tacit encouragement of China to join the TPP, and China's positive consideration of the possibility, appears rather sudden given the mutual diplomatic uneasiness of both countries during President Obama's first term in office. Much as the recent developments might have happened quickly and taken most by surprise, there are several reasons behind the precipitous turn in events. One of the most important of these is the change in personalities in the Chinese leadership. President Xi's assumption of office is particularly important in this regard. President Xi visited China in his capacity as the vice-president in February 2012, at a time, when the United States was gradually getting into election mode and the Obama Administration was mindful of concerns that the average American workers in the manufacturing industries had over China's unfair trade practices (Landler and Wong 2012). While Xi had to encounter the US frustration over 'fair rules of trade', not only did he remain unprovoked, but also managed to strike a positive chord with his audience with his casual and down-to-earth personality.

A protégé of Jiang Zemin and known for his conviction in market-friendly economic strategies, Xi, upon becoming president, headed a seven-member standing committee of the politburo of the CPC, which includes veteran economic administrators like Zhang Gaoli and Wang Qishan. His team also has prominent experts and technocrats such as economist Zhou Xiaochuan, governor of the People's Bank of China for more than a decade, finance minister Lou Jiwei, who earlier headed the China Investment Corporation, and the

Harvard-educated Liu He, who is both the deputy director of the National Development Reform Commission and director of the Office of the Central Leading Group on Financial and Economic Affairs. Xi clearly has a team around him that is experienced in drafting economic policies and is capable of introducing far-reaching reforms. President Xi and Premier Li have been waxing eloquent about the need for greater economic reforms in several of their speeches. They realize the importance of greater opening up and restructuring of critical sectors like banking and insurance for reviving China's economic growth and maintaining economic progress. They also understand the importance of collaborating with the United States in this regard. The collaboration is not limited to bilateral initiatives like the BIT, but also an exhaustive RTA like the TPP. Staying out of the TPP in the medium term, from the Chinese leadership's perspective, means greater loss of economic opportunities. Xi and his team are happy to do 'business' with the United States on equal terms and are not averse to engaging with the United States for doing so, unlike the earlier leadership, which was markedly perturbed over the US 'rebalancing' towards Asia and apprehensive of cultural domination.

Both the United States and China appear to have realized the importance of downplaying the competition between the TPP and the RCEP and avoiding a strengthening of perceptions, as discussed in Chapter 4, identifying them as templates of strategic influences of the United States and China. The polarization of the two templates between the United States and China also has consequences for the Asia-Pacific region, particularly ASEAN, which is wholly in the RCEP and partly in the TPP, and within which opinions vary over joining the TPP in future. What is being defined as a 'benign race between two vastly different models of economic integration' (Emmerson 2013) might not actually remain so, making the Asia-Pacific a complex and divided region to manage for both China and the United States. Both the TPP and RCEP are likely to experience the prolongation of negotiations given the ambitious trade agenda of the former and the difficult objective of consolidating existing ASEAN+1 FTAs by the latter.[14] China's entry in the TPP can help in bringing the two agreements closer by a great extent, as Japan's entry in the TPP has done partially, and to help the TPP avoid the criticism of being a more Pacific and less Asian template, driven by US business and geo-political interests.

Japan's entry in the TPP has clearly been a game-changer and has influenced China's decision to rationally analyse the pros and cons of joining the TPP. Despite sharp differences of opinion within the ruling LDP and domestic interest groups, Japan's entry was precipitated by several imperatives: reviving economic growth through greater opening up, influencing trade rule-making in the Asia-Pacific, and hedging against a rising China by building stronger ties with the United States and other middle powers in the region (Cooper and Manyin 2013). Prime Minister Abe has two major challenges with respect to the TPP: convincing the domestic constituency of farmers about his sincerity in protecting their interests despite joining the TPP; and extracting the best deals out of the various issues being discussed in parallel with the United States. On the other hand, Japan's entry in the TPP has important implications for China. Japan has been dragging its feet on the trilateral CJK FTA, which China has been keen on pushing as an alternative to the TPP. For Japan, economic and strategic benefits necessitate greater focus on the TPP compared with the CJK FTA. Furthermore, given that China and Korea are part of the RCEP and that Korea is likely to join the TPP as well, Japan will get preferential access to both markets through the RCEP and TPP and therefore may not be keen on prioritizing the CJK FTA. That, however, is not good news for China, as the trilateral agreement will remain a non-starter and constrain its strategic influence in regional integration efforts. Figuring in both the RCEP and TPP along with Japan will help China in balancing its influence on both the negotiations and the evolutions of the frameworks. It will also help China in mitigating the strategic irritants, which Japan's presence at the TPP might produce, such as Prime Minister Abe's endorsement of Taiwan's entry in the TPP.[15]

China has been following the developments on the TPP closely and realizes the importance of joining the negotiations soon as a delayed entry will make the entry cost higher. Once negotiations are over and the framework is in place, China will have little option other than taking most of the TPP rules as given, and would have to rely heavily on bargaining with the United States and other large economies like Japan and Australia for obtaining exemptions from the commitments. There are also concerns over the preferential market access schedules in the TPP making production cheaper in some competing economies like Vietnam, Malaysia and Mexico and forcing the relocation of cost-effective export-oriented production from China. As the TPP expands by adding more members from Southeast Asia, such as Thailand, these relocations may increase, particularly with American and Japanese businesses preferring to relocate to other markets within the bloc for obtaining preferential treatment.[16] While trade distortion for 'squeezing' out China from the region by cutting its comparative advantages in low cost exports is a threat visualized by China from the TPP since the beginning, the best way of nullifying the threat, with China now poised to join the TPP, is to actually join soon so that Chinese companies can also avail the preferential accesses and Chinese businesses can also relocate within the TPP countries.

The Chinese leadership's positive overture towards the TPP has been accompanied by a strengthening of the view that the TPP provides China an excellent opportunity for deepening institutional reforms, similar to the chance that annexing to the WTO has offered China. Influential opinions in China justify its joining the TPP on the grounds of such a move enabling China to introduce reforms in critical areas like IP and having a greater say in the rule-making process in regional trade, notwithstanding the TPP's fulfilling the US agenda of returning to the Asia-Pacific in a significant manner (Wang 2013). Looking at the TPP as an 'opportunity' for kick-starting deeper reforms reflects a new pragmatic assessment of trade developments in the Asia-Pacific by the Chinese leadership. At the same time, doubts remain among experts and academics in China over the purported US strategic motives, particularly geo-political intentions, in pushing through the TPP.

One factor, though, which might provide a certain source of comfort to China, is the renewed US preoccupation with developments in the Middle East and West Africa. Ironically, greater preoccupation with the other part of Asia constrains the United States from playing as active a role in the Asia-Pacific as it would like to, much to the relief of China. Furthermore, while China would have sensed an almost obsessive urgency on part of the United States to return to Asia during President Obama's first term, given the unfurling of the TPP, signing the TAC with ASEAN and taking its seat at the high table of the EAS, the situation appears to be different now; not only are the Middle East and Africa major US priorities, its efforts to embark on an ambitious TPP-like RTA with the EU through the TTIP also assures China of the Atlantic remaining a priority for the United States, as it always has, and has not slipped in the pecking order compared with the Asia-Pacific. China also would have been amused by the US president's inability to attend the APEC summit at Bali in October 2013 due to domestic compulsions. President Obama's cancellation of the trip not only held back any conclusive announcements on the state of negotiations on the TPP, but also 'let down' the US allies in the region over its intention to act as an effective counterweight against China (Perlez 2013). While the United States is surely not withdrawing from its 'rebalancing' posture, the developments cast doubts on the ability of the US administration to manage the Asia-Pacific as effectively as its allies would wish it to, given the pressures of its commitments elsewhere in the world and at home. No other country could have been happier than China by the display of this visible weakness in the capacity of the US administration. This would encourage it to seek entry at the TPP on more emphatic 'equal' terms.

China's domestic politics: elitists, populists and the TPP

The shift in China's attitude towards the TPP is intricately connected to the change in leadership of the CPC. The change, from a larger perspective, not only reflects important transformations in China's approach to external trade and future reforms, it also mirrors the fundamental changes taking place in China's domestic politics. New political groups and leaders are beginning to dominate the CPC and their views are becoming significant in shaping China's economic policies and external engagement. At the same time, political groups with contrasting views continue to remain active in the CPC. The eventual direction of China's future economic policies, particularly the nature, extent and pace of reforms enabling China to meet commitments at the TPP, will be significantly influenced by the success of particular political coalitions in prevailing over the others.

President Xi represents a political coalition popularly referred to as the 'elitist' group in the CPC; the other major coalition within the CPC, represented by Li Keqiang, is the 'populist' group. The two coalitions represent varied socioeconomic and geographical characteristics as well as differences in expertise and experience (Li and McElveen 2013). The elitist faction owes allegiance to former President Jiang, while the latter include protégés of the last President Hu.

Several current leaders of the elitist group include 'princelings' – children of veteran revolutionaries and senior government officials – hailing from families with prosperous economic backgrounds and educated in the top institutions in China and the West. Most of the elitist coalition leaders also have long experiences of managing economic administration and handling businesses, mostly provincial but also some centrally-owned SOEs, in the economically advanced coastal provinces of China. The populist coalition, on the other hand, essentially comprises leaders who have risen through the ranks in the Communist Youth League and come from families with humble economic backgrounds, mostly from the hinterland and relatively backward provinces.

The fourth and fifth generation of Chinese leaderships – represented by Hu Jintao and Wen Jiabao, and Xi Jinping and Li Keqiang – represent the changing prominences of socio-political and economic viewpoints in China's politics as manifesting through the shifting influences of the two coalitions. The Hu–Wen leadership reflected the ideological characteristics of the populist coalition. It focused on reducing socio-economic inequality in the economy by emphasizing more on distribution as opposed to high economic growth, which was a hallmark of the third generation leadership under President Jiang and Premier Zhu. There was also a softer stance on privatization, again in contrast to the third generation's emphasis; a strong focus on indigenous innovation and development in backward areas, particularly the West; and stress on cultivating peaceful relations with the neighbourhood through the active exercise of soft power and public diplomacy (Sinha Palit 2010). While not abandoning market-oriented reforms, the Hu–Wen era did witness the rising prominence of SOEs, particularly in strategic sectors and in line with the emphasis on indigenous innovation. The revival of the strategic significance of the SOEs was in rather sharp contrast to the extensive reforms introduced in these enterprises in the 1990s, including painful restructuring through large-scale layoffs and retrenchments. Clearly, the Hu–Wen combination was a less ardent supporter and champion of market-based reforms for accelerating growth compared with the Jiang Zemin–Zhu Rongji team. The inclination to adopt populist policies for addressing China's deepening cleavages in economic and social equality and refraining from adopting aggressive reforms capable of accentuating these cleavages, showed in the era's trade policies too, which focused more on expanding China's traditional strengths in manufacturing and much less on conceding market access in the tightly-regulated SOE dominated service industries.

The influence of the populist faction on economic and social policies during the Hu–Wen period is likely to erode during the current fifth generation of leadership, which might, in some respects at least, revive the more aggressive reform spirit witnessed during Jiang and Zhu. The populist faction is in a minority in the standing committee of the Politburo with Premier Li as its sole representative. But even Premier Li, notwithstanding his roots in the Communist Youth League and close association with Hu Jintao for decades, is a strong advocate of reforms. He has been explaining China's economic policy transformations to global businesses at key summits like the World Economic Forum.

His address at the summer Davos opening ceremony of the World Economic Forum in September 2013 reiterated the importance that China attaches to 'steadfastly pursuing reform and opening-up with priority given to the stimulation of the market' and the leadership's conviction that 'China's modernization will not be accomplished without reform, nor will it be achieved without opening-up'.[17] As mentioned earlier, President Xi has gathered an accomplished team of experts for implementing the programme of economic reforms and opening up. To that extent, the difference in coalitional allegiance between him and Premier Li is not expected to adversely influence the reform orientation of China's highest decision-making body. Such differences, however, can be significant in deciding the role of the state sector in production and consumption in the domestic economy and the significance of SOEs in China's economy in determining long-term policies on the subject at the central committee of the CPC, where both factions are represented in large numbers.

The SOEs are palpable sources of tension in determining the quantum and quality of future reforms in China. Much of the tension in reforming them arises from the economic and political clout of SOEs managed by the State-owned Assets Supervision and Administration Commission (SASAC), which is the key regulatory agency for central SOEs following the consolidation of these enterprises across size after privatization reforms in the 1990s. The SOEs have grown into formidable economic entities courtesy of generous state subsidies and monopolistic command over strategic industries, such as financial services. These companies are resisting the enactment of anti-monopoly legislations and have contributed to the growth of the real estate bubble in the economy (Li and McElveen 2013). Along with their economic clout, they exert considerable political influence, with many high-ranked SOE executives being recruited as senior provincial leaders for managing local businesses and economic administration (Gore 2012).[18] The high ministerial status of several heads of SOEs has enabled them to exercise influence over regulatory authorities. SOE leaders in the central committee are visualized as a distinct interest group within the CPC, similar to other groups representing specific interests like provinces and the military (Brodsgaard 2012).

The economic and political clout of the SOEs makes them a major obstacle to reforms in various sectors, particularly those that the United States and other TPP members would demand from China, including greater foreign ownership in banking, insurance, telecom and communication services. The test for President Xi and his team will be the extent by which their envisaged market-oriented reforms include lessening the monopoly of SOEs. Indeed, for representatives of the elitist coalition the challenge will be to overcome turf issues within itself, as there will be many in the coalition who run, or have run the powerful SOEs, and might be reluctant to give up control. For the populist coalition too, the challenge will be to alter their own perspectives by rejecting the long-held notion that efficient distribution of public goods for reducing inequality and achieving key economic objectives like First World innovative capacities can be realized only through SOEs.

Unhappiness over the influence enjoyed by the SOEs in China is on the rise, particularly among the rising middle class, which visualizes the enterprises as limiting factors on privatization and new job opportunities. While the middle class has its representatives in the politburo and will ensure reflection of its grievances, the role of the 'princelings' will be interesting to watch. The West, particularly the United States, has been cultivating the princelings for several years, arguably for using their influential family networks and connections for making deeper inroads into China. Several princelings are admitted at the top-ranking elite institutions in the West and are subsequently recruited by leading corporates as part of sustained efforts to build strong ties with China's political elite for gaining access into the country's regulated markets (Pei 2013). The long-term interests of some of these princelings might be in preserving control, as this will retain their high values for Western businesses. Some though, might come under greater influence of Western corporates for abetting greater competition and liberalization.

The first few months of the new leadership indicates the unlikelihood of it adopting a confrontationist attitude towards the United States, particularly in trade and business. This is reminiscent of the relatively conciliatory position of the third generation leadership towards the United States. However, China has come a long way since the Jiang Zemin–Zhu Rongji days and is now a much greater and powerful strategic presence. At the same time, the financial crisis has exposed the institutional weaknesses in the US economy and has left it searching for sustainable long-term solutions. The new generation of Chinese leadership is showing signs of emulating the third generation, which had prepared the ground for China's acceding to the WTO, by making identical efforts for taking the country to the TPP. This time, though, China is in a stronger position to bargain with the United States and will resist offering such concessions as it offered while entering the WTO. The ease with which the new leadership can take China closer to the TPP through far-reaching reforms in domestic regulations will depend on the balance achieved between the vantage points of the two dominant political coalitions and other significant interest groups in pursuing SOE reforms. The third plenary session of the eighteenth central committee of the CPC, which has laid out the road map for economic policies in China, has reiterated its faith in markets and the importance of encouraging private sector development, while suggesting that SOEs will adhere to modern corporate practices.[19] As of now, however, these directions are tentative; to what extent China is able and prepared to embrace the market by pushing back the SOEs will be revealed in the future.

India and the geo-politics of TPP

India has been at a more distant periphery from the core of the TPP than China. Its participation in the RCEP negotiations has brought it closer to the TPP ambit given that both negotiations include some common members. China's impending entry in the TPP will add a new dimension to the evolving geo-economic scenario in the Asia-Pacific. For India, it has become imperative to closely follow the developments at the TPP for assessing their strategic implications.

Though India is not a member of the APEC, it is eligible for entry in the TPP given the latter's open annexation clause and provided it is capable of meeting the TPP bar. While the TPP is hardly discussed in India except in policy circles, opinions from the United States have already begun pitching for India's entry. The strongest official endorsement of India's joining the TPP, albeit in passing, came from the vice president, Joe Biden, when he deliberated on India's future role in the Asia-Pacific and emphasized on an 'open and fair' trade and economic partnership between the two countries (Bagri 2013).[20] From the US perspective, getting India in the TPP would be an 'economic coup' given its status as the world's largest democracy and a major member of the BRICS (West and Caplan 2013). It would vastly increase the credibility of the TPP as a model of new trade architecture in the Asia-Pacific, if India, one of the major critics of the US trade policy objectives at the WTO, were to join the TPP. Furthermore, the United States also stands to obtain geo-strategic benefits by having India and more ASEAN members in the TPP that will make the latter a more effective counterbalance to the economic and political hegemony of China in the region.[21] As far as India is concerned, till now, the reaction to the TPP has been non-committal. India's Prime Minister Singh's response to media queries on the subject has been to indicate that India is studying the implications of the TPP. In the same breath, though, he emphasizes that RTAs should not come up at the expense of the multilateral trade framework.[22]

While opinions are steadily increasing on the importance of India becoming a part of the TPP, and India too is focusing attention on the framework, unlike China, it enjoys the advantage of not having to assess the threat perceptions of the TPP. Such perceptions, for China, continue to remain important notwithstanding a positive official posture towards the TPP. Most of the Asia-Pacific region is expected to be positively inclined towards India joining the TPP, particularly those members with whom India either has operational bilateral FTAs, or is negotiating, such as Canada, Japan, Korea, Singapore, Malaysia, Australia, New Zealand and Chile. Indeed, India has good bilateral relations with the rest of the TPP members too and is expected to be a welcome strategic addition to the bloc. In fact, many members would actually welcome India as a counterbalance to an assertive China: these include, other than the United States, Japan, which has traditionally focused on the ASEAN+6 framework, compared with China's preferred ASEAN+3 template, and has preferred including India in Asian integration models for hedging against China. Vietnam too would be happy to see India in the TPP given the acrimony it has with China on territorial suzerainty in the South China Sea.

There is evidently a considerable degree of strategic goodwill that will back India's entry in the TPP club when the occasion arises. Viewed purely from a geo-political prism, India too would be happy to be in the TPP for various reasons: to preserve its strategic space in the region by playing a role in shaping its trade architecture, to collaborate with other regional 'middle powers' in balancing China, and to collaborate more with China itself within the well-defined domain of a regional economic framework. Being included in the TPP along with the RCEP will be a maturing of its 'Look East' policy that has guided its economic and diplomatic engagement with the region. What will be a much bigger problem for it though is to meet the TPP standards. Like China's problems in extracting more room for private business from the SOEs, India will face considerable difficulties in overcoming anti-reform and inward-oriented domestic interest groups, which, on several occasions, have successfully thwarted reforms. While enjoying a benign strategic image in the region, India also suffers from the adverse impression of being a difficult and defensive trade negotiator. The Asia-Pacific perceives India as a reluctant trade 'liberalizer' with a heavily defensive approach to conceding market access. These impressions have not been helped by India's frequent inflexible postures at the WTO. The main challenge for India, as discussed subsequently, will be to win the battle at 'home' by convincing stubbornly resistant domestic constituencies about the benefits of greater reform and opening up.

Indian politics: stalling reforms and opening up

India has, at best, been a hesitant liberalizer, with several domestic constituencies remaining unconvinced about the benefits of market-friendly policies and greater integration with the world economy. India's external trade policies reflect the hesitation. Its early FTAs, as mentioned in Chapter 4, were executed mainly for strategic and political benefits. Over time, the FTAs have expanded in coverage and scope, particularly with Southeast and Northeast Asian partners. Even then, on several WTO plus issues, India's commitments in FTAs with Japan and South Korea are mostly cooperative in nature and hardly match up to what the TPP is expected to demand.

Economic reforms in India have not progressed in a coordinated and synchronized fashion and have taken place in short bursts. Indian policymakers appear to have utilized occasions of economic slowdowns and impending crises as opportunities for introducing key reforms. This was evident in the early 1990s, when India responded to a major balance of payments crisis by introducing major changes in industrial and trade policies, and also in the early years of the last decade, when economic growth dropped to as low as 3.8 per cent, and India responded by unleashing more reforms in foreign investment, financial and fiscal management. The most recent episode of low growth and economic deceleration triggering reforms was in September 2012, when faced with an almost stagnating growth in industrial output and threat of downgrade by credit rating agencies, the government implemented a slew of policies. Clearly depressed economic conditions have been taken as good excuses by incumbent governments for introducing reforms and minimizing their adverse political implications (Palit 2012b).

Over the last few years, and particularly since the global financial crisis, India has shown a strange inertia to implementing economic reforms. Opinion in the country has been sharply polarized on decisions regarding allowing greater foreign ownership in key service industries like telecom, insurance, banking and retail trade. The polarization has been across the political spectrum, with some provincial governments, including those supporting the Congress Party-led coalition at the centre, heavily critical of the move to allow FDI in retail.[23] The issue has had sharp divisions within the central cabinet of ministers too, which has been split between 'pro-FDI' and 'anti-FDI' groups of ministers.[24] Political parties have vacillated in their stated positions on reforms, with the main opposition party, Bharatiya Janata Party, a proponent of FDI in domestic retail trade during its tenure in the government, reversing position to opposing the same in recent years. The political agitation over reform and foreign investment is largely driven by the desperation of political parties and individual leaders to retain hold over specific domestic constituencies such as the informal retail trades, labour unions in banking and insurance and farmers. The desperation to latch on to these constituencies has increased over time, with coalition governments in India becoming commonplace, and regional parties commanding weights in these coalitions far in excess of their vote shares, given the critical importance of parties with even miniscule numbers of elected representatives in mustering numerical majority in parliament. The situation shows little sign of changing in the foreseeable future, making India's economic reforms captive to the whims of a retrograde and fractured political economy. The circumstances are becoming counterproductive for India's external trade policy and FTA negotiations, as is evident from the India–EU FTA negotiations failing to conclude despite several rounds of discussions for more than five years.

The political polarization in India over reforms symbolises a larger intellectual polarization between groups advocating a more 'inclusive' flavour in India's economic growth strategy and those championing more aggressive market-based reforms. The former group, arguing for guarantee of greater economic rights and expansion of state subsidy programmes for improving distributive efficiency, have been influential in economic policymaking since the Congress-led United Progressive Alliance government under Prime Minister Singh assumed office from May 2004. Over the two terms of the United Progressive Alliance, India has introduced several measures for empowering the poor and improving their living standards. These include guaranteeing the right to employment for the rural population through the Mahatma Gandhi National Rural Employment Guarantee Act and an ambitious national food security programme aiming to provide food grain to around 800 million Indians, including three-quarters of the rural population and half of the urban population at subsidized rates (Palit 2013c). The latter programme has implications for India's trade policy and has already raised questions over whether it will result in India's exceeding the permitted ceiling on agricultural subsidies under the Agreement on Agriculture (AoA) at the WTO.[25]

While the social objectives of the above programmes are laudable, they have been criticized for imposing heavy fiscal burdens on the central government. Alongside these programmes, which, by the way, have hardly been politically criticized given their 'populist' appeal, the government has been noticeably slow in not only implementing market-based productivity-enhancing reforms, but also in turning around a depleting exchequer through prudent fiscal management. The frustrations in this regard manifested in a rather unprecedented situation with the finance minister, Palaniappan Chidambaram, criticizing his own government's handling of the fiscal situation during 2009–2011 as the reason for the economy's poor shape.[26] The pro-reform, pro-market, fiscal discipline-conscious Chidambaram's anguish was clearly directed against his predecessor and India's current president, Pranab Mukherjee, who is perceived less market friendly and cautious in his approach to economic management.[27] The divergence in views between two of India's most senior economic administrators highlights the angst among market-based sentiments in the government, and in the country, over reforms being seemingly abandoned. The almost unbridgeable gap between pro-market and pro-state subsidy inclusive growth proponents also affects India's preparedness in envisioning entry in high standard trade agreements like the TPP, as these entail major changes in domestic regulations, which, needless to say, are difficult given the sharp divide among policy ideologies and lack of consensus within the government.

India's business lobbies and trade negotiations

Ideology and politics apart, other influences also shape India's positions on market access commitments at international trade negotiations. These include the role of business lobbies and industry associations. On most occasions, these groups have had defensive interests and have lobbied for protecting their home turfs by keeping import tariffs high. India's FTA negotiations with the ASEAN are a case in point, where plantation lobbies, particularly palm oil, rubber and spices protested against lowering of import tariffs on these items. Similar protests on lowering of import duties on automobiles and textiles have also frequently been lodged with the government by industry associations representing specific interests such as the Society of Indian Automobile Manufacturers and various export promotion councils promoting specific exporter interests like cotton textile, chemicals and engineering. On many occasions, industry lobbies, particularly those representing the greater interests of farmers and small industries, have been able to mobilize political support for pressurizing the government on negotiations. It is difficult for the incumbent coalition governments to ignore these pressures given their own inherent fragility, necessitating the accommodation of various interest groups. At the same time, it is equally difficult to overlook the objections raised by major industry groups like the Society of Indian Automobile Manufacturers, and India's largest dairy cooperative, Amul, which have urged for not granting greater market access in India's ongoing negotiations with the EU.[28]

There have also been occasions when industry groups and associations have lobbied with offensive interests. Automobile assemblers and original equipment manufacturers in India, mostly MNCs, have lobbied for lowering import duties on semi-finished and intermediate products from the region, particularly South-east Asia, for cutting production costs. Processed food manufacturers have made similar demands for import of intermediate products. These are examples of tariff liberalization demanded by domestic producers due to their integration with regional supply chains. More such demands can be placed before Indian negotiators at the TPP and RCEP if more multinationals begin taking advantages of India's more liberal foreign investment policies by locating parts of their pro-ductions in India and sourcing imports at preferential tariffs under the TPP and RCEP. Lobbying demands from industry associations in India appear to have been confined largely to imports, either for raising duties as a protective measure, or for lowering duties for securing access to cheaper imports for increasing value addition in domestic markets. Business groups have been successful in securing both, with the result that India's imports of intermediate goods and components have increased substantially from the relatively new FTA partners such as the ASEAN countries (Smitha and Murali 2013) while its agricultural markets have remained protected by high tariffs. Empirical studies also indicate that while Indian producers have benefitted from lower import duties in FTAs with South-east Asian countries, the agreements have made hardly any difference to exports.[29] The finding has implications for India's future trade negotiations. It is worth wondering whether political and lobbyist pressures for preserving import duties has deflected negotiating attention from securing greater access for manu-facturing exports in FTA negotiations – a point driven home by the disappoint-ment of India's knitwear exporter manufacturers over the stalling of India–EU FTA talks.[30] The knitwear example also reflects the relative strength of different business lobbies in influencing opinions. A parliamentary committee examining India's engagement in FTAs and inviting submissions from industry groups appears to have been more influenced by defensive demands from influential lobbies like the Society of Indian Automobile Manufacturers and Amul for maintaining high import tariffs and urged the government not to rush into the EU FTA; the stalling of the FTA talks successfully obliterated the export pro-spects of knitwear manufacturers, presumably a weaker lobby in influencing the legislature.

The more comprehensive coverages in India's recent FTAs, such as those with Japan and Korea, show greater tendency of reflecting India's export interests. These, however, are mostly in services, which is not unexpected given India's fairly strong comparative advantage in some services. It also reflects the increas-ing weight of India's new generation industry associations like the National Association of Software and Service Companies (NASSCOM) – the apex body for India's IT and IT-enabled products and services – in exerting influence on trade negotiations. NASSCOM has been advocating for a quick conclusion of India's FTA with one of the leading TPP members – Australia – and has also been pushing for an open IT services market in the FTA with EU.[31] India's greater proficiency in service exports, particularly IT, has influenced its FTA negoti-ations, particularly in demanding greater mobility for IT professionals. These demands have stretched beyond IT to cover a wide range of professionals with various specializations and areas of expertise. It is also noticeable that India's negotiations are increasingly influenced by domestic firms and business lobbies having strong linkages with MNCs (Smitha and Murali 2013), which could again reflect greater association of domestic firms with global supply chains. Foreign businesses are acting with their Indian partners for lobbying changes in domestic regulations: one of the most active sectors in this respect has been pharmaceuticals, where giant US drug multinationals like Pfizer and Merck have been lobbying with the Indian government for stronger patent laws. However, there are also examples of defensive lobbying in services, such as local resistance to the entry of foreign professionals in legal and accountancy services.[32]

The combination of comparative advantage in services, and the growing presence of foreign businesses and their affiliates in the country, has resulted in India becoming more liberal in granting market access in services and investment in its recent FTAs, and also in pushing offensive export interests in trade talks. More exhaustive adoption of this approach may lead to India making deeper WTO plus and GATS plus commitments in its future trade agreements. However, it must be noted that the new lobbies with export interests in services are yet to gain as much political traction as other lobbies with defensive interests in both manufacturing and services. The political balance is still in favour of the latter groups and is unlikely to change substantively in the medium term.

Final thoughts

The growth of the TPP and the evolving trade architecture in the Asia-Pacific has implications for both the regional political economy as well as the domestic political economies of countries in the region. This applies to both China and India, who are focusing increasingly deeper on the TPP for examining the possibilities of joining the agreement, by taking note of its economic and strategic implications.

China's perspective on the TPP has changed from a primarily hostile view to a more accommodating and positive posture. The geo-politics of the TPP has fashioned China's views as has the transformation in leadership at home. China's initial misgivings on the TPP were intricately connected to the US 'pivot' strategy towards Asia. Coming on the heels of the global financial crisis, the United States was desperate to increase economic sustenance and fell back on exports for reviving economic growth through greater economic and commercial integration with the Asia-Pacific. The strategy, manifesting through the TPP, was interpreted by many Chinese experts as a US attempt to marginalize China's strategic influence in the region and displace it from its seat of prominence in regional integration efforts. While 'containing' China geo-strategically might not have been the primary objective of the TPP, given the vigorous push by the United States to its rebalancing strategy in Asia and its simultaneous commitment to the TPP, it was difficult for the latter to be viewed as simply an economic initiative without geo-strategic ambitions. For China, these perceptions gathered strength as its relationship with the United States entered a somewhat rocky phase with President's Obama entry in office. Trade disputes and the American unhappiness over China's unfair trade practices were at the bottom of the ticklish bilateral ties that often resulted in diplomatic spats. The bad blood spilled on to the TPP, colouring it as a foreign policy and security agenda of the United States crafted for relegating China.

The impending possibility of the Asia-Pacific experiencing a turf battle for consolidating strategic influence between the United States and China appears to have been avoided for the time being. The Chinese leadership under President Xi has focused on deepening and widening business ties with the United States. One of the key components of this expansive strategy has been the possibility of China joining the TPP, which now appears not only strong, but also likely in the near future. The United States too, on the other hand, appears enthusiastic about the possibility of China joining the TPP. A conscious deviation of the United States from its high-pitch trade diplomacy diatribe against China also reflects its intention of not letting the TPP become a tool for driving a wedge between itself and China at a time when China is keen on doing 'business'. On China's part, apart from the pragmatic decision of working closely with the United States and entering the TPP for maximizing its own growth prospects, it has become increasingly reassured about preserving its strategic influence in the region. This is due to the Obama Administration's renewed strategic preoccupation with West Asia and pressing domestic circumstances demanding priority over the Asia-Pacific, such as the government shutdown in early October that forced the president to cancel his trip to the region.

Notwithstanding China's veering closer to the TPP, the latter will continue to remain a source of geo-political discomfort for it. As more countries join the TPP, China will be wary of an alliance of democracies coming together in the TPP under US leadership. Furthermore, greater expansion will also increase the possibility of Taiwan joining the TPP, which will be difficult for China to resist given the support Taiwan might draw from existing members, and also because it is already a member of the APEC and the WTO. By joining the TPP, China will also take a calculated risk in giving up, at least partially, its strong commitment to the RCEP and the chances of fashioning an alternative framework to the TPP, with trade rules reflecting more of its preferences than those of the United States.

As of now, China appears to be reconciling to the prospect of joining the TPP club, where it will co-exist with several difficult neighbours. The decision, *inter alia*, has been prompted by the objective of increasing economic growth and hastening deeper reforms in the economy for abetting the development of modern services industries. But whether and when it will eventually join will depend on the consensus President Xi and his team are able to secure from a CPC divided between the pro-market elitist faction and the inclusive and social development-minded populist faction. The standing committee of the politburo – the topmost decision-making body in the country – appears determined to introduce bold economic reforms, some of which will be the initial steps for joining the TPP. The toughest challenge for the leadership will be to loosen the control exercised by the SOEs. Reforming state enterprises will imply cracking the incentive structure and patronage existing between these enterprises and the provincial and federal arms of the CPC: a formidable task under any circumstances. The doubts in this regard are particularly strong given the dichotomy the Chinese leadership is attempting to maintain between its economic and political objectives: while it is keen on expanding the scope of private enterprise and competition in different sectors, it is not showing signs of matching economic liberalization with political liberalization. Whether the former is achievable without some movement on the latter will only be revealed over time.

Unlike China, India does not find itself walking a strategic tightrope on the TPP. It is still a fair distance away from considering itself a candidate. Other than China, there is no other TPP member with whom it shares a delicate strategic chemistry peppered by geo-political irritants in the form of outstanding territorial disputes or any other contentious matter. From a regional geo-political perspective, joining the TPP is a welcome choice for India given the opportunity of playing an active role in regional economic rule making that it offers. The problem for India is in meeting the entry conditions of the TPP. While China will also face similar difficulties, India's problems are expected to be greater given the retrograde effect that its domestic political economy has had on its reform and opening up efforts.

Pro- and anti-market policy constituencies exist in both China and India. The constituencies make their presence felt in the political cores of both countries: through the CPC politburo in China and the legislature in India. China's top-down centralized decision-making process, while allowing for different opinions to exist within various layers of the CPC, does not encourage them to inhibit decision-making at the top, which is usually irreversible and unaffected by alternative perceptions. India, however, is very different. The world's largest democracy has of late begun experiencing the downsides of a fractured polity where local interests and political groups have acquired the capacity of stalling federal decisions on economic reforms. Also, unlike China, where business associations hardly affect economic decisions, India has business groups lobbying hard for securing their agendas in economic policy decisions, including international trade negotiations. On several occasions the defensive pressures of lobbies have held negotiators back from making additional market access commitments in trade talks, which, in turn, prevent India from securing reciprocal commitments in its areas of export interests. While certain defensive interests are justified by the vulnerabilities persisting in the Indian economy, many others are purely protectionist, and pressurize the state for discouraging competition. India's political parties have displayed the disturbing tendency of encouraging such demands. Even the government, at its topmost decision-making level, has not been able to agree on a common perspective for economic reforms. The result has been policy inertia, with injurious outcomes for the economy. While India does not have to worry about geo-strategic threat perceptions from upcoming frameworks like the TPP, it should be worried over obstructive mindsets at home and the regressive state of the country's domestic politics, which have seriously crippled the ability of the government to be decisive on economic policies.

Notes

1 'The United States in the Trans-Pacific Partnership', Office of the United States Trade Representative (USTR), November 2011, online, available at: www.ustr.gov/about-us/press-office/fact-sheets/2011/november/united-states-trans-pacific-partnership (accessed 30 October 2013).

2 At the APEC meeting at Hawaii in November 2011, where the TPP leaders announced the outlines of the agreement, President Obama commented:

> The TPP will boost our economies, lowering barriers to trade and investment, increasing exports, and creating more jobs for our people, which is my number-one priority. Along with our trade agreements with South Korea, Panama and Colombia, the TPP will also help achieve my goal of doubling U.S. exports, which support millions of American jobs.
> (*White House Blog*, 13 November 2011, online, available at: www.whitehouse.gov/blog/2011/11/13/president-obama-asia-pacific-economic-cooperation-apec, accessed 31 October 2013)

3 'Chinese President Outlines Four-point Proposal on Asia-Pacific Economic Development', *Xinhua*, 13 November 2011, online, available at: http://news.xinhuanet.com/english2010/china/2011-11/13/c_122271144_2.htm (accessed 31 October 2013).

4 Trade disputes between the United States and China have covered numerous issues including rare earth, chicken parts, automobile parts, warm water shrimps and solar cells. See Isidore (2012) for more details.

5 Specific contentious issues with South Korea include China's removal of historical references to the Goguryeo kingdom and dispute over a submerged rock between Korea's Mara island and China's Tongdao island. China–Japan relations, on the other hand, have traditionally been difficult and have occasionally reached flashpoints in recent years over territorial disputes in the East China Sea involving the Senkaku islands.

6 The three countries agreed to expedite the trilateral FTA at their annual summit talks in May 2012. However, the meeting between the heads of states was marked by lack of warmth particularly between Japan and China with President Hu and Prime Minister Noda avoiding meeting each other (Petrov 2012).

7 Secretary of State Clinton welcomed China and other Asian countries to join the TPP talks at a speech in Singapore in November 2012 on the eve of President Obama's visit to Southeast Asia. 'Clinton: China Welcome in the TPP', *Bangkok Post*, 17 November 2012, online, available at: www.bangkokpost.com/breakingnews/321762/clinton-welcomes-china-to-join-trade-pact (accessed 2 November 2013).

8 'Door to TPP is Open for China, Says US", *China Daily*, 22 March 2013, online, available at: www.chinadaily.com.cn/kindle/2013-03/22/content_16333136.htm (accessed 3 November 2013).

9 'Debate on China's TPP Role Regains Momentum', *China Daily*, 11 July 2013, online, available at: www.chinadaily.com.cn/cndy/2013-07/11/content_16760355.htm (accessed 2 November 2013).

10 'After Japan Joins Talks, China Considering TPP', *Japan Times*, 1 June 2013, online, available at: www.japantimes.co.jp/news/2013/06/01/business/after-japan-joins-talks-china-considering-tpp/#.UnWfHb-jDjA (accessed 3 November 2013).

11 'Positive' Sign on Free Trade Pact', *China Daily*, 7 July 2013, online, available at: www.chinadaily.com.cn/world/2013-07/03/content_16711073.htm (accessed 3 November 2013).

12 Ibid. Note views expressed by Arvind Subramanian from the Peterson Institute for International Economics, Washington, DC, and Matthew Goodman, Former White House Coordinator for the APEC.

13 As in Note 8 earlier; views expressed by Zhang Yunling, Director, Division of International Studies, Chinese Academy of Social Sciences (CASS).

14 'ADB Voices Concern over TPP Agenda', *Bangkok Post*, 24 October 2013, online, available at: www.bangkokpost.com/breakingnews/376145/adb-skepticism-about-tpp-rcep (accessed 3 November 2013).
15 'Japanese PM Supports Taiwan's TPP Bid', *China Post*, 9 October 2013 online, available at: www.chinapost.com.tw/taiwan/foreign-affairs/2013/10/09/390838/Japanese-PM.htm (accessed 3 November 2013).
16 Panasonic plans to shift sizeable parts of its production to Thailand from China with other manufacturers also suggesting similar dislocation to Vietnam and other economies. 'Chinese Factories to Face Strong Headwinds from Enlarged TPP', *China Daily*, 25 April 2013, online, available at: www.chinadaily.com.cn/kindle/2013–04/25/content_16447512.htm (accessed 3 November 2013).
17 'Li Keqiang's Speech at Summer Davos Opening Ceremony – Full Text', *Xinhuanet*, online, available at: http://news.xinhuanet.com/english/china/2013–09/12/c_125371685.htm (accessed 4 November 2013).
18 Many of the top SOE leaders also include 'princelings'. For details see Gore (2012).
19 'China Advances Diverse Forms of Ownership: Communique', *Xinhua*, 12 November 2013, online, available at: http://english.people.com.cn/90785/8454569.html (accessed 18 November 2013).
20 Views from the Indian strategic community also interpreted the vice president's address as an indirect invitation to India for joining the TPP. See Anand (2013).
21 'US Keen on India's Inclusion in the Trans Pacific Partnership', *Economic Times*, 20 August 2013, online, available at: http://articles.economictimes.indiatimes.com/2013–08–20/news/41429362_1_indian-ocean-myanmar-asean (accessed 5 November 2013).
22 'PM's Interview with the Japanese Media', Press Release, Prime Minister's Office, Government of India, 26 May 2013, online, available at: http://pmindia.nic.in/press-details.php?nodeid=1623 (accessed 5 November 2013).
23 The Trinamool Congress, a regional party running the provincial government in West Bengal and a partner in the Congress-led coalition, has been a vocal critic of foreign investment in retail. The party eventually pulled out of the coalition after a majority foreign equity was permitted in multi-brand domestic retail in September 2012.
24 'Cabinet Divided over FDI in Retail', *Deccan Herald*, 25 November 2011, online, available at: www.deccanherald.com/content/207439/cabinet-divided-over-fdi-retail.html (accessed 6 November 2013).
25 Aggregate domestic support measures including direct price support and production and input subsidies are capped at 10 per cent of the total value of agricultural production under the AoA at the WTO, online, available at: www.wto.org/english/tratop_e/agric_e/ag_intro03_domestic_e.htm (accessed 8 November 2013).
26 'FM Talks of 10-point Plan to Boost Growth', *Times of India*, 28 August 2013, online, available at: http://timesofindia.indiatimes.com/business/india-business/FM-talks-of-10-point-plan-to-boost-growth/articleshow/22109497.cms (accessed 6 November 2013).
27 Mukherjee justified the policies he took during his time as finance minister by referring to difficult circumstances like the global economic crisis as the reasons behind his expansive fiscal and monetary policies. See 'Mukherjee Defends Stimulus as Finance Minister', *Business Standard*, 4 October 2013, online, available at: www.business-standard.com/article/news-ians/mukherjee-defends-stimulus-as-finance-minister-113100400839_1.html (accessed 6 November 2013).
28 'EU India FTA: Political Opposition Gathers Momentum in India', *Third World Network*, 16 May 2013, online, available at: www.twnside.org.sg/title2/wto.info/2013/twninfo130507.htm (accessed 7 November 2013).
29 'India Inc Unable to Reap Benefits of Goods FTA with ASEAN: FICCI', *bilaterals.org*, 30 October 2013, online, available at: www.bilaterals.org/spip.php?article24084 (accessed 7 November 2013).

30 'Knitwear Exporters Upset over Panel Caution on Signing Trade Pact with EU', *Hindu*, 13 April 2013, online, available at: online, available at: www.thehindu.com/todays-paper/tp-national/tp-tamilnadu/knitwear-exporters-upset-over-panel-caution-on-signing-trade-pact-with-eu/article4613106.ece (accessed 7 November 2013).
31 See 'NASSCOM Wants Early FTA between India and Australia', *Economic Times*, 19 May 2012, online, available at: http://articles.economictimes.indiatimes.com/2012–05–19/news/31778038_1_trade-ties-india-and-australia-free-trade-agreement (accessed 7 November 2013); and 'NASSCOM Contribution to EU Public Consultation on a Future Trade Policy', online, available at: http://trade.ec.europa.eu/doclib/docs/2010/september/tradoc_146656.pdf (accessed 7 November 2013).
32 The Supreme Court of India has directed the Reserve Bank of India to refrain from allowing foreign law firms to set up liaison offices in India, which would allow temporary movement of foreign law professionals into India on a mode 4 service supply basis. The Supreme Court's judgment was in response to a petition filed by the Bar Council of India protesting a verdict allowing the temporary movement of foreign lawyers by the Madras High Court. 'Don't let Foreign Firms In: SC', *Times of India*, 5 July 2012, online, available at: http://articles.timesofindia.indiatimes.com/2012–07–05/india/32551147_1_foreign-lawyers-foreign-law-firms-advocates-act (accessed 9 November 2013).

6 China and India

How far from the TPP?

As the TPP negotiations draw to a close, China and India must anticipate the developments and study the feasibility of their joining the TPP. There are several areas where the TPP's aspirations will set high benchmarks that are difficult for both to meet given the current market access limitations they have in different segments of their economies as outcomes of their extant regulations. Some of the liberalization demands of the TPP, while being difficult to comply with might still be easier for both to negotiate, given their prior experience of doing so at the WTO and other RTAs. These include the more traditional trade issues like tariff liberalization including S&D treatment for sensitive items particularly in agriculture; addressing NTMs like SPS and TBTs and streamlining ROOs. These issues have featured in almost all the ASEAN+1 FTAs and other bilateral agreements in which China and India have been parties. There are, however, issues that have begun to be discussed at their RTAs only recently. There are also issues that they have tried to avoid in their RTA negotiations and are inexperienced in handling. These include the 'Singapore' issues of investment, competition policy and transparency in government procurement,[1] and WTO plus and WTO extra subjects such as services, IP, SOEs, labour and environment. All these subjects as variously mentioned in the earlier chapters are integral to the TPP. The difficulties for both countries in negotiating these issues are not only in their relative inexperience, but more critically in reforming domestic regulations that have for years preserved discriminatory incentives for distinct interest groups; nonetheless, such reforms are necessary if China and India are to seriously consider entering the TPP. This chapter examines some of the critical areas involving WTO plus and extra issues from the Chinese and Indian perspectives and tries to identify the current state of domestic regulations in these areas for gauging the distances they need to cover for meeting the TPP's yardsticks.

Services

Market access in services has been a challenging issue for China and India in international trade negotiations. Several major services in both countries, such as energy, finance, transport and communication, continue to remain dominated by state-owned agencies. Both countries have taken advantage of the flexibilities allowed in the GATS for imposing limitations on the quantum of market access allowed to foreign suppliers in several domestic services, as well as on 'national treatment' obligations requiring non-discrimination between domestic and foreign service providers. Bilateral negotiations on services with other countries have created some complications for both, with negotiating partners often demanding more concessions than China and India have made at the WTO. These demands have been more from countries with offensive interests in services, such as Australia, Japan, Korea and Singapore. Similar demands are likely to be faced by China and India again at the RCEP from these countries. Indeed, commitment to greater liberalization in services is an essential imperative for both countries if they are to figure in the TPP or its expanded edition in the future.

From the perspective of the TPP, the key issue is to achieve substantial liberalization commitments over and above what the members have committed at the GATS. A major step to securing such commitments is the TPP's emphasis on a 'negative list' approach for discussing cross-border services. The P4 agreement used a 'negative list' approach and so does the United States in most of its FTAs (Fergusson *et al.* 2013, Cooper *et al.* 2011). China and India do not usually employ the 'negative list' approach in their FTAs and prefer using the 'positive list' approach of the GATS. The former implies including all sectors within market access commitments and extending them MFN treatment, except for a 'negative list', where countries mention specific industries where they wish to maintain restrictions. This is arguably a more liberal approach for trade liberalization than the 'positive list' approach, where countries mention industries where they allow market access and stipulate the degree of such access along with restrictions on national treatment (if any). A negative list not only assumes all sectors to be subject to a similar degree of liberalization unless specifically excluded, but also extends the liberal treatment to all new services developed subsequently.

Liberalization outcomes from a positive list, however, might not necessarily be sub-optimal to those from a negative list. South Korea's FTA with the EU is almost as comprehensive in coverage of services as its FTA with the United States despite the former using a positive list compared with the negative list approach of the latter. Indeed, long negative lists specifying several excluded services might defeat the larger objective of deeper liberalization. The new Shanghai FTZ, for example, is being criticized for having an unduly long negative list. For China and India, viewed from the perspective of entering the TPP, the demand for using a negative list can always be matched by the promise of substantive commitments in their respective positive lists and therefore might not be a major obstacle.

In some of their recent FTAs, as mentioned earlier, both countries have extended the coverage of services. The FTAs that both China and India have with Singapore are fairly comprehensive. China's commitments in the Singapore FTA include professional and business services, communication services (including telecommunication services), distribution services, educational services, financial services, tourism, transport and recreational services. A similar range of commitments is noted in India's FTA with Singapore.[2] India's FTAs with Korea and Japan with identical coverage have even lower restrictions on market access in several categories of business and professional services.[3] Indeed, the FTA with Japan also specifies India's commitments in retail services, a sector that has long been closed to foreign suppliers.[4] For China, on the other hand, after the FTA with Singapore, the two most comprehensive FTAs with wide coverage of services are those with Costa Rica and Taiwan. The agreement with Taiwan assumes particular significance given that Taiwan belongs to the APEC and has expressed interest in joining the TPP. Under the services segment of the Economic and Cooperation Framework Agreement, China has made commitments to opening up several services including financial securities, transportation, entertainment, health and social, distribution, construction and IT.[5]

While the inclination to make WTO plus commitments in recent FTAs takes China and India closer to the thrust and flavour of services negotiations in the TPP, the relatively low depth of market access commitments in some critical sectors is likely to maintain their distance from the TPP. Telecommunications and financial services are two major sectors in this regard. The TPP is expected to have separate chapters on both, indicating the importance it attaches to these. The United States has active interest in both services evident from the fact that its initiation into the TPP was through the telecom and financial services negotiations with the P4. Several other TPP members with strong comparative advantages in global services trade such as Japan and Singapore (and Korea once it joins) will also be eyeing export prospects for these sectors keenly in China and India. The telecommunications chapter in the TPP is aiming to increase the access of foreign telecom service suppliers to TPP member markets and to allow suppliers of member countries to have reasonable network accesses of each other. Transparency of regulations is an important aspect of the negotiations, as they are in financial services, along with non-discrimination.[6] How do China and India fare with respect to these emphases?

Telecommunications

Both countries continue to maintain restrictions on foreign equity participation in telecommunications, which can be construed as market access limitations. China caps foreign equity participation in basic telecommunication services at a maximum of 49 per cent and does so at 50 per cent for value-added telecommunication services.[7] India, however, has recently revised regulations to allow 100 per cent foreign equity participation for all telecom services including basic, cellular and value-added services.[8] This is an improvement over the access allowed in its FTA with Japan, which was up to 74 per cent. But some procedural issues might still be considered as limitations on access such as taking prior government approval for all proposals involving foreign equity of more than 49 per cent, and observance of licensing and security conditions. Some of the latter

– testing requirements for imported information and communications technology lab equipment, allowing service providers and government agencies to inspect vendor's production facilities – have been irksome for the United States, as has been India's protected satellite services market (USTR 2013). Objections over lack of transparency and discrimination might also arise from the greater wireless spectrum held by the SOEs. This, however, is a policy over which India is unlikely to yield much given that it treats spectrum allocation as a major security issue to be safeguarded in national interest. Indeed, in this respect, it is expected to retain the sentiments reflected in its FTA with Japan even if it amounts to affecting the quantum of service suppliers.[9] The FTA also has limitations on national treatment in terms of majority directors on the boards of foreign service providers being required to be Indian citizens in line with India's policy guidelines for foreign investment in telecom.

China has far greater limitations on market access in telecom as are evident from its restrictive domestic regulations. The basic telecom services market is entirely dominated by SOEs, with China Telecom and China Unicom providing fixed line services across the country, and also providing mobile services along with China Mobile. Current policies allow foreign joint ventures only with these existing domestic providers, which reduces the possibilities of new entrants, further restricted by substantive capitalization requirements of more than US$100 million (USTR 2013). Much like in India, a protected satellite services market and limited access to broadband spectrum are market access limitations in China too, as are issues connected to non-transparent procedures such as the ambiguity over the range of value-added services that foreign service suppliers can offer to customers.

China and India are the world's two largest telecom markets with ample potential for further growth. China currently has around 280 million fixed line subscribers with 20.6 subscriptions for every 100 inhabitants. Its mobile subscriptions are at 1.1 billion with around 81 people in every 100 having mobiles. India's fixed line subscribers are at a much lower level of 31 million with around 2.5 lines per 100 people. Its mobile penetration, however, has grown rapidly, with the country now having around 865 million mobile subscriptions translating to 69 subscriptions for every 100 persons.[10] Given that population sizes are expected to increase in both countries, particularly India, in the medium term, the opportunities for growth in both markets are phenomenal. Foreign telecom service suppliers may be eyeing these growth opportunities in all FTAs and RTAs figuring China and India. These include the RCEP that both countries are currently negotiating, and the TPP, which they might negotiate in the future. While India has taken more proactive steps in expanding market access for foreign suppliers, China's telecom market continues to remain considerably restricted. This is a sector where future multilateral negotiations are expected to demand much greater liberalization from China.

Financial services

Obtaining greater access in member markets for establishing a commercial presence for foreign suppliers is a key objective in financial services negotiations at the TPP. The US demand in this respect is to not only ensure regulations allowing 100 per cent foreign owned service suppliers to operate in member markets, but also to achieve the seamless cross-border transaction of financial services without a commercial presence (Schott *et al.* 2013). Future negotiations with China in this regard are expected to focus on the restrictions China maintains on foreign equity levels for external service providers. Foreign banks, for example, are licensed to operate either as wholly funded foreign banks, or as joint ventures with domestic banks. However, the ceiling on foreign equity is capped at a maximum of 25 per cent of the total equity capital of domestic banks (Hansakul *et al.* 2009, USTR 2013). In addition to the restriction on foreign ownership, access for foreign banking suppliers is further cramped through specific eligibility requirements mandating only foreign funded banks having representative offices in the mainland for two years and with total assets of around US$10 billion to be eligible for incorporation. Furthermore, branches of foreign-funded banks are required to deposit one-third of their working capital with domestic banks and maintain a 75 per cent loan–deposit ratio. These various restrictive regulations indicate China's reluctance to open up domestic banking. Measures amounting to inflexibilities on capital use for foreign banks put them at significant comparative disadvantage vis-à-vis their domestic counterparts and do not conform to national treatment obligations.

India is similar to China in terms of having a banking sector dominated by state-owned banks. However, India does allow foreign banks to establish wholly owned subsidiaries with parent suppliers holding 100 per cent of the total paid up capital. But in joint ventures with private banks foreign equity ownership is capped at 74 per cent; for state-owned banks the ceiling is at 20 per cent.[11] Even though India allows greater foreign ownership levels in a commercial presence (mode 3 of service provision in GATS) than China, there are specific capitalization requirements for establishing branches by foreign banks. The norms are applicable for foreign banks both in establishing branches as well as setting up subsidiaries. In both of its FTAs with Japan and Korea, India has agreed to give preferential treatment to applications from Japanese and Korean banks. However, specific conditions for granting licences to foreign banks pertaining to caps on the proportions of assets they hold in India with respect to their total assets are again limitations on access granted.

Grant of licences is also an elaborate and lengthy process for foreign banks in China particularly the extensive documentation and justification procedures for retail banking functions like issuing credit cards and extending personal loans. China has removed the market access limitations on geographical coverage for foreign banks since 2006,[12] allowing them to carry out multiple functions in local currency – accepting deposits, lending (including consumer and mortgage credit), financial leasing, trading, payment and money transfer services (including credit cards, debit cards, traveller's cheques and bank drafts), trading for customers and dealings in foreign exchange – anywhere in the mainland. Nonetheless, local currency business requires foreign banks to fulfil specific eligibility conditions, including a past record of profitable business in foreign currency. On the whole, China's cautious and calibrated policy of liberalizing its state-enterprise dominated banking sector has resulted in stricter regulatory requirements for foreign banks and their being confined to mostly wholesale and commercial banking operations as opposed to retail banking (Hanskul *et al.* 2009).

Banking is not the only financial service where restrictive regulations will entail China and India facing challenging negotiations. Insurance will also create similar difficulties. The main limitations to market access on a commercial presence in domestic insurance services in China are in life, health, pension/annuities insurance and services auxiliary to insurance. For foreign insurers providing non-life and life services, majority equity participation is capped at 51 and 50 per cent respectively; and 50 per cent is also the ceiling for foreign entities in joint ventures in brokerage for large scale commercial risks. As in banking, China has progressively withdrawn geographic restrictions on foreign insurers. Foreign non-life insurance suppliers can serve both foreign and domestic clients in the mainland and offer a variety of insurances on property, liability, credit, health and pension/annuities in addition to reinsurance for life and non-life services subject to capitalization requirements. Licensing requirements for foreign suppliers remain tough, both for opening new businesses as well as in branch expansion. Though national treatment limitations such as not allowing foreign insurers to have mandatory third party liability for automobile insurance have been revised, critical segments like the political risk insurance market continue to deny access to foreign suppliers (USTR 2013).

Insurance remains a relatively restricted sector in India too given the limits on foreign equity ownership. Unlike banking, where foreign banks can have subsidiaries and joint ventures with majority equity up to 74 per cent, such equity ceiling in insurance is permitted only up to 26 per cent. The only services permitting foreign equity up to 51 per cent are services auxiliary to insurance such as actuarial and risk assessment, as specified in the India–Japan FTA.[13] The high restriction in insurance is unusual given that India has allowed much higher foreign equity in all other financial services, including banking and asset reconstruction services. A bill proposing increasing the foreign equity limit to 49 per cent in insurance has recently been introduced in the Indian parliament and is yet to be approved. Nationalist political sentiments opposed to the greater presence of foreign insurers have been the major obstruction to lowering of access barriers in insurance.[14] As a result, it continues to remain a heavily under-insured market. India, like China, is a net importer of insurance services and has vast needs for diverse insurance products for its large population. Trade negotiations such as the TPP, involving substantive GATS plus commitments, would see both countries pressured for allowing greater access to foreign service producers in insurance given that till now in their domestic regulations, and as reflected in the recent FTAs, they have not been able to move much beyond their original GATS commitments.

Both countries are aware of the importance of liberalizing their financial sectors. India has been able to open up financial services by a considerable extent, except insurance. It needs to address the issues connected to licensing procedures for foreign banks, particularly the requirements imposed by the Reserve Bank of India. For China, however, majority ownership for establishing a commercial presence in the country remains a substantive hurdle for foreign providers, as current regulations insist on foreign entry only through joint ventures with local partners. Compared with India, China too has a heavily regulated capital market. Foreign securities institutions, again, are allowed only through joint ventures with local partners in domestic securities fund management businesses, with foreign equity capped at 49 per cent.[15]

Given the restrictive regulations, and the expectations from other countries, including TPP members, regarding the GATS plus commitments that China must offer, financial sector reforms are a high priority for China, as emphasized by Premier Li (Anderlini 2013). China has begun taking steps in this regard, particularly after the new leadership assuming office in March 2013. These are reflected in the proposed services pact with Taiwan, where Taiwanese financial securities firms have been offered the opportunity to set up branch offices in Shanghai, Shenzhen and the Fujian province.[16] Furthermore, reforms aiming to create more depth in the domestic capital market, such as issuing local government bonds, allowing select foreign hedge funds to mobilize capital from the mainland and the possibility of non-banking finance corporations to open private banks (Rabinovitch 2013), are cautious but distinct measures towards granting more private and foreign access to a sector under heavy state control, till now. The most important step towards financial sector liberalization, according to many, is the launching of the Shanghai FTZ in September 2010. The FTZ is expected to be the first move towards complete liberalization of the mainland's financial services industry, including radical measures like full convertibility of the Chinese Yuan in the capital account (Bo 2013). China appears to be following the typical 'Chinese' style of calibrated liberalization in opening up a sector that it knows will be almost impossible to keep closed if it wants to enter high quality trade agreements such as the TPP.

Other services

Domestic regulations continue to constrain access for foreign suppliers in many other service industries in China and India. There are, however, distinct variations between the two countries in this respect. Distribution services are a case in point. China has a long history of allowing foreign retailers to establish a commercial presence for providing wholesale trade and retail services.[17] China's commitments at the GATS allowed foreign distributors to have majority equity in all joint ventures and to open stores in all provincial capitals within two years of its accession to the WTO, with geographical restrictions and most product-specific prohibitions to be phased out over time. These are indeed no more except for capitalization norms specifying minimum registered capital requirements for collaborative enterprises in wholesale trading and retail services (Ying 2010). In marked contrast to the foreign ownership restrictions prevailing in telecom and financial services, 100 per cent foreign shareholding is allowed in wholesale trade and retail. Hong Kong retailers were among the earliest to benefit from the mainland's liberal measures in distribution services as they could avail these through the bilateral FTA signed with the mainland in 2004. The major market access limitation continuing to exist on distribution services pertains to their expansion, with foreign retail chains operating more than 30 stores in the mainland being subject to equity restrictions (USTR 2013).

India, in contrast, has taken much longer to liberalize distribution services. It is interesting to note that neither country has large SOEs dominating domestic wholesale and retailing. While such absence enabled China to open the sector more briskly and without political ramifications, India faced much greater resistance, with the informal retailers mobilizing substantive political support and opposing the entry of foreign retailers. Nonetheless, India has covered considerable ground, and currently permits 100 per cent foreign equity ownership for cash-and-carry services, wholesale trading, and single-brand retail trading. It also allows majority foreign equity ownership of up to 51 per cent on multiple brand retailing, subject to conditions that can be deemed as limitations on market access and national treatment: minimum investment ceiling of US$100 million, mandatory deployment of half of the capital in developing the back-end supply chain infrastructure and sourcing at least 30 per cent procurement from small enterprises.[18] The procurement condition also applies to majority foreign equity single-brand retailers though they can source from any local enterprise irrespective of size. These rather restrictive conditions explain why foreign retailers are yet to establish notable presences in the Indian market, and also point to the demands India can expect to face at major trade negotiations in the future.

Audio-visual services present another contrast between the degree of market access offered by India and China. The distribution of motion pictures and videos is an important segment of the domestic market, where some TPP members, particularly the United States, have considerable export interest. India treats the representative offices of foreign motion picture distributors as branches of foreign firms and allows a commercial presence and distributorship. China, however, has strong restrictive policies for the number of films to be imported and the frequency of screenings, in addition to specific censorship reviews. Foreign filmmakers are required to obtain licences for making films in China, with co-production ventures most encouraged, similar to joint ventures in the telecom and financial services mentioned earlier. Importing foreign films in China continues to remain the sole prerogative of the China Film Group, the largest state-owned studio. China agreed to raise the import quota of 20 foreign films to 34 in February 2012, provided they were in IMAX or 3D formats, and also agreed to a higher revenue share of 25 per cent for foreign filmmakers.[19]

The distribution of films, however, remains monopolized by the China Film Group and Huaxia. The restrictions on the foreign ownership of theatres result in foreign films having limited screenings, and high print and advertising costs for distributors. Furthermore, China follows considerably restricted policies for television programme quotas, which are further complicated by the insistence that prints are to be obtained from local laboratories (USTR 2013).

There are other policies in both countries that are restrictive for service suppliers, such as China's Internet regulation policies and India's prohibition of e-commerce through single and multi-brand retail trade. Both countries also have restrictions on commercial presences in domestic civil aviation services. A variety of other sector-specific restrictions that handicap market access in varying degrees are possible to identify through industry-specific regulations. On the whole, however, both countries have come a long way from their initial commitments at the GATS. These strides are reflected in some of their recent FTAs that have GATS plus commitments in services. Nonetheless, 'docking' on to the TPP will entail considerably deeper reforms.

It is noticeable that the restrictions maintained by both countries are mostly for mode 3 of service provision – commercial presence – pertaining to the physical presence of foreign suppliers in the host countries. There are relatively less market access limitations maintained through modes 1, 2 and 4, though in GATS and other FTAs, China and India prefer keeping their commitments 'unbound' in these modes, which enables them to contemplate future regulations, if necessary. Cross-border service supplies should not be a major problem for either country in the TPP and RCEP negotiations; but difficulties will arise for mode 3. The latter again are intricately connected to national investment policies, competition laws and treatment for SOEs. Market access in mode 3 for foreign suppliers cannot be improved significantly unless these issues are simultaneously addressed.

Investment

The overwhelming emphasis of the investment negotiations at the TPP is on securing the rights of foreign investors. The negotiations have two main goals: ensuring foreign investors get across-the-board access to manufacturing and service industries in TPP member territories without discrimination and obligatory performance requirements; and guaranteed legal protection for investments by establishing appropriate and binding dispute settlement provisions, particularly investor–state settlements.

For China and India, allowing uninhibited access to foreign investors in all sectors of their economies is a difficult proposition given that they have historically followed selective policies of restricting foreign capital in certain industries. Some of these have been mentioned in the earlier section. China maintains a fairly long list of industries prohibited for FDI in spite of considerably pruning restrictions in its amended catalogue for foreign investment issued in January 2012. Some of the key prohibited sectors include the mining of radioactive mineral and rare earth elements, specific beverages like China's traditional green tea, traditional Chinese medicines (permitted in cultivation, not manufacturing), weapons and ammunition, specific electrical machinery (e.g. open lead acid and nickel cadmium cells), coal-fired steam plants (less than 300,000 KW), air traffic control, postal services, stem cell research, news agency services, publishing and printing books, radio and television stations, satellite up-linking and gambling.[20] China also restricts foreign investment in a significant segment of one of its cutting-edge industries – batteries for use in new energy vehicles (USTR 2013). The US administration and businesses have been particularly unhappy over the restrictions that China maintains in its steel production policies, where not only are foreign investors not allowed controlling stakes, but they are also expected to possess proprietary knowledge in production. The steel policy also incentivizes local content use by offering price subsidies to projects using domestic equipment (USTR 2013). China continues to restrict foreign ownership in several activities in a variety of manufacturing industries including farming, mining, tobacco, petroleum processing, pharmaceuticals, chemical fibre, transport and communication facilities, power grids, water supply and sewage networks in large cities, telecommunication companies, banking, insurance and real estate.[21]

Prohibitive sectors for foreign investment in India's current FDI policy include gambling and betting, lottery, chit funds,[22] real estate business, tobacco manufacturing, and in areas specifically reserved for the state like atomic energy and railway transport.[23] India has a fairly restrictive policy for foreign investment in agriculture and does not allow FDI in sectors other than floriculture, horticulture, pisiculture, aquaculture and the development of seeds and planting material; recently, however, India has allowed 100 per cent FDI in tea plantations. With respect to agriculture, both China and India have been cautious in not allowing foreign capital in segments where it can hurt the interests of domestic cereal and crop producers, and have tried to channelize investments by a greater degree in processing and value-added activities. Both are unlikely to budge on demands for greater access for foreign investors in core farming activities such as cereal production. Such reluctance, at least on the part of India, will also prevail in opening up more plantation sectors, with the decision to increase FDI in tea plantation having generated a political backlash.[24] While protective sentiments hold back opening the door wider for foreign investors in farming, the unwillingness to let the latter have prominent control over the management and distribution of precious resources has encouraged specific restrictions in mining activities. Like China's prohibitions in radioactive minerals and rare earth mining, India, while allowing 100 per cent FDI in several mining activities, imposes specific conditions for foreign investors in the mining of titanium-bearing minerals and ores, requiring the establishment of value-addition facilities and transfer of technology. These are again areas where, despite the strong investment interests of some TPP members, China and India are unlikely to compromise much.

India also regulates foreign investment in micro, small and medium enterprises (MSMEs) with caps on majority foreign equity, and imposes specific performance conditions in the form of export obligations on enterprises that are not classifiable as MSMEs, but nonetheless produce items 'reserved' for MSMEs.[25] FDI limits are also capped at minority levels in defence production, cable networks, terrestrial broadcasting, up-linking of news and current affairs television channels, publishing of newspapers and periodicals and Indian editions of foreign magazines on news and current affairs.[26] While Indian policies on foreign investment in audio-visual industries are more liberal than China's, in several segments of such services, India allows only limited presence of foreign enterprises despite allowing unrestricted access to domestic private agencies. The 'generosity' shown towards domestic private entities as opposed to their foreign counterparts reflects the success of the former in lobbying hard for protecting their home turfs. There are other sectors and services such as banking, insurance, civil aviation and distribution, where, as mentioned earlier, market access for foreign investors continue to remain restricted and subject to specific conditions.

Investment has been a high priority for the United States in its FTAs; specifically the provision relating to ISD mechanisms allowing foreign investors to arbitrate against national country governments over violations of investment rules (Fergusson *et al.* 2013). There is little doubt about the difficulties in incorporating such a provision, given the fears that member governments negotiating the TPP will have over the disproportionate rights that foreign investors might get over domestic investors in territorial investment matters, and also the limitations it might impose on sovereign authorities in regulating foreign investment, as discussed in Chapter 2. The downside effects of such a provision also include the excessive caution that can grip domestic regulatory authorities, forcing them into policy inertia (Schott *et al.* 2013). While the NAFTA does include such a clause, pushing the same through in the TPP has not been easy, given the strong resistance from dominant members such as Australia.

Neither China, nor India, have favoured strong ISD mechanisms in their FTAs or the large number of BITs that they have signed with various countries. China has BITs with five of the members negotiating the TPP – Australia, Brunei, Canada, Chile and Vietnam. It has just begun negotiating a BIT with the United States. TPP members having BITs with India include Australia, Brunei, Malaysia, Mexico and Vietnam.[27] Most of the BITs signed by the two countries are relatively dated, which is not difficult to explain, given that the more comprehensive recent FTAs include provisions on investment. While the initial BITs signed by both countries were relatively narrow, given the circumspection of both countries in allowing strong rights to investors, they have become more definitive in seeking investor protection provisions in recent years, as investors from both countries have begun investing overseas significantly, leading to their becoming exporters of capital (Sornarajah 2010).

China has had little involvement in international arbitrations in ISDs. The domestic system for addressing foreign investor grievances in China is usually through administrative reconsiderations; and only when investors are unhappy with the administrative decisions of the relevant governments and agencies can they approach the local courts. While normally the scope of judicial review for local courts in administrative matters is limited, China's terms of accession to the WTO stipulated to its agreeing to subject all government actions to judicial review, giving considerable local judicial authority in reviewing matters relating to foreign investment (Wang 2011). Culturally, litigation is discouraged as an instrument for settling disputes in China, and amicable methods are espoused as best solutions. The Chinese government has institutionalized specific administrative mechanisms such as complaint centres and mediation panels for resolving foreign investor disputes (Wang 2011), which are handled with particular care for not 'ruffling feathers', and explains why China has been able to avoid international arbitrations. China's relative unfamiliarity with international arbitration has also resulted in its focusing on settling ISDs in host country courts rather than taking recourse to international forums such as the International Centre for Settlement of Investment Disputes. However, the trend is increasingly reversing, with China becoming sensitive to protecting the overseas investments of its own nationals. China's more recent BITs appear to have been influenced by those of the United States and contain provisions such as a minimum standard of treatment and clearer definition of national treatment clause, which are prevalent in the BITs signed by the United States and other NAFTA members (Berger 2013); these traits underline China's efforts to take greater measures for protecting its overseas investments.

Compared with China, India has had a different experience in international arbitrations on ISDs. There have been several instances of India being dragged into arbitrations by investors citing relevant provisions in the different BITs that India has signed.[28] This has led to considerable consternation in India, forcing a serious rethink on the ISD provisions in its various BITs and demands for refraining from BITs that might award excessive protection to foreign investors, such as the one India is negotiating with the United States (Gopakumar 2013). Indeed, India is not the only country experiencing such difficulties, with other major emerging markets like Brazil and South Africa also facing similar problems (Jung 2012).

India's discomfort with the ISD provision appears to arise from a strong 'pro-investor' bias in several of its treaties, allowing foreign investors greater bargaining strength in ISD arbitrations. These include the essentiality of investor consent in initiating ISDs, non-requirement on the part of investors in exhausting local administrative remedies for initiating arbitration, protection of ISDs from public scrutiny and allowing arbitration rules to review the judicial decisions awarded by host countries on the basis of their laws (Dhar *et al.* 2012). There is also ambiguity in India's different BITs over the interpretation of 'indirect expropriation' allowing investors to expeditiously initiate arbitration claims. Furthermore, the treatment of investment in India's bilateral FTAs in terms of allowing greater market access to foreign investors in specific sectors appears to be running into conflict with many of the existing BITs that India has with its FTA partners. Binding market access commitments in its FTAs with Japan and Korea, for example, may invite the invocation of ISD provisions in line with its parallel BITs, if India effects changes in its FDI policies that are not consistent with the investment measures in these FTAs (Smitha and Murali 2013). The inconsistency between the treatment of investment in India's FTAs and BITs is also reflected in the similar disconnect between the latter and India's domestic regulations on foreign investments, with the domestic policy guidelines on sector-specific foreign investment ceilings and associated requirements hardly reflecting the qualitative and quantitative contents of India's BITs (Ranjan 2010). India's market access and national treatment commitments on foreign investment at bilateral FTAs and RTAs are usually made on the basis of its domestic policy guidelines and there is little surprise in the former not taking note of the BIT implications.

Though the Chinese and Indian experiences are markedly different with respect to ISD arbitrations, they are likely to be circumspect in agreeing to provisions allowing foreign investors greater leverage in bringing claims against host governments. At the same time, their efforts to ensure investment protection for their own overseas investors will also be an important concern. The concern for both countries in the TPP, as well as in the RCEP and their forthcoming BITs, will be to ensure that ISD provisions are accompanied with appropriate safeguards, particularly when it comes to defining investment and contentious concepts like indirect expropriation.

IP

China and India's anticipated difficulties in responding to the IP framework of the TPP primarily emanates from a difference in perceptions on IP issues between countries that are net exporters and importers of IP. The United States, as an example of the former, has offensive interests in IP negotiations. As a result, it is pushing for substantially high TRIPS plus commitments in the TPP and bargaining for stronger effective protection for IP. China and India are net importers of IP. While they have begun taking important strides in innovation, they continue to rely on imported technology and innovative products. The reliance is particularly heavy for China, which has a considerably large outgo on payments of royalties and licence fees. While strong IP protection has important cost implications for both countries, it is also a deterrent to their indigenous innovation efforts. India has been particularly sensitive towards longer patent protections for pharmaceuticals since it affects its development of generic drugs and their commercial introduction.

As mentioned in Chapter 2, both China and India figure on the 'Priority Watch List' of the USTR, reflecting US concerns over the lack of adequate protection of IP and weak enforcement of IP rights in both countries.[29] The USTR notes a variety of shortcomings in China, ranging from cyber theft, online piracy, leaking of trade secrets and large-scale counterfeits.[30] Piracy in China is exacerbated due to restrictions on imported entertainment products such as films, as well as caps on the entry of foreign books and printed material. While the inadequacies reported by the USTR mostly pertain to weak enforcement, the United

States has strong reservations on Chinese domestic regulations that, in its view, impede the market access of IP-intensive products and services. These mostly pertain to regulations favouring greater state purchase of products using locally developed IP (USTR 2013). Nonetheless, the Special 301 Report of the USTR acknowledges the efforts being made by China in improving its legal framework for protecting IP, including the higher incidence of criminal enforcement in trademark counterfeiting cases.[31] The effective enforcement of patents for protecting inventions has also been noted by the USTR as a serious problem in India, along with restrictions on patent rights for imported products and their licensing to third parties. As in China, online copyright piracy has been flagged as a serious concern in India, along with policies encouraging indigenous innovation such as the drug pricing policy.[32]

China and India's reluctance in agreeing to TRIPS plus commitments and accepting stronger IP rules in RTAs can be substantially explained by their thrust on developing indigenous innovation. Chinese policies during the last decade identified home-grown innovation as a priority, which was articulated in the Medium and Long Term Plan for development of Science and Technology in 2006.[33] The thrust has strengthened, with the emphasis on the growth of strategic emerging industries (SEIs).[34] While it was initially motivated by the sizeable technology gap between China and the developed world and China's critical dependence on imported technology, the current policies, particularly for innovation in the SEIs, are geared towards making China the global leader in innovations in strategic industries. This is also consistent with China's long-term objective of moving its industries away from predominantly low-end and largely assembling functions in the value chains to more value-added higher-end functions.

India's emphasis on developing national innovation and R&D systems was prominently reflected in its Science and Technology Policy of 2003. The latest Science, Technology and Innovation Policy of 2013 emphasizes on creating a 'robust national innovation system'.[35] Alongside these specific policies encouraging national innovation, both countries have also been encouraging grassroots-level innovations, mostly among farmers and small entrepreneurs, driven by the urge for devising cost-saving techniques. Such efforts have also witnessed institution-based cooperation between China and India (Palit 2012a). Patenting incremental innovations through utility models and design patents is provided in China's Patents Law of 1984. The law provides an expansive interpretation of patents, where both substantive and incremental inventions are considered patentable. India's Patent Act of 2005, on the other hand, takes a sharper view on innovations that are non-patentable, with the result that several incremental grassroots innovations may not always qualify for patents. Agencies like the National Innovation Foundation of India made great efforts to obtain patents for these innovations with a view to encouraging them.[36] In contrast, Chinese law has been more supportive of utility patents, as has been the Chinese state, which has encouraged greater use of products imbibing indigenous innovations through price and procurement preferences.

Given the importance that both countries attach to the development of national innovation systems through indigenous efforts, the US proposals tabled at the TPP, if finally incorporated in the agreement, will be difficult for China and India to accept. Provisions regarding longer periods of data exclusivity, mandatory patent registration linkage empowering patent holders to act against the introduction of similar products, patentability rights on new uses of existing products, and limited national flexibilities in administering domestic prices of patented drugs, are mostly unacceptable to China and India given their adverse impact on encouraging domestic innovation and national public health concerns (Palit 2013a). India's patent laws, while not entirely supportive of utility models, have safeguards for preventing 'evergreening' of patents and do not encourage data exclusivity and patent linkages. China's patent laws on the other hand encourage utility models, as do domestic laws in other TPP members such as Australia, Chile, Japan, Malaysia, Mexico, Peru and Vietnam. South Korea's patent laws also accommodate utility models. At the same time, strong copyright and trademark protections have implications for higher education prospects in China and India, given the proliferation of online teaching and distance learning programmes in the two countries and the importance of ensuring IP sanctity for the contents of these programmes. As a result, China and India, like several other TPP members, are expected to substantially differ on the US-proposed patent proposals, in keeping with their postures on indigenous innovation and impact on public health and other segments of society. Indeed, this is probably the reason why China and India's more recent and comprehensive FTAs, while including IP provisions, have hardly gone beyond a reiteration of their TRIPS commitments and cooperation with the partners in honouring such commitments.

The emphasis on encouraging and incentivizing domestic innovation in both countries, however, also encourages change in their domestic IP regulations. Both countries have aspirations of becoming major global innovators and owners of IP. In its Medium and Long Term Plan for Science and Technology declared in 2006, China highlighted R&D and indigenous innovation as essential for its becoming an 'innovation oriented society' by 2020 and a world leader in science and technology by 2050.[37] The plan also mentioned China's intentions to improve its IP system by creating an appropriate legal environment for IP protection and stricter action against IP infringement. President Hu echoed similar sentiments, reflecting China's efforts to enhance IP protection at the APEC summit in November 2011.[38] China not only expects its strategic industries to become its main industrial foundation for the future, but also expects innovations in these industries to contribute to a 'home-grown' pool of IP. On the other hand, India's STI policy of 2013 declares its goal of becoming a global scientific power propelled by innovations, with the current decade being christened India's 'decade of innovation'. India's draft national IPR strategy is emphatic in the need to improve the capacity of institutions granting IP rights as well as in ensuring better enforcement of these rights.[39]

There is therefore, a clear imperative on the part of both countries to reform domestic regulations in a manner that helps them safeguard the IPs of their own innovators in their eventual quest for becoming net IP exporters. The dilemma they face in this regard is qualitatively similar to that on ISDs mentioned earlier, where, while having strong reservations on sacrificing sovereign rule-making space to foreign investors, they cannot afford to overlook such provisions in the RTAs and FTAs they negotiate, given the importance of protecting their own overseas investments. Both realize the importance of having effective domestic IP laws with strong enforcement characteristics for achieving global comparative advantages in IP-intensive goods and services. The challenge for both will be to reform domestic regulations for incentivizing domestic innovation on the one hand, while ensuring greater IP compliance on the other.

Government procurement

The issue of government procurement has long been under discussion at the WTO. Though the GPA at the WTO came into force from 1 January 1996, several WTO members have refrained from annexing to the agreement. Among the TPP negotiating members, Canada, Japan, Singapore and the United States are members of the GPA, while Australia, Chile, Malaysia, New Zealand and Vietnam are observers. The latter includes China and India as well. Some observers, such as China and New Zealand, are negotiating annexation to the GPA. China began negotiating its accession to the GPA from 2007, while India decided to become an observer in 2010.

Government procurement has been a sensitive issue for both China and India given the large sizes of their state sectors and the built-in incentives for several local industry groups that such procurement enables. China's government procurement market was around US$180 billion in 2011 by conservative estimates, amounting to more than 10 per cent of its aggregate annual fiscal expenditure (USTR 2013).[40] The size of the Indian procurement market on the other hand is estimated at around US$300 billion, including both central and state-level procurements (CUTS 2012), which is almost a third of India's GDP. Clearly, changes in regulations in government procurement and commitments given by both countries in their respective RTAs and FTAs, have important ramifications for market access.

Public procurement in China is administered at two levels. The first pertains to state organizations and public institutions, whose procurement is governed by the Government Procurement Law (GPL) of 2003. While the GPL encourages greater procurement of locally manufactured goods by both central and provincial governments, it does not include procurement by SOEs. It also excludes bidding for public works and state-owned infrastructure projects. To this extent, a crucial aspect of China's market access commitments in government procurement will be the treatment of procurement by SOEs. Indeed, procurement by SOEs, along with greater coverage of provincial entities, and lower thresholds for domestic products in public procurement, are the areas in which China's GPA accession at the WTO continues to run into trouble.[41] Prying open provincial procurement markets is going to be a challenge given the long tradition of preferences extended by provincial government agencies to local industries in procurements (Lynch 2010). However, despite these constraints and the noticeable lack of transparency in several aspects of procurement, China has gradually allowed the degree of discrimination in procurement between domestic and foreign investors to ebb over time. Creating more uniform national treatment conditions include allowing products manufactured by foreign-invested enterprises in China to be treated as 'domestic' and issuing draft regulations under GPL specifying circumstances enabling the former enterprises to compete in procurement (Matechak and Gerson 2010).

Unlike China, India does not have the equivalent of a GPL. Nonetheless, procurement across government departments, organizations and agencies are geared to act discriminatively in favour of products manufactured by small enterprises and central SOEs. The discrimination is exercised through price preference as well as reservation of specific products for manufacture by certain industries. India's national manufacturing policy of November 2011 specifies greater local content requirements in government procurement in some industries (IT and renewable energy). There has been ample debate and criticism in India over the lack of transparency in government procurement processes and the abetment of corruption by the same. These are reportedly being addressed by the draft legislation on public procurement currently pending in the Indian parliament, which proposes regulating large government contracts by specifying the process of tendering and participation in the tenders. On the whole though, except for the selective preferences awarded to small enterprises and SOEs, India does not have exclusive policies discriminating between domestic and foreign producers in national treatment. While it is yet to begin negotiations for acceding to the WTO's GPA, its strong likelihood of doing so in the future is evident from the specific treatment of government procurement in its FTA with Japan that other than non-discrimination also commits to further bilateral negotiations on a 'Comprehensive Chapter on Government Procurement' when India aspires to join the GPA of the WTO.[42]

China appears to be in a greater state of preparedness in opening up its government procurement market. It submitted a revised offer at the WTO at the end of 2013, albeit with modest improvements. India, on the other hand, has begun embarking on the initial steps through its agreement with Japan and the new public procurement bill. Both, though, are expected to progress at their own calibrated paces, given the enormity and complexities of their procurement processes, and the preferences they have developed over time. The TPP, as mentioned earlier, appears to be a split bloc on government procurement between the GPA members and those with large state procurement programmes like Malaysia and Vietnam. The balance that government procurement regulations eventually achieve between these two groups at the TPP would be the standards that China and India must watch out for. The difference in this regard with respect to the GPA is that while the WTO might be expected to be more accommodating in allowing lower thresholds and longer exemptions, the TPP is unlikely to be.

Competition policy and SOEs

A major challenge for China and India in envisioning their prospects for joining the TPP, or any other regional trade and economic agreement with an equivalent range of countries and diversity of issues, is to prepare for changing domestic regulations in connected spheres. The changes in government procurement regulations, for example, cannot be considered in isolation from similar changes in competition laws and treatment for SOEs. Given that procurement markets in both countries are functional outcomes of the significant roles that the state continues to play as producer and consumer in the two economies, the indispensability of SOEs as state entities in extending preferential treatments in procurement, and the flexibility in national competition rules allowing them to do so, imply the near impossibility of reforming public procurement regulations without concurrent efforts in competition laws and SOE policies.

The competition law related negotiations in the TPP focus on the creation of 'a competitive business environment, protect consumers, and ensure a level playing field for TPP companies'.[43] The SOE proposals are expected to reflect most of the characteristics connected to SOEs in various US FTAs – national treatment, non-discrimination and transparency – without marginalizing their importance in national economies. While competition policy has been a feature of global and regional trade negotiations, including in the WTO, the SOEs are new creatures. As far as India and China are concerned, while competition law does find mention in some of their FTAs, SOEs do not. Even by WTO standards, competition policy is a new issue and has been dropped from the Doha agenda. Thus negotiating competition policy and SOEs will be new challenges for China and India.

Several sectors – electricity, civil aviation, telecommunications, postal services, railways and banking – are heavily restricted in competition in China, though the situation has changed with the notification of the Anti-Monopoly Law in 2008 (USTR 2013). The law addresses monopolistic tendencies on the part of business operators as well as monopoly agreements and the growth of administrative monopolies. There are, however, ambiguities over how the anti-monopoly law will regulate government monopolies and SOEs. This is particularly a concern given the conflict that the objectives of competition policy, in terms of curbing monopoly formation and practices and increasing consumer welfare, runs into with China's industrial policy objectives, where SOEs continue to remain dominant, particularly in the SEIs (Bush and Yue 2011). SOEs continue to hold about a third of total assets in industry and service sectors in China,[44] with their significance in the national economy having increased considerably following the thrust on indigenous innovation and post-crisis fiscal expansion (Palit 2012a). As discussed in Chapter 5, reforming SOEs by curbing their monopoly statuses and making them more attuned to functioning in competitive conditions is one of the biggest challenges facing China's new leadership. The significant political and economic clout enjoyed by the SOEs and the state-patronized business groups they represent will be one of the biggest hurdles to deeper institutional reforms in China.

Notwithstanding the Indian Constitution abhorring the concentration of economic power and its misuse, business monopolies in India were recognized institutionally till the economic reforms of the early 1990s. During the last decade, India established a new competition law in 2002, which also paved the way for the establishment of a regulator in form of the Competition Commission of India. Weak enforcement, remains a major challenge for India's competition regulator (Singh 2011). Nonetheless, there are continuous efforts to upgrade and refine competition laws, which are evident from the new Competition Amendment Bill introduced in parliament that is expected to facilitate enforcement through easier 'search and seizure' processes and to underpin industry-specific turnover thresholds for pre-merger notifications.[45] Indeed, modern competition law in India appears more advanced than that in China on the grounds of market environment, government commitment and institutional support, as well as the flexible common law approach (Zhang Xian-chu 2010). These changes, however, cannot extend their influence across all sectors of the economy unless the SOEs are also brought under the purview of anti-competitive measures. Though India has reduced exclusive state participation to only atomic energy and railways and has allowed private and foreign investment even in a hard-core strategic sector like defence, SOEs dominate several sectors and account for almost a quarter of the country's GDP (Palit 2012a). The preponderance of these enterprises in core economic activities and their large sizes may make the effects of new competition laws somewhat vacuous in both China and India – a fact that can hardly escape attention of other parties in international trade negotiations such as at the GPA of the WTO and the TPP. Much of how India and China fare at future negotiations will depend on how significant are the roles they visualize for SOEs in their respective economies and by what extent they continue to support these SOEs with subsidies and other preferences. The market domains of the SOEs in both countries are large spaces that other country producers and investors wish to gain access to. However much both countries yield on procurement and competition, in the absence of clearer turf demarcations for SOEs, other countries at multilateral and regional trade negotiations will remain sceptical on the competitive neutrality between SOEs and private firms in China and India.

Labour and environment

The outlines of the TPP as announced in its leaders' meeting in November 2011 does not contain specific suggestions on the issues being discussed in drafting the chapter on labour, except for incorporating commitments on protecting labour rights and cooperation on improving workplace practices.[46] As with several other issues being discussed at the TPP, labour is an important agenda for the United States, and the negotiations are influenced accordingly. Labour has figured in several US bilateral FTAs. The emphasis in the TPP, as can be intuitively drawn from the treatment of labour issues in other US FTAs, will be on strengthening and implementing workers' rights in the member countries, along with enhancing their collective bargaining capacities; sub-optimal enforcements in these areas, US businesses apprehend, might encourage continuing with low wage and poor standard practices in member countries, putting the US domestic workers at comparative disadvantages (Fergusson *et al.* 2013). What could, however, be a difficult demand for countries like Vietnam, and by extension China and India, is subjecting violations from labour standards to binding dispute settlement procedures, as it is in several US FTAs. Both countries will also be worried over such violations inviting punitive actions from other trade partners, such as sanctions or bans on labour-intensive exports suspected of encouraging the violations.

Both China and India are yet to ratify the International Labour Organization's (ILO) conventions 87 and 98. These conventions pertain to freedom of association of workers and their rights to organize and collective bargaining. While in China workers do not have the rights to join trade unions of their choice, in India, notwithstanding such rights, employers are not legally bound to recognize unions and collective bargaining. While both countries have ratified conventions on equal remuneration and discrimination, China has ratified conventions on the worst forms of child labour and minimum age, which India has not; India on the other hand has ratified conventions on forced labour, contrary to China.[47]

From a TPP perspective, and particularly that of the United States on labour issues, China and India fail to meet the bar because of their non-ratification of ILO conventions 87 and 98. They also, individually, fall short on the requirements of child labour (India) and forced labour (China). The common problem for both countries is that ratification of the ILO conventions does not ensure their full honouring in the absence of adequate enforcement mechanisms. Given the large sizes and complexities of both economies, including their informal sectors and designated economic enclaves like the Special Economic Zones where labour laws have been deliberately kept flexible for attracting investments, enforcement is not only up against the challenge of scale, but also discrimination. The sharp division between industry and labour bodies on the question of stronger worker rights has also influenced policy postures, with both countries struggling to achieve the optimal balance between industry's vocal call for flexible labour policies enabling easier 'hire and fire' and the legitimate rights of workers to collective bargaining and better workplace conditions. The dilemma is affecting the quality of policies and enforcement in both countries and is also manifesting in their hesitation to agree to stronger labour rights provisions in their FTAs, particularly if the latter are linked to enforceable dispute mechanisms.

Unlike labour, environment has been more widely discussed at the WTO in terms of the relationship between trade and environment protection. And like labour, environment has featured prominently in several US FTAs, implying the importance of the issue being included in the TPP from an environment perspective. Indeed, the emphasis on labour and environment can be traced back to the 'May 10th Agreement',[48] whose provisions have influenced the drafting of the recent US FTAs. The similarity between labour and environment provisions in terms of the thrust of the US posture can be found in the insistence on adherence to multilateral agreements on environment and strict enforcement provisions in the event of the lowering of agreed environment standards for attracting investment.

Both China and India have introduced a variety of domestic regulations in recent years for minimizing pollution and carbon emissions. With both countries among the world's largest carbon emitters, their roles have been significant in discussing both mitigation and adaptation options at multilateral forums such as the United Nations Forum on Conservation and Climate Change. But with respect to the TPP again, the dilemma for both countries will be in agreeing to binding commitments. Given that such commitments can entail the activation of dispute settlement procedures as well as unwarranted actions on 'harmful' subsidies, China and India will be wary of deep commitments. Their uneasiness will be further compounded by the rather large agenda of the environment chapter at the TPP, which includes marine fisheries, biodiversity, alien species and environmental goods and services.[49]

Final thoughts

During the last decade, China and India have engaged in trade negotiations at different forums. They have remained active at the WTO for successful implementation of the DDA. On the other hand, they have vigorously pursued RTAs and FTAs, both as part of the larger economic regionalization efforts in Asia, as mentioned in Chapter 4, as well as bilaterally with countries in and outside Asia. At the WTO, their emphasis has been on ensuring the implementation of the 'development' dimension of the DDA, which found them locking horns with developed countries, particularly the United States. In terms of issues and priorities, the focus of China and India at the WTO, has primarily been on traditional trade issues of market access in agriculture and non-agricultural products. So has been their focus in many of their bilateral RTAs and FTAs, except some recent ones. These foci have led to their relatively lesser experience in negotiating 'WTO plus' issues such as services, investment, competition, government procurement and IP. Quite a few of these issues are 'Singapore' issues and were excluded from the DDA discussions. It is only recently that both countries have begun taking up these issues in trade negotiations – China through its bilateral agreements with Taiwan and Costa Rica, and India in its FTAs with Japan and Korea. But even in these agreements, the formal content of commitments on issues like government procurement and IP, are hardly substantive. It is evident that both countries are yet to be comfortable and clear in their negotiating strategies on the Singapore issues, which occupy significant chunks of the TPP agenda and are also likely to come up at the RCEP. The lack of negotiating experience and exposure on even more 'new generation' issues like labour, environment and SOEs, are going to be tougher challenges. Due to a lack of negotiating experience, both countries might end up taking obtrusive and defensive positions on these subjects. The possibility of 'docking' on to the TPP in the future therefore presents formidable negotiating challenges for both countries.

The TPP is seeking WTO plus commitments in all the issues discussed in this chapter. The abilities of China and India to respond positively depend largely upon their progress in reforming domestic regulations. GATS plus commitments in services are critical in this regard. Several countries in the TPP have offensive interests in service exports and would welcome greater market access concessions from China and India. Such expectations are also likely to manifest at the RCEP through common members like Australia, Japan and Singapore. Negotiations on the cross-border supply of services in modes 1 and 2 are unlikely to create problems. The biggest difficulties will arise in mode 3, which is intricately linked to investment liberalization, and will depend on the extent by which both countries relax restrictions on foreign equity ownership in services such as banking, insurance, telecommunications, audio-visual and entertainment services and distribution. Market access demands from negotiating partners are likely to be higher on China given its insistence on allowing foreign entry through collaborations with local partners and its reluctance to incorporate 100 per cent wholly owned subsidiaries of foreign companies. China is likely to be pressurized even at the RCEP for opening up its telecom and financial services markets to more foreign investments given the latter's focus on WTO plus commitments in services. Recent policy changes in India have resulted in its lifting several caps and facilitating majority foreign ventures in telecom and finance. Nonetheless, its insurance sector continues to remain heavily protected, as does China's. Given the size and depth of these markets in China and India, and the scope of opportunities that the United States and other service exporters envisage in the markets, China and India will find it hard to resist greater market access demands in services and investment policies.

History and economic structures have been crucial in influencing China and India's negotiating postures at multilateral and regional negotiations and will continue to do so even at the TPP and the RCEP, not to mention the WTO. Restrictions on foreign investments in key services and preferential discriminations for domestic investors and industries are part of the historical legacies of both countries, where SOEs remain dominant economic entities and the state a major player in national production and consumption. The prominence of the SOEs and the state sector not only encourages limitations on foreign entry, but also creates a mutually reinforcing system of incentives, where the enterprises and select groups of domestic producers benefit from well-defined buyer–seller relationships. Commitments at international trade negotiations must be backed by assurances of change in domestic regulations, which, in both countries, need to overcome the roadblocks created by the SOE-based system of incentives. This explains why despite several revised submissions China's offers at the GPA continue to largely exclude procurements by local governments and SOEs; and why India's latest draft public procurement legislation continues to justify preferential procurement for domestic industries (Sengupta 2012).

A major challenge for China and India in negotiating 'high standard' agreements like the TPP will be in meeting the latter's demands on transparency and enforcement on various issues. Transparency in awarding licences in major service sectors requires both countries specifying underlying norms and setting them on par with the OECD and global standards. The same is expected of China and India in the tendering and bidding processes as well. While there is no reason for doubting the sincerity of both countries in outlining transparencies, the quality of results in this regard is influenced by their large economic sizes and structural complexities, including significant informal sectors and differences in systems and capacities within their federations. Enforcement, again, is a tricky issue for both countries, making them reluctant to commit to binding dispute settlement provisions in areas like ISD, IP, labour and environment, given that the federal governments in neither country have complete control over disaggregated enforcement mechanisms and practices. It is probably enforcement and transparency that will consume maximum time and space for China and India at critical trade negotiations since the United States and other OECD TPP members have been rather critical of the two countries' track records in enforcing existing provisions.

The gap between China and India – and an agreement like the TPP – is essentially in the perspectives on external trade between influential movers of the TPP such as the United States, and those of China and India. The US and most of the OECD members in the TPP have comparative advantages in global trade in services, particularly those that are innovation and IP-intensive. They are keen on obtaining greater access in foreign markets in these sectors and realize the importance of correcting domestic regulations that are 'behind the border' handicaps on market access. China and India are yet to develop clear visions of their strategies when it comes to obtaining access in foreign markets in services, except for demanding greater concessions in mode 4. It is important for both countries to visualize and articulate their positions on the 'new generation' issues objectively. Unlike the WTO, which offers considerable flexibilities and where China and India could get away with defensive and occasionally obstructive postures, RTAs like the TPP and RCEP are unlikely to allow such latitude.

Notes

1 The WTO's first ministerial conference at Singapore in 1996 set up working groups and work agendas on trade and investment, trade and competition policy, transparency in government procurement and trade facilitation. These were also included in the DDA. Apart from trade facilitation, the other three were dropped from the DDA as there was no consensus among members on the modalities. 'Investment, Competition, Procurement, Simpler Procedures', WTO, online, available at: www.wto.org/english/thewto_e/whatis_e/tif_e/bey3_e.htm (accessed 29 October 2013).
2 Annex 5 – Part A, 'China's Schedule of Specific Commitments on Services', China–Singapore FTA, online, available at: http://fta.mofcom.gov.cn/topic/ensingapore.shtml (accessed 19 October 2013) and Annex 7A, 'India's Schedule of Specific Commitments', Comprehensive Economic Cooperation Agreement between the Republic of India and the Republic of Singapore, online, available at: http://commerce.nic.in/trade/ceca/anx7a.pdf (accessed 19 October 2013).
3 'Annex 6B – Schedule of Specific Commitments for Korea', India–Korea CEPA; ch. 6, pp. 94–137; Ministry of Commerce, Government of India, online, available at:

http://commerce.nic.in/trade/INDIA%20KOREA%20CEPA%202009.pdf   (accessed
19 October 2013).

4 Annex 6, 'Comprehensive Economic Partnership Agreement between the Republic of
India and Japan', Ministry of Commerce, Government of India, online, available at:
http://commerce.nic.in/trade/IJCEPA_Basic_Agreement.pdf (accessed 19 October
2013).

5 'Services Pact: TSU Knocks Cross-strait Service Trade Agreement', *Taipei Times*, 23
June 2013, online, available at: www.taipeitimes.com/News/front/archives/2013/06/
23/2003565441 (accessed 20 October 2013).

6 'Outlines of the Trans-Pacific Partnership Agreement', Office of the United States
Trade Representative (USTR), online, available at: www.ustr.gov/about-us/
press-office/fact-sheets/2011/november/outlines-trans-pacific-partnership-agreement
(accessed 20 October 2013).

7 Value added services include electronic mail, voice mail, online information and database retrieval, electronic data interchange, value-added facsimile services, code and
protocol conversion and online information and data processing.

8 Press Note no. 6 (2013 series), 22 August 2013; Department of Industrial Promotion
and Policy (DIPP), Ministry of Commerce and Industry, Government of India, online,
available at: http://dipp.nic.in/English/acts_rules/Press_Notes/pn6_2013.pdf (accessed
20 October 2013).

9   Each Party retains the right to exercise its spectrum and frequency management
policies, which may affect the number of suppliers of public telecommunications
transport networks or services, provided that it does so in a manner that is consistent with this Agreement. Each Party also retains the right to allocate frequency bands taking into account current and future needs.

(Annex 5, Section 14, p. 896; as in Note 3 above)

10 International Telecommunications Union (ITU) Statistics, online, available at: www.
itu.int/en/ITU-D/Statistics/Pages/stat/default.aspx (accessed 21 October 2013). The
figures are for 2012.

11 'Consolidated FDI Policy (effective from 5 April 2013)', pp. 74–75; Department of
Industrial Promotion and Policy, Ministry of Commerce and Industry, Government of
India, online, available at: http://dipp.nic.in/English/Policies/FDI_Circular_01_2013.
pdf (accessed 21 October 2013).

12 The geographical limitations were specified in China's commitments at the GATS.

13 As in Note 3 above, p. 913.

14 'Against Openness', *Indian Express*, 7 August 2013, online, available at: www.indi-
anexpress.com/news/against-openness/1152007/ (accessed 22 October 2013).

15 Foreign funds can have joint ventures for underwriting 'A' shares and underwriting
'B' and 'H' shares along with managing government and corporate debts. The foreign
equity ceiling in such ventures is capped at 33 per cent. 'A' shares are those in which
most Chinese companies are listed in Shanghai and Shenzhen stock exchanges and
where foreign investors were not allowed to trade. The latter could trade only in 'B'
shares and 'H' shares – a much smaller basket of shares compared with 'A'.

16 As in Note 4 above.

17 Foreign retailers established a presence in the mainland even before China acceded to
the WTO in 2001, mainly through their discussions with provincial governments
(Ying 2010).

18 As in Note 10 above.

19 'Boost for Hollywood Studios as China Agrees to Ease Quota on US Films',
Guardian, 20 February 2012, online, available at: www.theguardian.com/world/2012/
feb/20/china-eases-import-quota-hollywood-films (accessed 22 October 2013).

20 'Catalogue for the Guidance of Foreign Investment Industries (amended in 2011)',
Ministry of Commerce, People's Republic of China; Policy Release, 21 February

2012, online, available at: http://english.mofcom.gov.cn/article/policyrelease/aaa/201203/20120308027837.shtml (accessed 23 October 2013).

21 Ibid.

22 Chit funds are savings schemes, fairly popular in India, where the chit fund company enters into agreements with a group of people for collecting specific sums of money in periodic instalments. The incentive on the part of the contributors is the promise of prize money from the pooled savings, determined by auction or tender.

23 As in Note 10 above.

24 'Will Not Allow FDI Caps in Plantation in TN: Jaya', *Business Standard*, 23 July 2013, online, available at: www.business-standard.com/article/politics/will-not-allow-fdi-caps-in-plantation-in-tn-jaya-113072300274_1.html (accessed 23 October 2013).

25 Though the list of items reserved for manufacture by MSMEs has been progressively pruned over time, there are still several items that are reserved, including food products, wood and wooden products, paper products, chemicals, glass and ceramics, and mechanical engineering equipment. See 'List of Items Reserved for Exclusive Manufacture by Micro and Small Enterprise Sector (As at 31 July 2010)', Development Commissioner (MSME), Ministry of Micro, Small and Medium Enterprises, Government of India, online, available at: www.dcmsme.gov.in/publications/reserveditems/reserved2010.pdf (accessed 23 October 2013).

26 As in Note 10 above.

27 'Full List of Bilateral Investment Agreements Concluded', 1 June 2013; China, India; United Nations Conference on Trade and Development (UNCTAD), online, available at: http://unctad.org/Sections/dite_pcbb/docs/bits_china.pdf and online, available at: http://unctad.org/Sections/dite_pcbb/docs/bits_india.pdf (accessed 23 October 2013).

28 The most discussed instances have been one of India's major SOEs – Coal India Limited – being called into arbitration by the Australian firm White Industries under the India–Australia BIT and disputes with the Vodafone International Holdings BV (Dutch subsidiary of the UK-based Vodafone Plc) and Children's Investment Fund Management of the United Kingdom under BITs with Netherlands and the United Kingdom respectively. See Dhar *et al.* (2012) and Gopakumar (2013) for more details.

29 China has also figured in the USTR's 'out of cycle' review of notorious markets.

30 '2013 Special 301 Report', Acting United States Trade Representative Demetrios Marantis, Office of the United States Trade Representative, May 2013, online, available at: www.ustr.gov/sites/default/files/05012013%202013%20Special%20301%20Report.pdf (accessed 25 October 2013).

31 Ibid.

32 Ibid.

33 'China Issues Guidelines on Sci-Tech Development Program', 9 February 2006, online, available at: www.gov.cn/english/2006–02/09/content_184426.htm (accessed 26 October 2013).

34 Premier Li is credited with the coinage. The seven SEIs are new energy auto industry, energy-saving and environmental protection industry, new generation information technology industry, biology industry, high-end equipment manufacturing industry, new energy industry, and new material industry. 'China Releases 12th Five Year plan for National Strategic Emerging Industries', *China Briefing*; 25 July 2012, online, available at: www.china-briefing.com/news/2012/07/25/china-releases-12th-five-year-plan-for-national-strategic-emerging-industries.html (accessed 26 October 2013).

35 'Science, Technology and Innovation Policy 2013', Ministry of Science and Technology, Government of India, online, available at: www.dst.gov.in/sti-policy-eng.pdf (accessed 26 October 2013).

36 A detailed discussion of the issues surrounding utility patents in India is available in a discussion paper on the subject prepared by the Department of Industrial Promotion and Policy (DIPP), Ministry of Commerce and Industry, Government of India, online,

available at: http://dipp.nic.in/English/Discuss_paper/Utility_Models_13May2011.pdf (accessed 26 October 2013).

37 As in Note 32 above.

38 'Chinese President Outlines Four-point Proposal on Asia-Pacific Economic Development', cctv.com, 13 November 2011, online, available at: http://english.cntv.cn/20111113/102225_1.shtml (accessed 29 October 2013).

39 'Invitation of Views on the Draft National IPR Strategy as Prepared by the Sectoral Innovation Council on IPR', Department of Industrial Promotion and Policy (DIPP), Ministry of Commerce and Industry, Government of India, online, available at: http://dipp.nic.in/English/Discuss_paper/draftNational_IPR_Strategy_26Sep2012.pdf (accessed 29 October 2013).

40 Other estimates indicate the procurement market to be as large as US$500 million (Lynch 2010).

41 'China Tables Revised Government Procurement Offer', International Centre for Trade and Sustainable Development (ICTSD), 12 December 2012, online, available at: http://ictsd.org/i/news/bridgesweekly/151470/ (accessed 27 October 2013).

42 Article 113 of the India Japan CEPA, as mentioned in Note 3.

43 As in Note 5 earlier.

44 'State Owned Enterprises in China: How Big are They?', Posted by Gao Xu, 19 January 2010, online, available at: http://blogs.worldbank.org/eastasiapacific/state-owned-enterprises-in-china-how-big-are-they (accessed 27 October 2013).

45 'India Update – Significant Changes Proposed by India's Competition Bill Amendment 2012', International Institute for the Study of Cross-border Investment and M&A, 27 February 2013, online, available at: http://xbma.org/forum/india-update-significant-changes-proposed-by-indias-competition-bill-amendment-2012/ (accessed 27 October 2013).

46 As in Note 5 earlier.

47 See 'Internationally Recognised Core Labour Standards in the People's Republic Of China', Report for the WTO General Council Review of the Trade Policies of the People's Republic Of China, International Trade Union Confederation (ITUC), Geneva, 10–12 May 2010, online, available at: www.ituc-csi.org/IMG/pdf/Chinal_Final-2.pdf (accessed 28 October 2013); and 'Internationally Recognised Core Labour Standards In India', Report for the WTO General Council Review of the Trade Policies of India, International Trade Union Confederation (ITUC), Geneva, 23–25 May 2007, online, available at: www.ituc-csi.org/IMG/pdf/India_report_final-2.pdf (accessed 28 October 2013).

48 The 'May 10th Agreement' refers to a statement issued by the Bush Administration on 10 May 2007 underlining the core principles on workers' rights, environment, IP and investment to be incorporated in all FTAs signed by the United States. These have subsequently been incorporated in the American FTAs signed with Colombia, Peru, Panama and South Korea. See Fergusson *et al.* (2013) for more details on this agreement.

49 As in Note 5 above.

7 Strategies and alternative alignments

In a sense, the TPP, is fait accompli for China and India; while they did nothing to contribute to its evolution (except perhaps in the far-fetched and cynical sense of creating the deadlock at the WTO by not agreeing to the demands of the United States and other developed countries for lowering safeguards on agricultural imports, which convinced the United States about its inability to shape multilateral trade rules according to its preferences), they are, nonetheless, unable to be indifferent towards its progress and ramifications. Their frustrations in witnessing trade rules in what is their home turf – the Asia-Pacific – being rewritten without their voices being heard will only increase over time as the TPP negotiations near completion.

Frustrations notwithstanding, China and India's strategic and economic prominence in the current world order compels them to contemplate strategies for responding to the TPP. Part of these strategies is aimed at reducing the distance between their trade policies and domestic regulatory structures vis-à-vis those expected at the TPP. Another part comprises exploring non-TPP alternatives. The ambiguity over the final shape of the TPP framework, uncertainty over the date of its completion and ratification by member country legislatures, and the complicated domestic political economies of both countries, are major constraints on their formulating tangible policies. They can at best frame tentative responses anticipating certain outcomes. Such strategizing, for both of them, is not made easier by their simultaneous involvement in multiple trade negotiations.

China has embarked on a more decisive strategy compared with India. Its strategy has been influenced by the new leadership's motivation to consider the TPP as a major opportunity for undertaking far-reaching, external integration and competition enhancing comprehensive reforms in the economy. India does not appear to have worked out a strategy yet. This chapter examines the key features of China's initiatives for preparing for the TPP, particularly the BIT with the United States, the launching of the Shanghai FTZ and seeking entry at the TISA. It argues that much of China's success in converting the initial steps to a full-fledged outward-oriented reform agenda depends on the new leadership's ability to overcome domestic political opposition. In examining India's possible strategies for joining the TPP, the chapter takes a critical view of its approach to trade negotiations and argues for a new and objective outlook backed by adequate institutional capacities and greater coordination between official agencies. Finally, the chapter examines two non-TPP alternative alignments – the BRICS and the WTO – and argues that notwithstanding their strategic and economic commitments to these frameworks, China and India cannot afford to deprioritize the TPP.

China and TPP: initiatives and constraints

Developments over the last few months suggest China is not averse to joining the TPP. Several influential opinions from China, as discussed in Chapter 5, argue for China's entry to the TPP. Most of these feel that entering the TPP offers China an excellent opportunity for introducing new economic reforms by effecting deeper changes in domestic regulations. They also feel that joining the TPP early will be better for China as it will help it in contributing effectively to the TPP's rule-making process. Delaying the process will force China to accept the TPP conditions as they are dictated and will reduce China's bargaining capability.

Pro-TPP opinions in China consider it to be the next best opportunity for market-based reforms, coming a little more than a decade after China's entry in the WTO. Accepting the WTO's commitments did indeed spur widespread regulatory change in China, with more than 2,000 central regulations and around 20,000 local regulations changing to honour the WTO commitments (Wang 2013). China also opened up several of its services industries, albeit with entry conditions, and gave up administered pricing practices in several sectors. The most significant commitments were the slashing of tariffs on agricultural imports by more than half within three years of accession, and capping subsidies for farmers (Gertler 2002). The concessions, substantive by any standards, were endorsed by China's political elite, particularly the third generation leadership under Jiang Zemin and Zhu Rongji, who visualized considerable economic benefits from joining the WTO by implementing large scale domestic reforms (Lim and Wang 2009). A similar endorsement of the TPP by China's mainstream political elite under the leadership of President Xi and the elitist group of leaders owning allegiance to Jiang Zemin is now in command. As discussed in Chapter 5, the new fifth generation leadership has been instrumental in implanting pro-TPP thinking in China. The leadership has in mind the WTO annexation example and its effect on regulatory reform efforts in China. Indeed, in this regard it is interesting to note Commerce Minister Deming's comments on the WTO and the Asia-Pacific trade agreements within two years of each other. Deming described China's entry at the WTO as a 'courageous and tough choice' producing 'win–win' outcomes, at the World Economic Forum in Davos in January 2011, marking ten years of China in the WTO.[1] The minister, as mentioned in Chapter 5, has also indicated China's willingness to participate in all regional cooperation efforts being conducted on the basis of equality and in a transparent fashion.[2] Taken together with the Ministry of Commerce's assertion that it was studying the pros and cons of joining the TPP,[3] there is little doubt of the WTO accession's reform-inducing experience being a major determinant of the current leadership's posturing towards the TPP. It is also indicative of the relatively lesser hope that China's pro-market reform community now has in the ability of the WTO to spur greater domestic reforms, given the stagnancy over the DDA. China is looking at the TPP and other RTAs such as the RCEP for providing the next 'big push' for reforms by taking up the 'WTO plus' issues.

In the last few months and with the new leadership's assuming office, China has taken a few decisive steps that could be considered significant for moving towards the TPP. The first of these is resumption of talks on a bilateral investment agreement with the United States. At its last and fifth strategic economic dialogue with the United States in July 2013, China announced its decision to take up bilateral investment discussions with the United States.[4] The significance of the decision is not only in agreeing to resume talks that were suspended for a few years, but also in China agreeing to adopt the US approach to negotiating BITs based on the US model BIT text. These include, *inter alia*, China's agreeing to bring all sectors under the purview of investment, as opposed to its earlier demand of excluding several service industries, which had led to the stalling of talks. The BIT talks, from a Chinese perspective, are considerably radical given that they are expected to include WTO extra issues such as labour and investment. In a significant shift of its negotiating approach, China has agreed to pursue a negative list approach to the negotiations. The BIT is also expected to include 'pre-establishment' market access features. This would imply the non-imposition of performance requirements on foreign enterprises for investing in particular sectors and treating them on par with domestic enterprises.[5] In the Chinese business context specifically, coverage of all services in the BIT and adhering to the US approach may imply that China will eventually remove the current restrictions on foreign entry in key service industries such as telecom and finance, which are currently mandatory through collaborations with local partners and capitalization norms. These would indeed be significant and far-reaching reforms. If achieved under the US BIT prior to joining the TPP, the reforms would entail China satisfying some of the major 'entry conditions' of the TPP.

Taking an exhaustive attitude to reforms in the US BIT, with an emphasis on greater market access and investment protection, underpins China's willingness to negotiate bilateral investment provisions in line with those emphasized by the United States and EU in their BITs. The salient features of the United States' BIT negotiations are expected to rub off on investment discussions in China's ongoing FTAs, including the RCEP, and in future at the TPP. While China's willingness to embrace radical market access talks in the US BIT might have surprised many, it can be rationalized by China's emergence as a major global exporter of capital. This has inspired China to become attentive towards protecting its investments in the different BITs it has signed in recent times (Sornarajah 2010). The 'protection' aspect has now become imperative for its investments in the United States given that China has around US$20 billion direct investments in the United States and also holds a sizeable chunk of the US Treasury bills.[6] China realizes the importance of imbibing 'high quality' OECD country regulatory characteristics in its BITs and FTAs; without such features it will not be reassured about the security of its overseas investments in the United States and other OECD countries, if the latter themselves are wary of the security of their investments in China, and the trust deficit continues to exacerbate. Graduating to US BIT models is therefore a necessity for China, and, in the process, it is also able to narrow its gap with the TPP.

A second important measure taken by China for introducing deep and extensive reforms in the domestic economy, particularly in financial services, is the opening of the pilot FTZ in Shanghai. Through the FTZ, China aims to take decisive steps in changing domestic regulations on both traditional trade issues as well as the new generation WTO plus and WTO extra issues. As far as traditional market access issues are concerned, the FTZ is expected to eliminate tariffs on an exhaustive range of merchandise imports, including agricultural products. With respect to WTO plus and WTO extra issues, the Shanghai zone is expected to lead the way in domestic reforms in three critical areas: stronger IP rights, removal of preferential treatment for specific industries and SOEs, and liberalizing the financial services industry by allowing full convertibility of the yuan in capital account transactions (Bo 2013). The zone is also expected to work towards an assurance of labour and environmental safety standards in line with international norms. Importantly, the Shanghai FTZ is expected to grant pre-entry national treatment and work on the basis of a negative list approach; both these are conditions premising talks at the TPP and the US–China BIT. The selection of the emphases and objectives of the FTZ leave little doubt about its eventual intention in extensively reforming domestic regulations and preparing China for joining the TPP. The Shanghai FTZ is to be the first in a series of such zones expected to come up in different parts of the mainland as part of a long-term policy for implementing next generation reforms in pilot zones, as endorsed by the CPC at the third plenary session of the central committee in November 2013.[7]

Another decisive step by China for opening up its tightly regulated service sectors, and one that should be seen as a part of a series of moves for introducing deeper reforms and facilitating its journey towards the TPP, is its recently expressed interest in joining the TISA. The TISA, as mentioned earlier, is a plurilateral agreement negotiating GATS plus commitments. The EU, United States, and 21 other countries accounting for more than 70 per cent of the global trade in services are negotiating the TISA.[8] Its objective is notionally similar to the TPP: 'negotiate a high-quality and comprehensive agreement, which is compatible with the World Trade Organization (WTO) General Agreement on Trade in Services, will attract broad participation, and will support and feed back into multilateral trade negotiations'.[9] The TISA includes several TPP members: Australia, Canada, Chile, Japan, Mexico, New Zealand, Peru and the United States, and also includes Korea. The negotiations at TISA are expected to broadly converge to those at the TPP, as well as the ongoing GATS plus talks at the RCEP, given the presence of common members in all frameworks. China clearly wishes to stay abreast of the negotiations by participating in the TISA talks for maintaining a core position at the negotiations.

China's current strategy for joining the TPP seems to be guided by specific policy choices. The first of these is the economic motivation: revive economic growth and facilitate the transformation of its economy to accommodate greater role of services and new generation 'strategic' industries in national production. Trade and exports will continue to remain vital for the long-term growth prospects of the Chinese economy, but they may, if the course correction in policy works in the desired fashion, have more contributions from innovative strategic industries and services, replacing the dominance of low-cost exports in China's trade profile. The new leadership is convinced about the importance of deeper structural reforms for enabling greater integration with the world economy and accelerating such exports. The TPP is being taken as the ideal framework for carrying out such reforms. The second strategic motivation guiding China's increasingly positive slant towards the TPP is the urge to retain its position of prominence in regional integration efforts in the Asia-Pacific. Given the strategic discomforts China has with some TPP members, and the United States' proximity to these countries (e.g. Japan, Vietnam), China's absence from the TPP is likely to intensify the 'ring fencing' around it by drawing more anti-China countries into the TPP. The shaping of such an alliance is not a welcome prospect for China. Tackling the adverse ramifications of such a coalition – already taking shape at the TPP – is probably best attempted by being within the TPP rather than outside it. Indeed, China's entry to the TISA is also probably prompted by consternations over it including Hong Kong and Taiwan.

But there are downsides to China's current strategy of getting close to the TPP, particularly from an economic perspective. The success of China's incremental strategy of transiting to the TPP – through bilateral and plurilateral accessions (the BIT with the United States and the TISA) and the experimental launching of the next generation of ambitious reforms through the Shanghai FTZ – is heavily dependent on the political consensus that President Xi and his team are able to secure for the next generation of reforms. The deep factional divide in China's domestic politics and the pervasive influence of the SOEs and their top executives in deciding (or blocking) the introduction of competitive economic policies might result in the country implementing reforms in a piecemeal fashion; that is obviously not what the new leadership wants, nor also what the TPP and its members would demand from China. Addressing 'behind the border' issues is the core mandate of the TPP and all next generation trade agreements being currently negotiated. For China, it is impossible to take on these issues without political consensus. The recently concluded third plenary has provided broad directions to reforms by iterating the importance of more competitive markets and the greater need of private and foreign capital, but has avoided mentioning the specifics. It is in the specifics, and particularly at the provincial levels, where implementation will face political and systemic challenges. Indeed, this is where concerns are also arising over the approach adopted by the Shanghai FTZ, in terms of whether the results it achieves by implementing major services reforms are extendable to the rest of the country. What is possible in a heavily globally integrated and business-friendly territory like Shanghai, might be far more difficult in other parts of the mainland that remain more inward-looking and insulated. In addition to political support, extending the Shanghai FTZ model to the rest of the country also calls for developing appropriate modern service industry infrastructures elsewhere, for handling complex transactions related to currency operations, for example. Whether China's state-dominated banking sector, accustomed to traditional banking practices and unfamiliar with complex operations, will be able to perform sophisticated financial sector transactions at province and local levels, notwithstanding political goodwill, is questionable. Questions are also being raised over the content of reforms being pushed through the Shanghai FTZ, given its rather long negative list (Yiping 2013), which hardly reflects much substantive difference from China's current foreign investment guidelines.[10]

In its effort to join the TPP, China also aims to consolidate its efforts at negotiating other RTAs in the Asia-Pacific. Two of these are especially important to China: the RCEP and the CJK FTA. China's negotiating strategy in the RCEP would be largely conditioned by its perceptions on the TPP. As China draws closer to the TPP and undertakes far-reaching reforms at home for progressing on WTO plus issues, particularly GATS plus milestones in services, it is expected to bring commensurate pressures at the RCEP negotiations for negotiating similar commitments. At the same time, it will continue to emphasize on greater market access for manufactured products for retaining its comparative advantages. Given its strategic eagerness to leave the ASEAN centrality and ASEAN FTA characteristics undisturbed at the RCEP, it is expected to uphold S&D treatment for economically backward members at the RCEP. From a geostrategic perspective, engaging Southeast Asia is a major imperative for China for ensuring that it does not complicate the strategic dynamics between China and the United States in the region (Palit 2013d). Much as China is engaging the United States bilaterally through the BIT, and also multilaterally through its increasingly positive posture towards the TPP, the new leadership is conscious of the United States' 'pivot to Asia' and its ability to curb China's strategic command in the region. There has, therefore, been a vigorous push on the part of the Chinese leadership to engage Southeast Asia. This was evident from President Xi's recent visits to Indonesia and Malaysia – the two largest Southeast Asian economies – where he emphasized on the importance of consolidating bilateral trade and business links, and also at the APEC, where trade was again highly emphasized including transparency and openness in ongoing trade negotiations. The push on engaging Southeast Asia has encouraged experts to view the current decade as the 'decade of diamond' in China–ASEAN relations following the 'decade of gold' earlier (Qian 2013). There is little doubt that China will remain strongly committed to the RCEP and will push for a trade compact that preserves the core features of Asian regionalism while accommodating additional commitments in some specific WTO plus areas.

Much as China would like to proceed with the CJK FTA, uneasy relations with Japan remain a problem. Japan on the other hand is keen on preserving its strategic space vis-à-vis China, and is unlikely to prioritize the FTA. Indeed, Japan's entry to the TPP and its simultaneous figuring at the RCEP, might have made the CJK somewhat irrelevant. From a Japanese perspective, the RCEP is expected to be a greater trade order subsuming the CJK FTA; Japan will expect the TPP to be an even larger and strategically balanced framework given that Korea is expected to join the TPP soon and China is also clued to the agreement. For Korea too, the RCEP and the TPP might be superior alternatives to the CJK FTA. Indeed, China needs to decide how much negotiating and strategic priority it wishes to award to the trilateral agreement given that both Japan and Korea appear to be drifting towards larger regional compacts. Nonetheless, China is expected to continue its efforts to engage partners in the neighbourhood by exploring the possibilities of new bilateral FTAs (including a possible bilateral with Korea for establishing one arm of the CJK FTA) and expanding the scope of existing ones. This includes striking new deals with Southeast Asian countries and improving economic partnership frameworks like the one with Taiwan. China's greater economic cooperation with Taiwan on IP, SPS and TBT, and financial cooperation, are important components of its strategy of establishing deeper economic links with the rest of the world in new areas. Furthermore, China is fully conscious of the importance of bilateral FTAs as strategic CBMs and is happy to occasionally negotiate these even without substantive economic benefits.

From an economic perspective, China is aware of the difficulty it will face in negotiating all demands at the TPP. To that extent, by joining the TPP it expects to carry along with it other members who will experience similar difficulties and try to develop intra-TPP blocs with issue-based alternative agendas. In this respect, it is likely to have considerable support on WTO extra issues such as labour and environment, and also in IP. Some TPP members, feeling burdened by the US pressure at the TPP negotiations, might be enthused by the prospect of China's presence at the negotiating table and the 'counterbalancing' effect of such a presence. At the same time, on a number of issues specific to its own economic interests and circumstances, China is likely to request parallel consultations, similar to those going on between the United States and Japan. China is expected to work on achieving a 'hybrid' template for the TPP, combining both the US and ASEAN FTA features, which are representative of the Pacific and Asian approaches to regional integration. Such a framework will enable China to retain certain characteristics of the Asian FTA regulations; embrace OECD trade standards in several areas by aligning domestic regulations accordingly; and also balance its geostrategic space in a region experiencing greater US attention.

India and the TPP: imperatives of new approach and outlook

India is yet to unfold a specific strategy for joining the TPP. This is presumably because India is much further away from the TPP than China. It is not a member of the APEC. With the initial TPP membership expanding through the APEC club, India is yet to envisage itself as a distinct candidate for the TPP. But as discussed earlier, in Chapter 5, the steady growth of opinions favouring India's entry, including tacit encouragement from the highest levels of the US administration, reflect the rapid pace of the evolving circumstances in the Asia-Pacific, dragging India closer to the TPP. At this point in time though, India's strategy towards the TPP has to be largely anticipatory, manifesting through its engagement in the RCEP and other RTAs and FTAs in the region.

The RCEP has brought India closer to the TPP. Japan's entry has increased the number of common members between the RCEP and TPP, and China's entry will increase it further. The rest of the non-TPP RCEP members include, other than India, three economically backward ASEAN members – Laos, Myanmar, and Cambodia – and three members of the original ASEAN-5 – Indonesia, the Philippines and Thailand. The first three are not members of the APEC, while the latter three are. Thailand is willing to join the TPP and the United States will be keen on including Indonesia and the Philippines too in the long run. Among the non-ASEAN economies having bilateral FTAs with ASEAN and participating at the RCEP, Korea and China's entries at the TPP will leave only India outside the TPP. The possibility of all RCEP members featuring in the TPP, barring Cambodia, Laos, Myanmar and India is distinct in the foreseeable future. Cambodia, Laos and Myanmar are unlikely to be invited soon, given the institutional deficiencies in their economies and the difficulties they will face in accepting the TPP's conditions. But if almost all major economies at the RCEP join the TPP, the former is likely to become a connected template to the latter. Much of such an outcome will materialize whenever China and Korea join the TPP. The enlargement of the TPP in this fashion will make India isolated in the trade architecture of the Asia-Pacific. It is therefore important for India to develop its strategies with the eventual objective of joining the TPP.

Proceeding towards the TPP requires a combination of economic and strategic priorities. For India, the underlying assumption in this respect is to integrate more closely with the Asia-Pacific, both for long-term economic benefits emanating from deeper presence in the region's production networks and supply chains, and for strategic dividends sourced from an active geo-political presence in the region. By today, India could have been a much bigger economic presence in the region had it not been for its historical neglect of Southeast and Northeast Asia due to the Cold War-driven strategic and ideological compulsions during the Asia-Pacific's economic take-off beginning from the 1960s. Even the economic engagement propelled by India's Look East Policy since the early 1990s has acquired momentum only since the last decade through a step-up in negotiations with various countries in the region. The region is poised to be integrated in the plurilateral trade framework of the TPP, which will aim to maximize growth opportunities from new industrial structures, supply chains and business models, by connecting both sides of the Pacific. India can ill afford to be left out of the next phase of growth and expansion in the Asia-Pacific. In order to avoid this, it must step up its diplomatic efforts to become a member of the APEC.

Though India has a 'back door' entry in the APEC territory through its membership at the EAS and RCEP, pitching a claim to join the APEC would convince the Asia-Pacific community, and particularly important APEC members like Australia, Japan and the United States about India's intentions of becoming a part of the new rule-based trade framework in the region.

Acceding to the TPP requires satisfying several conditions of extensive liberalization. While some of these might be too extensive and binding for India to comply with at this point in time, there are others, particularly WTO plus issues like services, competition policy, IP and government procurement, where it needs to objectively review its negotiating positions. With more RCEP members likely to join the TPP, and with tacit efforts from this large group of common members to take the RCEP closer to the TPP, India should look at the RCEP as an opportunity for carrying out more reforms. Like China visualizing the TPP as an opportunity for introducing more reforms, India can take the RCEP as the means to an end rather than being an end by itself, and can use it as a forum for addressing some of its 'behind the border' trade barriers. The RCEP gives India an opportunity for viewing its own comparative advantages and disadvantages in the region objectively and to initiate measures for digging deeper into the regional supply chains, both in goods and services, and narrow the gap between the TPP's expected regulatory framework and India's domestic regulations.

It is important for India to realize that modern world trade will increasingly be run by rules going well beyond the WTO's current structure. The Asia-Pacific and the TPP are showing the way in this regard with RTAs becoming the preferred option for achieving deeper integration. Sooner or later, the Asia-Pacific will imbibe 'high quality' trade rules covering 'WTO plus' issues through the TPP, and individual countries might also begin insisting on these in their bilateral FTAs. India's existing FTAs with TPP members such as Chile and Japan (as well as Korea and Thailand) and ongoing negotiations with Australia and New Zealand, might experience demand for revisions in line with the new rules coming in at the TPP. India should anticipate the possibility and prepare itself accordingly. The RCEP should be taken as a forum where India can up the bases of its existing bilateral FTAs with ASEAN and other countries through greater liberalization so that it is not perpetually identified as a country incapable of integrating deeper in the trade architecture of the region because of ineffective regulations and policy hesitancy. The imperative of deeper economic integration with the Asia-Pacific in its own long-term economic interests and the opportunity of doing so through the RCEP should be utilized as an excuse for convincing protectionists and initiating moves on reforming domestic regulations.

As discussed in Chapter 3, Asian members of the TPP such as Malaysia and Vietnam, are likely to experience considerable gains from the TPP given the preferential access they will obtain in the US and NAFTA market. This is where India might be at a relative disadvantage given the lesser preferential access it will get in these markets post-TPP. China's imminent entry to the TPP along with other Southeast Asian countries such as Thailand will accentuate the disadvantage. If India does not join the TPP soon enough, the only possibility of avoiding the trade diversion losses in the near and medium term is to work towards bilateral FTAs with the NAFTA members. India is negotiating an FTA with Canada. Speedier completion of the FTA will help India to gain partial access in the NAFTA market. More critical and necessary though, is an FTA with the United States. Such an agreement while offering India deeper market access in goods might involve it committing to greater liberalization in domestic services, particularly in mode 3 service supplies. Given the recent reforms India has introduced in its foreign investment policies, particularly in politically sensitive sectors like multi-brand retail and telecommunications, it might not find the liberalization efforts too difficult to accommodate. Negotiations are expected to be challenging on 'WTO plus' issues like IP and government procurement, as they were in India's talks with the EU; nonetheless, citing the precedent of less stringent US FTAs such as those with Peru and Chile, as well as bargaining for exemptions in some areas while conceding others, is a possible negotiating option. Comprehensive FTAs with the United States and Canada can compensate considerable market access loss and prepare the Indian economy for closer integration with a high quality twenty-first century Asia-Pacific trade agreement like the TPP or the FTAAP. Given that the United States is also working on the TTIP with the EU, a bilateral deal with the United States can also help India in securing greater market access across the Atlantic.

At a time when India's economic growth has dropped to one of its lowest in recent years and might drop further to less than 5 per cent in 2013, greater integration with the world economy is imperative. India's strategy towards the TPP and external economic engagement should be guided by the motive of maximizing economic gains. This requires India to change its negotiating approach towards RTAs and FTAs. The first point to note in this regard is the pointlessness in having a hard focus on tariffs. Globally, MFN tariffs have been declining at a consistent pace. The Asia-Pacific region, particularly, has experienced maximum reduction in tariffs due to the numerous FTAs and RTAs competing with each other for securing additional preferential access. India's tariffs have also reduced on a variety of items. But many of its tariffs continue to remain high in sensitive products such as agriculture and automobiles. Negotiations on tariffs with other partners hardly yield much additional access for India because its own tariff base is higher than those of its partners. As a result, India cuts its tariffs further, giving exports from the latter greater access. Also, India's insistence on retaining too many exemptions from tariff cuts makes partners reluctant in offering reciprocal market access commitments. It is important for India to revise its outlook by reducing its focus on tariffs as the core point of negotiations and by shifting from an obsessively defensive position. India's FTA interests must become more offensive by focusing on its export advantages in manufacturing and services. Services will increasingly occupy greater space in negotiations as India takes up more RTAs with the OECD countries as well as members of large negotiating blocks like the TPP. But in services too, India appears to be focused on gaining access only in mode 4, i.e. more short-term access for its skilled professionals. While this can be persisted with, exhaustive mode 4 access cannot be obtained without mutual recognition agreements on professional qualifications. In this respect, India cannot expect foreign country professional bodies to recognize its professional certifications unless it reciprocates. Along with more liberal attitudes towards the recognition of foreign certifications and the entry of foreign professionals in its domestic turf, India must also focus on more offensive export interests in mode 3 (Singh and Pachouri 2013), given the growing presence of Indian MNCs abroad. At the same time, India must also decide whether it merely wishes to pay lip service to the WTO plus and WTO extra issues in the new FTAs it is negotiating or if it is keen on objectively reviewing these issues in the light of the developments in standard-setting on these subjects. Most importantly, India must understand the importance of approaching international negotiations as a composite package of traditional and WTO plus issues, and not as discussions where discrete objectives of liberalization in goods and services can be traded off.

Domestic circumstances and priorities are always important in deciding the quantity and quality of external engagements. They will continue to influence foreign and trade policies of India, as much as they will for China, the United States and other TPP members. But India's external engagement policies suffer from an inexplicable lack of policy coordination, which often make them suboptimal. India's early FTAs were mostly driven by foreign policy considerations with little care for economic rationale. Over time, the assessment of economic benefits has become more important. This has led to a greater role of the Ministry of Commerce in India's external economic engagement. As India is drawn into more external negotiations, it must be clear about the factors determining its choice of FTA partners and negotiating groups. India is currently involved in multiple negotiations. These include reviewing and expanding the scope of some existing FTAs (e.g. Singapore, Thailand, Sri Lanka, Chile) and negotiating new ones (e.g. Australia, Canada, New Zealand, Indonesia, Mauritius, Gulf Cooperation Council). In addition to these, India is negotiating at the RCEP and the WTO. There are also agreements like the EU–India FTA, which are at an advanced stage of negotiations, but suspended for lack of consensus on some key issues with little clue on when and how the disagreements will be dissolved. A close look at the FTAs that India have signed till now, and the ones it is involved in, shows that most of these have been initiated by foreign policy considerations and have shallow coverages, requiring that they are taken up again to be made more comprehensive (e.g. Sri Lanka, Thailand, Chile). The lack of synergy between strategic and economic motives is leading India to commit to multiple negotiations that often produce narrow FTAs with negligible economic benefits, and also stretch its negotiating capacities to the utmost, leading to long delays in concluding negotiations and reflecting the tendency to avoid 'difficult' issues. Matters are not helped by the almost complete inconsistency between India's FTAs and BITs, the latter being handled by the finance ministry, which seems to look at the BITs without being in sync with the foreign and commerce ministries.

India's negotiating skills and techniques will be tested severely in all its forthcoming FTA and RTA talks because of the internal lack of coordination between departments and ministries on negotiations. In most OECD countries, as well as in China, foreign and commercial policy making agencies work in close coordination. This is natural since commercial and economic interests drive a considerable part of modern diplomacy. India seems immune to the imperative of such integration. Its foreign policy and trade policy do not show signs of close convergence, certainly not in their institutional characteristics. Indian diplomats and diplomatic missions hardly have the economic and commercial expertise necessary for anticipating and responding to fast-evolving economic circumstances and their impacts on India's commercial interests. This is a serious limitation in perceiving the circumstances that may determine India's role and participation in trade talks. It is also a limitation in prioritizing engagements such as whether to give precedence to RTA talks over FTAs. For participating in the TPP and the RCEP, India must overcome its own institutional limitations for more meaningful outcomes.

Alternative alignments: BRICS and WTO

Though China and India are increasingly becoming conscious of the TPP and the imperatives for joining it, they cannot, at least hypothetically, discount the possibility of the TPP moving ahead without them for quite some time in the near future. This possibility should encourage them to explore alternative alignments in world trade. Even if they eventually join the TPP, their significant strategic and economic presences in the Asia-Pacific and multilateral trade and economic forums like the WTO, G20 and the UN, will ordain them to remain engaged in the non-TPP world in a constructive fashion.

From the perspectives of both countries, deep and sustained engagement with two configurations is significant. These are the BRICS and the WTO. The BRICS are the world's most significant non-TPP and non-OECD economic grouping. The WTO is, to date, the most comprehensive and influential trade order in the world, including almost all countries. China and India have had extensive involvement with both the BRICS and the WTO. The BRICS has been particularly active in international affairs since the global economic crisis in 2008. As a sub-group with the influential G20,[11] the BRICS is desirous of playing a much larger role in global financial and economic management. Successive BRICS summits since the first in Russia in 2009 have emphasized the importance of large emerging market developing countries working out mechanisms for avoiding a global liquidity crunch, which could affect their growth potential adversely, like the transatlantic financial crisis of 2008. China and India, along with other BRICS members, are working on establishing a BRICS development bank for funding the infrastructure needs of its members, as well as a contingent reserve arrangement for addressing short-term liquidity requirements.[12] On the other hand, the involvement of China and India has been long and extensive at the WTO. While India has been a member of the multilateral trade club since its inception, China annexed to the WTO as its 143rd member in December 2001. Both countries have adopted a pro-developing country posture at the WTO on several issues – often criticized by the United States and EU as obstructive positions halting progress. The occasional common agenda and united defence of both against developed country demands have produced dead-locks at multilateral trade talks, particularly since 2008, and reflect the strategic economic clout acquired by both countries at multilateral discussions, which makes it impossible for the United States and other developed countries to push their preferred trade agenda at the WTO.

Though the BRICS is yet to conceive the possibility of a FTA, China has already voiced the need.[13] Opinions in China conceive the need of a BRICS FTA in the light of the growth of the TPP and the TTIP and the possibility of these trade deals re-writing global trade rules in a manner reflecting the preferences of the United States, the EU and other developed countries.[14] The views were expressed on the occasion of the fifth and last BRICS summit at Durban in March 2013. Since then, China's official views towards the TPP have changed significantly. However, from a Chinese perspective, keeping engaged with the BRICS is vital given that it visualizes itself as the 'leader' of the BRICS prim-arily on the basis of its greater economic strength in the group.[15] The BRICS is also expected to enlarge in the future by adding more emerging market eco-nomies such as Indonesia, Turkey, Mexico and Egypt to its fold. The BRICS is already a sizeable group, accounting for almost US$15 trillion GDP; proportion-ally, the five BRICS members currently account for 20.4 per cent and 27.0 per cent of global GDP in nominal and PPP terms, and more than 40 per cent of the world population. With more large emerging markets entering its fold, the eco-nomic size and significance of the BRICS may well match up to the TPP. There is little surprise in China aiming to provide leadership to such an economically and strategically prominent bloc.

At present though, there are discernible limitations on the part of the BRICS in emerging as a coherent trade framework as an alternative to the TPP. Apart from lacking geographical contiguity – an important condition for shaping as a regional trade bloc – the BRICS is yet to galvanize into a strategic whole, largely due to the discomfort that members like India would have in accepting China's leadership of the bloc. It is also important to note that none of the BRICS members, unlike the United States and the EU, have the experience of having contributed substantively to global rule-making on new-generation trade issues, particularly the WTO plus and WTO extra issues. Neither do they have bilateral FTAs between themselves, underlining a further lack of experience in negoti-ating with each other on bilateral trade concerns. It is therefore difficult to visu-alize the ability of the BRICS to embark on a mega-regional trade deal like the TPP. Nonetheless, the geo-strategic significance of the BRICS is undisputed. Both China and India are likely to treat the configuration as a priority and to maintain their sustained engagement with the forum. As of now, however, the BRICS clearly lacks the wherewithal to present an alternative trade template to the TPP.

The multilateral trade system of the WTO has been affected by a crisis of confidence for some time now due to the lack of progress on the DDA. China and India's proclivities towards bilateral FTAs and RTAs have been a result of the stagnancy at the WTO. The growth of the TPP too, as discussed in Chapter 2, has been largely influenced by the deadlock at the WTO. As such the inability of the WTO to move forward, particularly on the DDA, might mean an end of trade liberalization under the multilateral framework and put the onus of such liberalization entirely on regional and bilateral trade deals (Panagariya 2013). For China and India, there is little choice other than accepting the fact that a considerable amount of the future world trade involving their interests is likely to be run by rules decided outside the WTO framework and within large RTAs like the TPP. If the majority, and more significant trade partners of both countries, particularly the United States and the large Asia-Pacific economies, show greater commitment to a regional trade framework like the TPP as opposed to the WTO, China and India must also assess objectively their prospects of focusing more on the WTO vis-à-vis RTAs, and whether they stand to benefit more from a contrary focus.

A well-functioning rule-based multilateral trade framework is a superior alternative to RTAs in terms of its positive trade creation effects. However, the past decade has seen RTAs coming back with a vengeance, particularly in the Asia-Pacific. The United States' disenchantment with the WTO in terms of its failure to implant its preferred characteristics in several aspects of WTO regulations along with the failure to include WTO extra issues in the multilateral trade agenda is expected to see it committing more to plurilateral frameworks outside the WTO like the TPP, TTIP and the TISA and work towards their eventual regulatory convergence as an alternative to the WTO. For China and India, as well as several other emerging markets, joining these agreements imply accepting difficult conditions. They are likely to opt for a middle path: a 'hybrid' approach combining both US FTA regulatory features as well as their own FTA characteristics. In this respect, both countries should look at the WTO as an enabling platform for achieving greater liberalization in WTO plus areas like services, IP and government procurement. They should also play an active role in expanding the WTO's agenda by taking on new issues – an aspect noted by the WTO itself as one of the major challenges for the multilateral trade framework (WTO 2013).

Final thoughts

Compared with India, China has more specific strategies for moving towards the TPP, at least at this point in time. These involve increasing its preparedness for accepting the high standards of the TPP by undertaking significant changes in domestic regulations. The most conspicuous efforts are in liberalizing market access in domestic services, and implementing new modalities in investment rules. China is attempting to achieve these through a series of apparently discrete, but intrinsically connected steps, such as negotiating a BIT with the United States and experimenting deeper financial sector reforms in the Shanghai FTZ. While all these highlight the Chinese leadership's intention to make the economy more market-oriented, to achieve greater integration with the world economy in services, and, in the process, to get closer to the yardsticks of the TPP, there are some doubts over the success of the strategy. Initiatives like the Shanghai FTZ appear narrow in scope and restrictive in approach for creating new standards and rules for transactions in business and financial services that are adaptable across the country. Furthermore, to date, China has not made any specific moves on introducing greater reforms in competition policies, restructuring SOEs and liberalizing government procurement. WTO extra issues like labour and the environment have also not featured in China's domestic reform agenda. China's ability to introduce deep and wide market-oriented policy changes for making itself TPP 'compliant' will be significantly determined by the new leadership's capacity in overcoming opposition to reforms from domestic interest groups.

India's strategy for moving towards the TPP, which has been ambiguous till now, needs to begin at the RCEP, which offers the scope for incremental liberalization. In quite a few respects, particularly policies relating to foreign investment, India's current guidelines are more liberal than China's. India's biggest problem is in conceiving a trade negotiation strategy that puts the highest emphasis on maximizing economic benefits as opposed to achieving cosmetic strategic gains. At the RCEP, as well as the TPP whenever it participates in the future, India's negotiations should stop focusing only on the defensive protection of tariffs and should pursue offensive interests in enhancing exports, particularly in services through business expansion overseas. It is also imperative for India to ensure greater coordination between its different ministries and departments – foreign affairs, commerce and finance – for pursuing focused negotiations. Spreading limited negotiating capacities thinly on multiple negotiations, some of which scarcely entail economic gains, is counterproductive and avoidable.

Strategically, the current international dynamics do not present China and India distinctly superior alternatives to the TPP. Preserving economic and strategic space in the Asia-Pacific necessitates their pursuit of the TPP through sustained liberalization. The growth of the TPP provides them a great opportunity for stepping up momentum on trade liberalization. The lack of progress at the WTO hardly presents much scope for trade liberalization at the multilateral level, leaving them with precious little option other than focusing on mega-regional trade blocs such as the RCEP and the TPP. An emerging market grouping like the BRICS, while geo-politically significant, is not ideally suited yet for providing an alternative trade template to the TPP. Neglecting upcoming trade compacts in the Asia-Pacific may be detrimental to the prospects of both economies in the long term. Much as they feel intimidated by the TPP for their own specific reasons, it is a reality they can hardly overlook. The challenge for both is to visualize it as an opportunity for maximizing national interests and take precipitate actions for doing so.

Notes

1 'China Prospers with World after WTO Accession', *China Daily*, 28 January 2011, online, available at: www.chinadaily.com.cn/bizchina/2011–01/28/content_11935664.htm (accessed 9 November 2013).
2 Source as in Note 10, Chapter 5.
3 Source as in Note 9, Chapter 5.
4 'US and China Breakthrough Announcement on the Bilateral Investment Treaty Negotiations', US Department of the Treasury, 15 July 2013, online, available at: www.treasury.gov/connect/blog/Pages/U.S.-and-China-Breakthrough-Announcement-.aspx (accessed 9 November 2013).
5 There are some ambiguities over the specific content of 'pre-establishment' national treatment in terms of whether it will extend to acquisitions such as in the US–Korea BIT and specific definitions of 'investors'.
6 The imperative was reiterated by the Chinese vice finance minister Zhu Guangyao at the US–China Strategic Economic Dialogue in Washington in July 2013. 'US, China Agree to Restart Investment Treaty Talks', *Reuters*, 12 July 2013, online, available at: www.reuters.com/article/2013/07/12/us-usa-china-dialogue-trade-idUSBRE96A0ZD20130712 (accessed 9 November 2013).
7 'China's FTZs Promise Flourishing Growth', *China.org.cn*, 19 November 2013, online, available at: www.china.org.cn/business/2013–11/17/content_30626521.htm (accessed 19 November 2013).
8 Apart from the EU (including Turkey) and the United States, the other TISA negotiating members are Australia, Canada, Chile, Taiwan, Colombia, Costa Rica, Hong Kong, Iceland, Israel, Japan, Liechtenstein, Mexico, New Zealand, Norway, Pakistan, Panama, Paraguay, Peru, South Korea and Switzerland. *Coalition of Services Industries*, September 2013, online, available at: https://servicescoalition.org/negotiations/trade-in-services-agreement (accessed 10 November 2013).
9 'Trade in Services Agreement (TISA)', Department of Foreign Affairs and Trade (DFAT), Australian Government, online, available at: www.dfat.gov.au/trade/negotiations/services/trade-in-services-agreement.html (accessed 10 November 2013).
10 The negative list refers to industries maintaining restrictions on foreign investments. These include agriculture, forestry, animal husbandry and fishery; mining; manufacturing; production and distribution of power, gas and water; construction; wholesale and retail; transportation, warehousing and postal service; IT, computer and software; finance; real estate; leasing and commercial service; scientific research and technical service; water conservation, environment and public facility management; education, health, culture, sports and entertainment. In addition, foreign investment continues to be banned in news agencies, radio and film production, newspaper, magazine and book publishing and Internet cafes. Restrictions also continue on telecommunication and satellite transmission services. 'Shanghai Releases "Negative List" for Foreign Investment in Shanghai Free Trade Zone', *China Briefing*, 30 September 2013, online, available at: www.china-briefing.com/news/2013/09/30/shanghai-releases-negative-list-for-foreign-investment-in-shanghai-free-trade-zone.html (accessed 10 November 2013).
11 The G20 is probably the world's most influential strategic and economic grouping, comprising OECD countries, emerging markets and the Bretton Woods institutions. The members include Australia, Argentina, Brazil, Canada, China, France, Germany, India, Indonesia, Italy, Japan, Korea, Mexico, Russia, Saudi Arabia, South Africa, Turkey, the United Kingdom and the United States. The EU is also a part of the group, along with the IMF and the World Bank, online, available at: www.g20.org/infographics/20121201/780989503.html (accessed 20 November 2013).
12 'Fifth BRICS Summit', Durban, South Africa, 26–27 March 2013, online, available at: www.brics5.co.za (accessed 12 November 2013).

13 'China Calls for Closer Trade Cooperation amongst the BRICS', *Agritrade*, 22 July 2013, online, available at: http://agritrade.cta.int/en/layout/set/print/Agriculture/Topics/ACP-FTAs/China-calls-for-closer-trade-cooperation-amongst-the-BRICS (accessed 12 November 2013).
14 'Experts Call for BRICS Free Trade Pact', *China Daily*, 27 March 2013, online, available at: www.chinadaily.com.cn/china/2013–03/27/content_16347695.htm (accessed 12 November 2013).
15 The vice chairman of the China Society for World Trade Organization Studies – a think-tank attached with the Ministry of Commerce – affirms China as 'the leader of the BRICS' and encourages China to initiate the BRICS FTA. Ibid.

Bibliography

Anand, V. (2013), 'Geopolitics of RCEP and TPP: Implications for India', Vivekananda International Foundation (VIF), India, 10 September, online, available at: www.vifindia.org/article/2013/september/10/geopolitics-of-rcep-and-tpp-implications-for-india (accessed 5 November 2013).

Anderlini, Jamil (2013), 'China Premier Li Keqiang Commits to Financial Reform', *Financial Times*, 11 September, online, available at: www.ft.com/intl/cms/s/0/43fb452e-1adf-11e3–87da-00144feab7de.html#axzz2iPdbqBwq (accessed 22 October 2013).

Armstrong, Shiro (2011), 'TPP Needs Less Haste, More Caution', *East Asia Forum*, 17 April, online, available at: www.eastasiaforum.org/2011/04/17/tpp-needs-less-haste-more-caution/ (accessed 8 October 2013).

Barfield, Claude (2013), 'Crunch Time for the TPP', *East Asia Forum*, 10 January, online, available at: www.eastasiaforum.org/2013/01/10/crunch-time-for-the-tpp/ (accessed 28 September 2013).

Bagri, Neha Thirani (2013), 'Biden Urges Closer Cooperation before India's Business Elite', *New York Times*, 24 July, online, available at: www.nytimes.com/2013/07/25/world/asia/biden-urges-closer-cooperation-with-indias-business-elite.html (accessed 5 November 2013).

Berger, Axel (2013) 'Investment Treaties and the Search for Market Access in China', *investmenttreatynews*, 3(4), International Institute for Sustainable Development (IISD), June, online, available at: www.iisd.org/pdf/2013/iisd_itn_june_2013_en.pdf (accessed 9 November 2013).

Bergsten, Fred C. (1997), 'Open Regionalism', Working Paper, 97–3, Peterson Institute for International Economics, Washington, DC, online, available at: www.iie.com/publications/wp/wp.cfm?ResearchID=152 (accessed 7 October 2013).

Bergsten, Fred C. and Schott, Jeffrey, J. (2012), 'China and the Trans-Pacific Partnership', *APEC Currents*, RMIT University, March 2012, online, available at: www.apec.org.au/docs/currentsRMIT/2012–1/index.html#3 (accessed 31 October 2013).

Bo, Chen (2013), 'Pilot Free Trade Zone in Shanghai to Build Open Economy', *East Asia Forum*, 19 October 2013, online, available at: www.eastasiaforum.org/2013/10/19/pilot-free-trade-zone-in-shanghai-to-build-open-economy/ (accessed 22 October 2013).

Brodsgaard, Kjeld Erik (2012), 'Politics and Business Group Formation in China: The Party in Control?', *China Quarterly*, 211, pp. 624–648.

Bush, Nate and Yue, Bo (2011), 'Disentangling Industrial Policy and Competition Policy in China', *theantitrustsource*, online, available at: www.antitrustsource.com, February, online, available at: www.americanbar.org/content/dam/aba/migrated/2011_build/antitrust_law/feb11_bush2_23f.authcheckdam.pdf (accessed 27 October 2013).

Capling, Ann and Ravenhill, John (2011), 'Multilateralising Regionalism: What Role for the Trans-Pacific Partnership Agreement?', *Pacific Review*, 24 (5), pp. 553–575.

Capling, Ann and Ravenhill, John (2012), 'Multilateralising Regionalism or the Securitization of Trade Policy?', in Lim, C.L., Elms, Deborah, and Low, Patrick (ed.) (2012), *The Trans-Pacific Partnership: A Quest for a 21st Century Agreement*, New York: Cambridge University Press.

Chiang, Min-Hua (2013), 'The Potential of China–Japan–South Korea Free Trade Agreement', *East Asia*, online, available at: http://link.springer.com/article/10.1007%2Fs121 40–013–9196–5# (accessed 8 September 2013).

Cooper, William H. and Manyin, Mark E. (2013), 'Japan Joins the Trans-Pacific Partnership: What Are the Implications?', *Congressional Research Service (CRS)*, 7–5700, online, available at: www.crs.gov, R42676, 13 August, online, available at: www.fas. org/sgp/crs/row/R42676.pdf (accessed 29 September 2013).

Cooper, William H., Jurenas, Remy, Platzer, Michaela D. and Manyin, Mark. E. (2011), 'The EU–South Korea Free Trade Agreement and its Implications for the United States', *Congressional Research Service (CRS)*, 7–5700, online, available at: www.crs. gov, R41534, 1 December, online, available at: www.fas.org/sgp/crs/row/R41534.pdf (accessed 19 October 2013).

CUTS (2012), 'Government Procurement in India: Domestic Regulations and Trade Prospects', Consumer Unity and Trust Society (CUTS) International, Jaipur, India, October, online, available at: www.cuts-citee.org/pdf/Government-Procurement-in-India_Domestic-Regulations-Trade-Prospects.pdf (accessed 27 October 2013).

Dhar, Biswajit, Joseph, Reji and James, T.C. (2012), 'India's Bilateral Investment Agreements Time to Review', *Economic and Political Weekly (EPW)*, xlvii (52), 29 December, Mumbai, India.

Du, Lan (2011), 'Comments on the US Strategy for Promoting Trans-Pacific Partnership', *China Institute of International Studies*, 3 August, online, available at: www.ciis.org. cn/english/2011–08/03/content_4380581.htm (accessed 31 October 2013).

Elms, Deborah (2012), 'Getting from Here to There: Stitching Together Goods Agreements in the Trans-Pacific Partnership (TPP) Agreement'; *Working Paper*, 235, S. Rajaratnam School of International Studies (RSIS), Singapore, 17 April, online, available at: www.tfctn.org.sg/pdf/2012–04–17%20WP235.pdf (accessed 2 October 2013).

Elms, Deborah and Lim, C.L. (2012), 'An Overview and Snapshot of the TPP Negotiations', in Lim, C.L., Elms, Deborah and Low, Patrick (ed.) (2012), *The Trans-Pacific Partnership: A Quest for a 21st Century Agreement*, New York: Cambridge University Press.

Emmerson, Donald (2013), 'Challenging ASEAN: The American Pivot in Southeast Asia', *East Asia Forum*, 13 January 2013, online, available at: www.eastasiaforum. org/2013/01/13/challenging-asean-the-american-pivot-in-southeast-asia/ (accessed 3 November 2013).

Fan, Ying and Tong, Sarah Y. (2012), 'The Trans-Pacific Partnership from China's Viewpoint: Perceptions, Realities and Uncertainties', *Background Brief*, 736, East Asian Institute (EAI), National University of Singapore, 13 July.

Fergusson, Ian F. and Vaughn, Bruce (2011), 'The Trans-Pacific Partnership Agreement', *Congressional Research Service (CRS)*, 7–5700, 12 December 2011, online, available at: www.crs.gov R40502; (accessed 11 October 2013).

Fergusson, Ian F., Cooper, William, H., Jurenas, Remy and Williams, Brock R. (2013), 'The Trans-Pacific Partnership Negotiations and Issues for Congress', *Congressional Research Service (CRS)*, 7–5700, online, available at: www.crs.gov, R42694, online, available at: www.fas.org/sgp/crs/row/R42694.pdf (accessed 28 September 2013).

Flynn, Sean, Kaminski, Margot E., Baker, Brook K. and Koo, Jimmy H. (2011), Public Interest Analysis of the US TPP Proposal for an IP Chapter', *PIJIP Research Paper Series*, Paper 21, online, available at: http://digitalcommons.wcl.americans.edu/research/21 (accessed 3 October 2013).

Frankel, S. (2012), 'The Intellectual Property Chapter in the TPP', in Lim, C.L., Elms, Deborah and Low, Patrick (ed.) (2012), *The Trans-Pacific Partnership: A Quest for a 21st Century Agreement*, New York: Cambridge University Press.

Gertler, J.L. (2002), 'What China's WTO accession is all about', World Bank, online, available at: http://siteresources.worldbank.org/INTRANETTRADE/Resources/gertler_china.pdf (accessed 9 November 2013).

Gopakumar, K.M. (2013), 'Civil Societies Demand Moratorium on US–India Treaty', *Third World Network (TWN)*, October, online, available at: www.twnside.org.sg/twnf/2013/4007.htm (accessed 23 October 2013).

Gore, Lance P. (2012), 'China Recruits Top SOE Executives into Government', *East Asian Policy*, East Asian Institute (EAI), National University of Singapore; 4 (1), World Scientific, January/March.

Gross, Donald (2013), 'Welcoming China to the Trans-Pacific Partnership', *Huffington Post*, 9 July, online, available at: www.huffingtonpost.com/donald-gross/trans-pacific-partnership-china_b_3562801.html (accessed 3 November 2013).

Guoyou, Song and Wen, Jin Yuan (2012), 'China's Free Trade Agreement Strategies', *Washington Quarterly*, 35 (4), pp. 107–119, online, available at: http://csis.org/files/publication/twq12FallSongYuan.pdf (accessed 24 September 2013).

Hansakul, Syetarn, Dyke, Steffen, and Karn, Steffen (2009), 'China's Financial Markets – a Future Global Force?', *Deutsche Bank Research*, 16 March, online, available at: www.dbresearch.com/prod/dbr_internet_en-prod/prod0000000000238901.pdf (accessed 21 October 2013).

Herreros, S. (2012), 'Coping with Multiple Uncertainties: Latin America in the TPP Negotiations', in C.L. Lim, Elms, Deborah and Low, Patrick (eds) *The Trans-Pacific Partnership A Quest for a Twenty-First-Century Trade Agreement*, New York: Cambridge University Press.

Hiebert, Murray and Hanlon, Liam (2012), 'ASEAN and Partners Launch Regional Comprehensive Economic Partnership', Centre for Strategic and International Studies (CSIS), Washington, DC, 7 December, online, available at: http://csis.org/publication/asean-and-partners-launch-regional-comprehensive-economic-partnership (accessed 15 October 2013).

Horn, Henrik, Mavroidis, Petros C. and Sapir, Andre (2009), 'Beyond the WTO: An Anatomy of EU and US Preferential Trade Agreements', Bruegel Blueprint 7, Bruegel Blueprint Series, VII, Bruegel, Brussels, Belgium, online, available at: www.bruegel.org (accessed 1 October 2013).

Isidore, Chris (2012), 'US vs. China: The Trade Battles', *CNN Money* 13 March, online, available at: http://money.cnn.com/2012/03/13/news/international/china-trade/ (accessed 2 November 2013).

Jiangyu, Wang (2010), 'The role of China and India in Asian Regionalism', in Sornarajah Muthucumaraswamy and Wang Jiangyu (eds), *China, India and the International Economic Order*, New York: Cambridge University Press.

Jiangyu, Wang (2011), 'China and East Asian Regionalism', *European Law Journal*, 17(5), pp. 611–629.

Jianmin, Jin (2012), 'China's Concerns Regarding TPP No More than Empty Worries?',

Fujitsu Research Institute, 11 January, online, available at: http://jp.fujitsu.com/group/fri/en/column/message/2012/2012–01–11.html (accessed 31 October 2013).

Jianmin, Jin (2013), 'RCEP vs. TPP', *Fujitsu Research Institute*, 22 February, online, available at: http://jp.fujitsu.com/group/fri/en/column/message/2013/2013–02–22.html (accessed 31 October 2013).

Jie, Huang (2012), 'TPP versus ECFA: Similarities, Differences, and China's Strategies', *China Review*, 12 (2), pp. 85–110.

Jung, Eun-joo (2012), 'India Plans to Abolish ISD Clause in FTAs', 6 April; *bilaterals. org*, online, available at: www.bilaterals.org/spip.php?article21295 (accessed 25 October 2013).

Kawai, Masahiro and Wignaraja, Ganeshan (2010), 'Free Trade Agreements in East Asia: A Way toward Trade Liberalization?' *ADB Brief*, 1, June, Manila: Asian Development Bank.

Khalifah, Noor Aini (1992), 'International Trade of the East Asian Economic Caucus', *Jurnal Ekonomi Malaysia*, 25, pp. 19–45, June, online, available at: www.ukm.my/fep/jem/pdf/1992–25/jeko_25–2.pdf (accessed 7 October 2013).

Kim, Sangkyom, Park, Innwon and Park, Soonchan (2011), 'Regional Economic Integration in the Asia-Pacific Region: Is an FTAAP the Catalyst for One Community?', *APEC Study Series*, 11–01, Korea Institute for International Economic Policy (KIEP), Seoul, Korea, 29 December.

Landler, Mark and Wong, Edward (2012), 'With Edge, US Greets China's Heir Apparent', *New York Times*, 14 February, online, available at: www.nytimes.com/2012/02/15/world/asia/us-seeks-to-size-up-chinas-heir-apparent-during-visit.html?pagewanted=all&_r=0 (accessed 3 November 2013).

Lewis, Meredith Kolsky (2009), 'Expanding the P-4 Trade Agreement into a Broader Trans-Pacific Partnership: Implications, Risks and Opportunities', *Asian Journal of WTO and International Health Law and Politics*, 4 (2), pp. 401–422, online, available at: http://heinonline.org (accessed 3 October 2013).

Lewis, Meredith Kolsky (2011), 'The Trans-Pacific Partnership: New Paradigm or Wolf in Sheep's Clothing?', *Boston College International and Comparative Law Review*, 34 (27), pp. 27–52.

Li, Cheng and McElveen, Ryan (2013), 'Can Xi Jinping's Governing Strategy Succeed?', *Current History*, online, available at: www.brookings.edu/~/media/Research/Files/Articles/2013/09/LiCurrent%20History.pdf (accessed 4 November 2013).

Li, Chunding and Whalley, John (2012), 'China and the TPP: A Numerical Simulation Assessment of the Effects Involved', Working Paper 18090, *National Bureau of Economic Research (NBER)*, Cambridge MA, May, online, available at: www.nber.org/papers/w18090 (accessed 9 September 2013).

Lim, C.L., Deborah Elms and Patrick Low (2012), 'Conclusions', in C.L. Lim, Elms, Deborah and Low, Patrick (eds) *The Trans-Pacific Partnership A Quest for a Twenty-First-Century Trade Agreement*, New York: Cambridge University Press.

Lim, C.L. and Wang, J.Y. (2009) 'China and the Doha Development Agenda', working paper prepared for presentation at the World Trade Organization (WTO) Forum, Geneva, 28 September, online, available at: www.nsi-ins.ca/english/pdf/China%20at%20Doha.pdf (accessed 9 November 2013).

Lynch, Elizabeth M. (2010), 'Pencils, Staplers and Pens, Oh My! China Submits Government Procurement Bid to WTO Body', *China Law and Policy*, 2 August, online, available at: http://chinalawandpolicy.com/2010/08/02/pencils-staplers-pens-oh-my-china-submits-government-procurement-bid-to-wto-body/ (accessed 27 October 2013).

McNicol, Hamish (2013), 'China Trade Surplus Close', *stuff.co.nz*, 11 July, online, available at: www.stuff.co.nz/business/industries/8903323/China-trade-surplus-close (accessed 20 August 2013).

Manzano, George and Bedano, Myrene (2009), 'Revisiting Sectoral Liberalization. An Alternative to the FTAAP? Implications on the Philippines', *Discussion Paper*, Series No. 2009–13, Philippine Institute for Development Studies, May, online, available at: http://dirp4.pids.gov.ph/ris/dps/pidsdps0913.pdf (accessed 8 October 2013).

Martin, Phillippe, Mayor, Thierry and Thoenig, Mathias (2010), 'The Geography of Conflicts and Regional Trade Agreements', *CEPR Discussion Paper*, 7740, 4 January, online, available at: www.cepr.org/pubs/dps/DP7740.asp (accessed 12 October 2013).

Matechak, Jason and Gerson, Brett (2010), 'Can China's Government Procurement Market be Cracked?', *China Business Review*, 1 May, online, available at: www.china-businessreview.com/can-chinas-government-procurement-market-be-cracked/ (accessed 27 October 2013).

Menon, Jayant (2013), 'How to Multilateralise Asian Regionalism' *East Asia Forum*, 6 January, online, available at: www.eastasiaforum.org/2013/01/06/how-to-multilateralise-asian-regionalism/ (accessed 9 March 2013).

Morrison, Wayne M. (2013), 'China–US Trade Issues', *Congressional Research Service (CRS)*, 7–5700, 17 July, online, available at: www.crs.gov RL33536; (accessed 1 November 2013).

Mulgan, Aurelia George (2013), 'Japan, US and the TPP: the View from China', *East Asia Forum*, 5 May, online, available at: www.eastasiaforum.org/2013/05/05/japan-us-and-the-tpp-the-view-from-china/ (accessed 29 September 2013).

Murdoch, Scott (2013), 'Richard Marles in 11th hour bid to seal FTA with China by year end', *Australian*, 25 July, online, available at: www.theaustralian.com.au/business/economics/richard-marles-in-11th-hour-bid-to-seal-fta-with-china-by-year-end/story-e6frg926–1226684619775 (accessed 6 September 2013).

Pakpahan, Beginda (2012), 'Will RCEP Compete with the TPP?', *East Asia Forum*, 28 November 2012, online, available at: www.eastasiaforum.org/2012/11/28/will-rcep-compete-with-the-tpp/ (accessed 9 March 2013).

Palit, Amitendu (2012a), *China India Economics: Challenges, Competition and Collaboration*, London and New York: Routledge, Taylor & Francis Group.

Palit, Amitendu (2012b), 'Economic Reforms in India: Perpetuating Policy Paralysis', *Working Paper*, 48, Institute of South Asian Studies (ISAS), National University of Singapore, 29 March, online, available at: http://ISAS_Working_Paper_148_Economic_Reforms_in_India_30032012163947.pdf (accessed 5 November 2013).

Palit, Amitendu (2012c), 'The Trans-Pacific Strategic Economic Partnership: Will it Divide the Asia-Pacific?', *Briefing Paper*, 6/2012, CUTS International, August, online, available at: www.cuts-citee.org/pdf/Briefing_Paper12-The_Trans_Pacific_Strategic_Economic_Partnership_Will_it_divide_the_Asia-Pacific.pdf (accessed 11 October 2013).

Palit, Amitendu (2013a), 'TPP and Intellectual Property: Growing Concerns', *Foreign Trade Review*, 48 (1).

Palit, Amitendu (2013b), 'Negotiating the Trans-Pacific Partnership: Possible Effects on the US–China Relationship in Asia', *China Current*, 12 (1), online, available at: www.chinacenter.net/negotiating-the-trans-pacific-partnership-possible-effects-on-the-u-s-china-relationship-in-asia/#more-2471 (accessed 1 October 2013).

Palit, Amitendu (2013c), 'India's Food Security Bill: Grave Digger or Game Changer?', *ISAS Insights*, 226, 4 September, online, available at: http://ISAS_Insights_226-_

India's_Food_Security_Bill_Grave_Digger_or_Game_Changer_04092013163457.pdf (accessed 6 November 2013).

Palit, Amitendu (2013d), 'For a New Regional Beginning', *China Daily*, 10 October 2013, online, available at: http://usa.chinadaily.com.cn/opinion/2013–10/10/content_17019283. htm (accessed 10 November 2013).

Panagariya, Arvind (2013), 'Challenges to the Multilateral Trading System and Possible Responses', *Economics: The Open-Access, Open-Assessment E-Journal*, 7, 2013–10, online, available at: http://dx.doi.org/10.5018/economics-ejournal.ja.2013–10 (accessed 12 November 2013).

Park, Cheol Hee (2012), 'Intra-regional Geopolitical Dynamics in Northeast Asia', in Dent, Christopher M. and Dosch, Jom (eds.) (2012), *The Asia-Pacific, Regionalism and the Global System*, Edward Elgar Publishing.

Pei, Minxin (2013), 'Wooing China's Princelings', *Project Syndicate*, 9 October 2013, online, available at: www.project-syndicate.org/print/jpmorgan-and-western-complicity-in-chinese-nepotism-by-minxin-pei (accessed 9 October 2013).

Perlez, Jane (2013), 'Cancellation of Trip By Obama Plays to Doubts of Asia Allies', *New York Times*, 4 October 2013, online, available at: www.nytimes.com/2013/10/05/world/asia/with-obama-stuck-in-washington-china-leader-has-clear-path-at-asia-conferences.html?_r=0 (accessed 7 October 2013).

Peter, A. (2012), 'Economics of the TPP and RCEP Negotiations', Pacific Economic Cooperation Council (PECC), 1 December, online, available at: www.pecc.org/resources/doc_view/1942-economics-of-the-tpp-and-rcep-negotiations (accessed 9 September 2013).

Petri, Peter A., Plummer, Michael G. and Zhai, Fan (2012), 'Note on Alternative TPP-Track Simulations', *asiapacifictrade.org*, 20 November, online, available at: http://asiapacifictrade.org/wp-content/uploads/2012/11/TPP-track-alternatives.pdf (accessed 9 September 2013).

Petrov, Leonid (2012), 'Northeast Asia: A Region without Regionalism', *East Asia Forum*, 23 May, online, available at: www.eastasiaforum.org/2012/05/23/northeast-asia-a-region-without-regionalism/ (accessed 30 October 2013).

Prasad, Eswar C. (2010), 'The US–China Economic Relationship: Shifts and Twists in the Balance of Power', US–China Economic and Security Review Commission Hearing on 'US Debt to China: Implications and Repercussions', 25 February (revised 25 March), online, available at: http://broookings.edu/testimony/2010/0225_us_china_debt_prasad.aspx (accessed 2 November 2013).

Qian, Liwei (2013), 'Double Implications of President Xi's Southeast Asia Tour', *China-USFocus*, 12 October 2013, online, available at: www.chinausfocus.com/finance-economy/double-implications-of-president-xis-southeast-asia-tour/ (accessed 10 November 2013).

Rabinovitch, Simon (2013), 'China Reforms Open Way for Short-Sellers', *Financial Times*, 17 September, online, available at: www.ft.com/intl/cms/s/0/39c64034–1f73–11e3-aa36–00144feab7de.html#axzz2iPdbqBwq (accessed 22 October 2013).

Ranjan, Prabhash (2010), 'Indian Investment Treaty Programme in the Light of Global Experiences', *Economic and Political Weekly (EPW)*, xlv (7), 13 February.

Rathus, Joel (2011), 'East Asian Free Trade Area: Bank on it', *East Asia Forum*, 11 December, online, available at: www.eastasiaforum.org/2011/12/11/east-asian-free-trade-area-bank-on-it/ (accessed 15 October 2013).

Schott, Jeffrey J., Kotschwar, Barbara and Muir, Julia (2013), 'Understanding the Trans-Pacific Partnership', *Policy Analyses in International Economics*, 99, January.

Sen, Amiti (2013), 'US Pharma Firms Lobby to Protect Patents in India', *Business Line*, 23 October 2013, online, available at: www.thehindubusinessline.com/industry-and-economy/us-pharma-firms-lobby-to-protect-patents-in-india/article5265436.ece (accessed 7 November 2013).

Sengupta, Ranja (2012), 'Government Procurement in the EU–India FTA: Dangers for India', *Economic and Political Weekly*, xlvii (28), 14 July.

Sinha Palit, Parama (2010), 'China's Soft Power in South Asia', Working Paper, 200, S. Rajaratnam School of International Studies, Singapore, 8 June, online, available at: www.rsis.edu.sg/publications/WorkingPapers/WP200.pdf (accessed 18 November 2013).

Singh, Ritesh Kumar and Pachouri, Anshul (2013), 'The Slack in Services Export', *Business Line*, 23 October 2013, online, available at: www.thehindubusinessline.com/opinion/the-slack-in-services-export/article5265189.ece (accessed 11 November 2013).

Singh, Vijay Kumar (2011), 'Competition Law and Policy in India; The Journey in a Decade', *NUJS Law Review*, 4, pp. 523–566, October–December, online, available at: www.nujslawreview.org/pdf/articles/2011_4/vijay-kumar-singh.pdf (accessed 27 October 2013).

Smitha, Francis and Murali Kallummal (2013), 'India's Comprehensive Trade Agreements: Implications for Development Trajectory', *Economic and Political Weekly (EPW)*, xlviii (31), 3 August, Mumbai, India.

Solis, Mireya (2012), 'The Trans-Pacific Partnership: Can the United States Lead the Way in Asia-Pacific Integration?', *Pacific Focus*, xxvii (3), pp. 319–341, December.

Sornarajah, Muthucumaraswamy (2010), 'India, China and Foreign Investment', in Sornarajah Muthucumaraswamy and Wang Jiangyu (eds), *China, India and the International Economic Order*, New York: Cambridge University Press.

Tajitsu, Naomi (2013), 'China bans New Zealand Milk Powder Imports on Botulism Scare: NZ Trade Minister', *Reuters*, online, available at: www.reuters.com/article/2013/08/04/us-newzealand-milk-idUSBRE97301K20130804 (accessed 20 August 2013).

Tanczos, Francis (2008), 'Unfair Play: Examining the US "Anti-Dumping" War against China', *Washington Undergraduate Law Review*, ii (3), pp. 78–92, online, available at: www.itssd.org/US-China_Antidumping_WULR_spr08_Francis_Tanczos.pdf (accessed 23 September 2013).

Tibung, Sheryl (2012), 'A Primer on the Trans-Pacific Partnership', *Stimson*, 9 October 2012, online, available at: www.stimson.org/summaries/a-primer-on-the-tpp/ (accessed 4 October 2013).

Tietje, Christian and Nowrot, Karsten (2011), 'Myth or Reality? China's Market Economy Status under WTO Anti-Dumping Law after 2016', *Policy Papers on Transnational Economic Law*, No. 34, Transnational Economic Law Research Center, School of Law, Martin Luther University, Germany, online, available at: http://tietje.jura.uni-halle.de/sites/default/files/telc/PolicyPaper34.pdf (accessed 22 September 2013).

Trumbull, Mark (2010), 'Obama Outlines Strategy to Boost US Exports – and Jobs', *Christian Science Monitor*, 11 March, online, available at: www.csmonitor.com/USA/Politics/2010/0311/Obama-outlines-strategy-to-boost-US-exports-and-jobs (accessed 30 October 2013).

USTR (2013), *2013 National Trade Estimate Report on Foreign Trade Barriers*, Office of the United States Trade Representative, online, available at: www.ustr.gov/about-us/press-office/reports-and-publications/2013/NTE-FTB (accessed 20 October 2013).

Villarreal, M. Angeles (2012), 'Mexico's Free Trade Agreements', *Congressional*

Research Service (CRS), 7–5700, online, available at: www.fas.org/sgp/crs/row/R40784.pdf (accessed 13 October 2013).

Wang, Guiguo (2011), 'Chinese Mechanisms for Resolving Investor–State Disputes', *Jindal Journal of International Affairs*, 1 (1), pp. 204–233, October.

Wang, Zhile (2013), 'TPP Can Benefit China', *China Daily*, 24 June, online, available at: www.chinadaily.com.cn/business/2013–06/24/content_16651594.htm (accessed 3 November 2013).

Wen, Jin Yuan (2012), 'The Trans-Pacific Partnership and China's Corresponding Strategies', *A Freeman Briefing Report*, Freeman Chair in China Studies, Centre for Strategic and International Studies (CSIS), Washington, DC, June, online, available at: http://csis.org/files/publication/120620_Freeman_Brief.pdf (accessed 11 October 2013).

West, Sean and Caplan, Jesse (2013), 'Bring India into the TPP', *Politico*, 8 January 2013, online, available at: www.politico.com/story/2013/08/bring-india-into-the-tpp-95049.html (accessed 5 November 2013).

Wignaraja, Ganeshan (2011), *Economic Reforms, Regionalism and Exports: Comparing China and India*, East–West Center, Policy Studies, 60, online, available at: www.eastwestcenter.org/publications/economic-reforms-regionalism-and-exports-comparing-china-and-india (accessed 12 October 2013).

Wignaraja, Ganeshan (2012), 'PRC and India: Pursuing the Same Approach to Free Trade Agreement', *Asia Pathways*, Asian Development Bank Institute, 24 October, online, available at: www.asiapathways-adbi.org/2012/10/prc-and-india-pursuing-the-same-approach-to-free-trade-agreements/ (accessed 10 October 2013).

Wu, Zhenglong (2010), 'Tackling Trans-Pacific Trade', *China Daily*, 16 October, online, available at: www.chinadaily.com.cn/opinion/2010–09/16/content_11309929.htm (accessed 30 October 2013).

WTO (2012), *Trade Profiles 2012*, Geneva, Switzerland.

WTO (2013), *World Trade Report 2013*, 'Prospects for multilateral trade cooperation', Part-II, E, pp. 266–290, online, available at: www.wto.org/english/res_e/publications_e/wtr13_e.htm (accessed 12 November 2013).

Xiaohui, Su (2012), 'Developments and Prospects of the RCEP', *China US Focus*, 22 November, online, available at: www.chinausfocus.com/foreign-policy/developments-and-prospects-of-the-rcep/ (accessed 9 March 2013).

Ying, Fan (2010), 'China's Liberalization of Trade in Distribution Services', Paper prepared for the conference on 'Regulatory Reforms and Liberalization in Services: Examining Impacts on Inclusive and Sustainable Development', jointly organized by ADBI and UNCESCAP-ARTNeT; 11–12 October, Bali, Indonesia online, available at: www.unescap.org/tid/artnet/mtg/reformservice_bp10.pdf (accessed 22 October 2013).

Yiping, Huang (2013), 'Can China's New Economic Reform Policies get in the Zone?', *East Asia Forum*, 20 October 2013, online, available at: www.eastasiaforum.org/2013/10/20/can-chinas-new-economic-reform-policies-get-in-the-zone/ (accessed 10 November 2013).

Yu, Peter (2012), 'The Alphabet Soup of Trans-border Intellectual Property Enforcement' Research Paper No. 12–13, Legal Studies Research Paper Series, Drake University, June, online, available at: http://papers.ssrn.com/sol3/papers.cfm?abstract_id=2054950 (accessed 3 October 2013).

Zhang, Xian-Chu (2010), 'An Institutional Race: A Comparative Study of the Competition Law Regimes in India and China', in Sornarajah Muthucumaraswamy and Wang Jiangyu (eds), *China, India and the International Economic Order*, New York: Cambridge University Press.

Zhang, Yunling (2010), *China and Asian Regionalism*, ch. 7, pp. 111–112, Singapore: World Scientific.

Zhang, Yunling and Shen, Minghui (2011), 'The Status of East Asian Free Trade Agreements', *Asian Development Bank Institute*, Working Paper Series, 282, May, online, available at: www.adbi.org/files/2011.05.17.wp282.status.east.asian.free.trade.agreements.pdf (accessed 15 October 2013).

Zheng, Yongnian, Lye Liang Fook and Chen Gang (2012), 'China's Foreign Policy: Coping with Shifting Geopolitics and Maintaining Stable External Relations', *East Asian Policy*, 4 (1), pp. 29–42, January/March.

Zilio, Michelle (2013), 'No Rush on Canada–India Trade Deal, says Canadian High Commissioner', *iPOLITICS*, 25 June, online, available at: www.ipolitics.ca/2013/06/25/no-rush-on-canada-india-trade-deal-says-canadian-high-commissioner/ (accessed 22 September 2013).

Index